CULLEN MURPHY

God's Jury

The Inquisition and the Making of the Modern World

PENGUIN BOOKS

PENGUIN BOOKS

Published by the Penguin Group
Penguin Books Ltd, 80 Strand, London WC2R 0RL, England
Penguin Group (USA) Inc., 375 Hudson Street, New York, New York 10014, USA
Penguin Group (Canada), 90 Eglinton Avenue East, Suite 700, Toronto, Ontario, Canada M4P 2Y3
(a division of Pearson Penguin Canada Inc.)
Penguin Ireland, 25 St Stephen's Green, Dublin 2, Ireland
(a division of Penguin Books Ltd)
Penguin Group (Australia), 250 Camberwell Road,
Camberwell, Victoria 3124, Australia (a division of Pearson Australia Group Pty Ltd)
Penguin Books India Pvt Ltd, 11 Community Centre,
Panchsheel Park, New Delhi – 110 017, India
Penguin Group (NZ), 67 Apollo Drive, Rosedale, Auckland 0632, New Zealand
(a division of Pearson New Zealand Ltd)
Penguin Books (South Africa) (Pty) Ltd, Block D, Rosebank Office Park, 181 Jan Smuts Avenue,
Parktown North, Gauteng 2193, South Africa

Penguin Books Ltd, Registered Offices: 80 Strand, London WC2R 0RL, England

www.penguin.com

First published in the United States of America by Houghton Mifflin Harcourt
Publishing Company 2012
First published in Great Britain by Allen Lane 2012
Published in Penguin Books 2013

1

Printed in England by Clays Ltd, St Ives plc

978-0-141-00009-1

GOD'S JURY

'Enormously enjoyable ... Murphy's touch, tone and emphasis a̶.̶ ̶ ̶ ̶er anything but sure and sane. This is popular history at its very best' Peter Stanford, *Independent*

'Fascinating, immensely readable' Samuel G. Freedman, *The New York Times*

'From Torquemada to Guantánamo and beyond, Cullen Murphy finds the 'inquisitorial impulse' alive, and only too well, in our world. His engaging romp through the secret Vatican archives shows that the distance between the Dark Ages and Modernity is shockingly short' Jane Mayer, author of *The Dark Side*

'When virtue arms itself – beware! Lucid, scholarly, elegantly told, *God's Jury* is as gripping as it is important' James Carroll, author of *Jerusalem, Jerusalem*

'The Inquisition is a dark mark in the history of the Catholic Church. But it was not the first inquisition, nor the last, as Cullen Murphy shows in this far-ranging, informed, and (dare one say?) witty account of its reach down to our own time in worldly affairs more than ecclesiastical ones' Margaret O'Brien Steinfels, Former Editor, *Commonweal*

'In his typically compelling style ... Murphy powerfully shows that the impulse to inquisition can quietly take root in any system – civil or religious – that orders our lives' *Publisher's Weekly*

'There will never be a finer example of erudition, worn lightly and wittily, than this book. As he did in *Are We Rome?*, Cullen Murphy manages to instruct, surprise, charm, and amuse in his history of ancient matters deftly connected to the present' James Fallows, National Correspondent, *Atlantic Monthly*

'Cullen Murphy's account of the Inquisition is a dark but riveting tale, told with luminous grace. The Inquisition, he shows us, represents more than a historical episode of religious persecution. The drive to root out heresy and sin, once and for all, is emblematic of the modern age and a persisting danger in our time' Michael J. Sandel, author of *Justice: What's The Right Thing To Do?*

'Entertaining, lively chronicle of the Inquisition, touching on a wide variety of issues across the centuries' *Kirkus Reviews*

Cullen Murphy is *Vanity Fair*'s editor at large and the author of *Are We Rome?* and *The Word According to Eve*. He was previously managing editor of *The Atlantic Monthly*.

For A.M.T

CONTENTS

GOD'S JURY

STANDARD OPERATING PROCEDURE

The Paper Trail

No one goes in and nothing comes out.

—A VATICAN ARCHIVIST, 1877

Theology, sir, is a fortress; no crack
in a fortress may be accounted small.

—REVEREND HALE, *THE CRUCIBLE*, 1953

The Palace

ON A HOT FALL day in Rome not long ago, I crossed the vast expanse of St. Peter's Square, paused momentarily in the shade beneath a curving flank of Bernini's colonnade, and continued a little way beyond to a Swiss Guard standing impassively at a wrought-iron gate, the Porta Cavalleggeri. He examined my credentials, handed them back, and saluted smartly. I hadn't expected the grand gesture, and almost returned the salute instinctively, but then realized it was intended for a cardinal waddling into the Vatican from behind me.

Just inside the gate, at Piazza del Sant'Uffizio 11, stands a Renaissance palazzo with the ruddy ocher-and-cream complexion of so many buildings in the city. This is the headquarters of the Congregation for the Doctrine of the Faith, whose job, in the words of the Apostolic Constitution, *Pastor bonus*, promulgated in 1988 by Pope John Paul II, is "to promote and safeguard the doctrine on faith and morals throughout the Catholic world." *Pastor bonus* goes on: "For this reason, everything which in any way touches such matter falls within its competence." It is an expansive charge. The CDF is one of nine Vatican congregations that together make up the administrative apparatus of the Holy See, but it dominates all the others. Every significant document or decision emanating from anywhere inside the Vatican must get a sign-off from the CDF.

The Congregation also generates plenty of rulings of its own. The Vatican's pronouncements during the past decade in opposition to cloning and same-sex marriage originated in the CDF. So did the directive ordering Catholic parishes not to give the names of past or present congregants to the Genealogical Society of Utah, a move that reflects the Vatican's "grave reservations" about the Mormon practice of posthumous baptism. The declaration *Dominus Jesus,* issued in 2000, which reiterated that the Catholic Church is the only true church of Christ and the only assured means of salvation, is a CDF document. Because the Congregation is responsible for clerical discipline, its actions — and inactions — are central to the pedophilia scandals that have shaken the Catholic Church. For more than two decades, the Congregation for the Doctrine of the Faith was headed by Cardinal Josef Ratzinger, now Pope Benedict XVI, who during his long reign as prefect was known as the enforcer and sometimes as the *Panzerkardinal* — bane of liberals, scourge of dissidents, and bulwark of orthodoxy narrowly construed. The Congregation has been around for a very long time, although until the Second Vatican Council it was called something else: the Congregation of the Holy Office. From the lips of old Vatican hands and Church functionaries everywhere, one still hears shorthand references to "the Holy Office," much as one hears "Whitehall," "Foggy Bottom," or "the Kremlin."

But before the Congregation became the Holy Office, it went by yet another name: as late as 1908, it was known as the Sacred Congregation of the Holy Roman and Universal Inquisition. Lenny Bruce once joked that there was only one "*the* Church." The Sacred Congregation of the Universal Inquisition was the headquarters of *the* Inquisition — the centuries-long effort by the Church to deal with its perceived enemies, within and without, by whatever means necessary, including some very brutal ones. For understandable reasons, no one at the Vatican these days refers to the Congregation as "the Inquisition" except ironically. The members of the papal curia are famously tone-deaf when it comes to public relations — these are men who in recent years have invited a Holocaust-denying bishop to return to the Church, have tried to persuade Africans that the use of condoms will make the AIDS crisis worse, and have told the indigenous peoples of Latin America that their religious beliefs are "a step backward" — but even the curia came to appreciate that the term had outlived its usefulness, although it took a few centuries.

It's easy to change a name, not so easy to engage in genetic engineering (which the Church would not encourage in any case). The CDF grew organically out of the Inquisition, and the modern office cannot escape the imprint. Ratzinger, when he was still a cardinal, was sometimes referred to as the grand inquisitor. New York's John Cardinal O'Connor once introduced the visiting Ratzinger that way from a pulpit in Manhattan — a not entirely successful way to break the ice. The epithet may have originated in "the fevered minds of some progressive Catholics," as a Ratzinger fan site on the Web explains, but it became widespread nonetheless. (In response to a Frequently Asked Question, the same site offers: "Good grief. *No, Virginia, Cardinal Ratzinger was not a Nazi.*")

The palazzo that today houses the Congregation was originally built to lodge the Inquisition when the papacy, in 1542, amid the onslaught of Protestantism and other forms of heresy, decided that the Church's intermittent and far-flung inquisitorial investigations, which had commenced during the Middle Ages, needed to be brought under some sort of centralized control — a spiritual Department of Homeland Security, as it were. Pope Paul III considered this task so urgent that for several years construction on the basilica of St. Peter's was suspended and the laborers diverted, so that work could be completed on the palace of the Inquisition. At one time the palazzo held not only clerical offices but also prison cells. Giordano Bruno, the philosopher and cosmologist, was confined for a period in this building, before being burned at the stake in Rome's Campo dei Fiori, in 1600.

When I first set foot in the palazzo, a decade ago, it was somewhat shabby and ramshackle, like so much of Rome and, indeed, like more of the Vatican than one might imagine. Outside, Vespas tilted against kickstands. In a hallway beyond the courtyard, a hand-lettered sign pointed the way to an espresso machine. A telephone on the wall dated to the 1950s. Here and there, paint flaked from ceilings and furniture. But the Congregation has a Web site now, and e-mail, and a message from Piazza del Sant'Uffizio 11 can still fray nerves in theology departments and diocesan chanceries around the world.

The Congregation for the Doctrine of the Faith inherited more than the Inquisition's institutional DNA and its place on the organizational charts. It also inherited much of the paper trail. The bulk of the Vatican's records are part of the so-called Archivio Segreto, and for the most part are stored in a vast underground bunker below a former observatory. (*Segreto*, though translated as "secret," carries the connotation "private" or "personal" rather than "classified.") But the Vatican's holdings are so great — the indexes alone fill 35,000 volumes — that many records must be squirreled away elsewhere. The Inquisition records are kept mainly in the Palazzo del Sant'Uffizio itself, and for four and a half centuries — up until 1998 — that archive was closed to outsiders.

At the time of my first visit, the Inquisition archive — officially, the Archivio della Congregazione per la Dottrina della Fede — spilled from room to room and floor to floor in the palazzo's western wing, filling about twenty rooms in all. It was under twenty-four-hour papal surveillance, watched over by a marble bust of Pius XII, a stern and enigmatic pontiff and now a candidate for sainthood, despite his troubling record in the face of the Holocaust. Pius was assisted in his duties by the sixteenth-century cardinal-inquisitor and papal censor Robert Bellarmine, whose portrait dominated a nearby wall, larger in oil than he was in life. The rooms were bathed in a soft yellow light. A spiral staircase connected upper and lower levels. Dark bookshelves stood in tight rows, sagging under thick bundles of documents. Many were tied up with string in vellum wrappers, like so much laundry. Others were bound as books. The spines displayed Latin notations in an elegant antique hand. Some indicated subject matter: "*De Spiritismo,*" "*De Hypnotismo,*" "*De Magnetismo Animale.*" Most were something else entirely. They contained the records of individual cases and also the minutes of the Inquisition's thrice-weekly meetings going back half a millennium. The meetings were held on Tuesdays, Thursdays, and Saturdays, and the pope himself presided once a week.

The cataloguing is by modern standards haphazard, even chaotic, reflecting centuries of handling and the peculiar organizational psychology of the Holy See. As one scholar has noted, the Vatican archives were arranged in a way that made sense for the curia, not for the convenience of modern historians. Pull down a bundle and you may stumble on internal deliberations over the censorship of René Descartes. Pull down another and you may discover some Renaissance cardinal-inquisitor's personal papers: the original handwritten records of all his investigations, chronologically arranged; a bureaucratic autobiography — he was proud of what he had achieved — with reflective comments scrawled in the margins; and here and there a small black cross indicating that a sentence had been duly carried out. Pull down a third bundle and you may find an account of a routine meeting, the sudden insertion here and there of several black dots by the notary indicating that the inquisitors had gone into executive session and the notary had been dismissed from the room — a more reliable procedure than the modern practice, employed by intelligence and law-enforcement agencies, of "redacting" a sensitive document with heavy black bars. No court order or Freedom of Information Act can unlock what the black dots conceal.

The atmosphere in the reading room is one of warmth and stillness. Hints of slowly crumbling leather hang in the air. A few scholars sit at tables. No one talks: *silentio* is the explicit rule. Espresso must be left outside. Smoking is prohibited. The physical experience is that afforded by any ancient library, enfolding and reassuring — which serves only to heighten a sense of psychic disconnection. When the Archivio was first opened, a Vatican official, Cardinal Achille Silvestrini, expressed the hope that it might contain "some pleasant surprises." But the record preserved on the millions of pages in these rooms is mainly grim: a record of lives disrupted and sometimes summarily put to an end; of ideas called into question and often suppressed; of voices silenced, temporarily or forever; of blind bureaucratic inertia harnessed to moral certainty and to earthly and spiritual power. It is a record of actions taken in the name of religion, though the implications go beyond religion.

Any archive is a repository of what some sliver of civilization has wrought, for good or ill. This one is no exception. The Archivio may owe its existence to the Inquisition, but it helps explain the world that exists today. In our imaginations, we offhandedly associate the term "inquisition" with the term "Dark Ages." But consider what an inquisition — any inquisition — really is: a set of disciplinary procedures targeting specific groups, codified in law, organized systematically, enforced by surveillance, exemplified by severity, sustained over time, backed by institutional power, and justified by a vision of the one true path. Considered that way, the Inquisition is more accurately viewed not as a relic but as a harbinger.

A 700-Year Trial

Say what you will about the Inquisition, but it was an unequivocal success in one respect: everyone knows its name. And everyone knows at least enough to throw its name around casually, to summon the Inquisition as a metaphor, to exploit it for entertainment, to wield it in argument as a quiet stiletto or a clumsy bludgeon.

"No one expects the Spanish Inquisition," cries Monty Python's Michael Palin, bursting into a room in a cardinal's robes. In the movie *History of the World: Part 1,* the Inquisition becomes a showstopping Mel Brooks dance number: "The Inquisition (What a show!). / The Inquisition (Here we go!)." You could compile a substantial monograph on just the Inquisition's contribution to the field of humor. An apt epigraph for it would be Woody Allen's observation that "Comedy is tragedy plus time."

On ABC's *Good Morning America,* the political commentator Cokie Roberts was asked about government officials who had become the focus of special investigations: "Cokie, you talk to these people a lot. Do they feel like they're targets of the Inquisition?" On Fox News, the anchorman Brit Hume described media scrutiny of Sarah Palin's record in Alaska as "the full Inquisition treatment." In *Fortune,* a column about captains of finance who were summoned to testify on Capitol Hill carried the title "The Inquisition Convenes in Washington."

Sometimes the references become more specific. In an interview with Kenneth Starr, whose investigations of President Bill Clinton's affair with Monica Lewinsky resulted in the exhaustive *Starr Report,* Diane Sawyer began by noting that Starr had been "compared to Saddam Hussein, Nero, to Torquemada, who was the head of the Inquisition." Starr replied, "I had to learn who Torquemada was. Yeah . . . that was a new one to me." Gore Vidal already knew, of course. Looking back on his life in an interview, the aging and acerbic writer attacked various members of the Kennedy family, as he had often done, singling out Bobby as "a phony, a little Torquemada." The columnist Taki Theodoracopulos, criticizing the tactics of Carla Del Ponte, the chief prosecutor of the International Criminal Tribunal for the former Yugoslavia, raised the specter of defendants' "being railroaded by a Swiss woman who thinks she's Torquemada, and looks like him to boot." The comparisons are often flip — but just as often deadly serious. Maureen Dowd, writing about the sex-abuse scandal that reaches to the highest levels of the Church, headlined a column "Should There Be an Inquisition for the Pope?"

No series of events in recent times has produced more invocations of the Inquisition than the prosecution of the war on terror since September 11, 2001. The enactment of tough new legal instruments, the use of extralegal surveillance, the detention without trial of suspected enemies, the reliance on torture in interrogations, the pervading atmosphere of religious suspicion: taken together, these developments help account for the fact that a Google search of "inquisition" today yields upward of eight million entries.

For all its familiarity as a reference point, the real Inquisition remains very little known. Few people can relate even a handful of basic historical facts about it. When did it start, and why? How long did it last? What countries did it affect? How was it conducted? What consequences did it have? How did it end? Does it, in various guises, reside with us still? And what, in the end, do we even mean by that word "it"? At best, common knowledge encompasses not much more than this: the Inquisition took place in the distant past, promoted persecution of the Jews, and notably employed torture and burning at the stake. All true enough, but just a small portion of the story.

Though its influence waxed and waned, the Inquisition continued in one form or another for more than seven hundred years. It

8

touched on episodes as diverse as the suppression of the Knights Templar and the siege of the heretic fortress at Montségur. It intervened in the lives of Galileo and Graham Greene. Associated most commonly with the persecution of the Jews, the Inquisition was in fact far more wide-ranging in its targets, and initially was not much concerned with Jews at all. Indeed, the Inquisition's specific warrant was to enforce discipline among members of the Church, not those outside it: people who had fallen into error, who had embraced heretical movements, or who had in some other way loosened the bonds of faith.

In the year 1231 Pope Gregory IX appointed the first "inquisitors of heretical depravity" to serve as explicit papal agents. Thus began what is called the Medieval Inquisition, which was launched to deal with the menace posed to the Church by Christian heretics, notably the Cathars of southern France. The newly established Dominican Order, whose priests and nuns are identifiable to this day by their white habits, was instrumental in combating the Cathar heresy. Its founder, Dominic Guzmán, is the man celebrated in the 1963 song "Dominique," by the Singing Nun (said to be the only Belgian song ever to hit No. 1 on the American charts). The inquisitors solicited denunciations and, as their name implies, conducted interrogations. Their efforts were highly localized — there was no central command. The inquisitors were aided in their work by the papal bull *Ad extirpanda*, promulgated in 1252, which justified and encouraged the use of torture, wielding philosophical arguments that have never wanted for advocates and that would eventually echo in the White House and the Justice Department. Within a century, the work of the Medieval Inquisition was largely done. One modern writer, reflecting on what makes inquisitions come to an end, calls attention to a simple reason: an eventual shortage of combustible material. The Dominicans were nothing if not thorough. As a Catholic growing up with many Jesuit friends, I remember hearing a comment about the difference between Dominicans and Jesuits: Both orders were created to fight the Church's enemies — Cathars in the one case, Protestants in the other. The difference: Have you ever met a Cathar?

A second chapter, the Spanish Inquisition, commenced in the late fifteenth century. As King Ferdinand of Aragon and Queen Isabella of Castile consolidated their rule, the Inquisition in a recently unified Spain pursued its targets independent of Rome. It was effectively an arm of the government, and the monarchs appointed its personnel. The Spanish Inquisition was directed primarily at Jews who had converted to Christianity and whose conversions were suspect — in other words, who were thought to be (or said to be) secretly "judaizing," or reverting to Judaism. It also focused its efforts on the many Christianized Muslims, who might likewise be reverting to the faith of their heritage. The first inquisitor general in Spain, Tomás de Torquemada, a Dominican monk, embarked on a career that made his name synonymous with the Inquisition as a whole, sending some 2,000 people to be burned at the stake within a matter of years. The Inquisition in Spain would lead to a cataclysm: the expulsion, in 1492, of unconverted Jews from the kingdom.

Because the domains of the Spanish sovereigns eventually extended to Asia and America, the Inquisition traveled far beyond Iberia. It was active in areas of what is now the United States — New Mexico, for instance. In Santa Fe, religious disputes in which the Inquisition played a role led to executions outside the Palace of the Governors, on the plaza, within sight of today's boutique restaurants and upscale art galleries. From Spain the Inquisition spread to Portugal and thence to the Portuguese Empire. It could be found operating in Brazil and India, and in places between and beyond.

The Spanish Inquisition ended at different times in different places. It survived in Mexico until 1820, when independence from Spain was just a few months away, and in Spain itself until 1834, when a royal decree abolished it once and for all. It conducted its last execution in 1826 — the victim was a Spanish schoolmaster named Cayetano Ripoll, who had been convicted of heresy. (He was hanged rather than burned at the stake.) In some ultraconservative Catholic precincts there are those who contemplate the record of the Spanish Inquisition with at most a shrug: Yes, the methods were perhaps too enthusiastic — but it was a different time. Let's not be anachronistic. And don't forget the threat to the Church! A group of Catholic clerics and activist laypeople are today pressing to have Queen Isabella declared a saint.

The third but not quite final chapter of the Inquisition, the so-called Roman Inquisition, began in the sixteenth century with the advent of the Reformation. This is the inquisition for which the palazzo was built. The main focus of the Roman Inquisition was Protestantism, but it did not spare Jews, homosexuals, people accused of practicing witchcraft, and certain kinds of quirky or annoying freethinkers and gadflies who might today be called "public intellectuals." With the Roman Inquisition, the inquisitorial process was for the first time lodged in an organ of state under direct papal supervision. It was a centralized bureaucracy overseen by a papal inquisitor general, whose job was often a stepping-stone to the papacy itself. In the latter half of the sixteenth century, no fewer than three grand inquisitors went on to become pope. The inquisitorial bureaucracy was a fertile recruiting ground for bishops and cardinals. It populated the curia the way the security services now staff the Kremlin. The operations of the Sacred Congregation of the Universal Inquisition were entwined with those of the Congregation of the Index, which oversaw censorship efforts — this at a time when the diffusion of the printing press had made ideas more dangerous, and censorship more difficult, than ever before. It was the Roman Inquisition that put Galileo on trial for his arguments about the heavens. In some ways it behaved like a modern institution — its rhythms and procedures, and even its inanities, will be recognizable to anyone with experience of a large bureaucracy. But the chief target was modernity itself, and the ideas and cast of mind that underlay it.

In 1870, the unification of Italy brought about the demise of the

Papal States, the domains where the pope ruled as a temporal monarch. Except for matters of purely internal Church discipline, which carry no threat of secular penalty or physical harm but which can stifle intellectual life and dissent all the same, the Roman Inquisition was at an end. It would take almost sixty years for the pope's dominion over the tiny walled 108-acre rump state of Vatican City to be recognized by Italy, in a concordat signed by Benito Mussolini and Pope Pius XI. By then, the Congregation of the Inquisition had disappeared into the organizational charts of the Roman curia, though as one historian observes, "No death certificate has ever been issued." The Congregation for the Doctrine of the Faith preserves the processes and functions of the Roman Inquisition in milder form. Until the 1960s, it remained in the business of censoring and banning books, though few took heed, and some of those who did pay attention did so for the wrong reasons. During my Catholic childhood, the relegation of a book to the Papal Index seemed to serve mainly as an inducement (though not always a reliable one, as those who tried reading Hobbes or Pascal under the covers with a flashlight will have discovered). Following the practice of the old Inquisition, the CDF still holds regular weekly meetings. It is to the Congregation that bishops, papal envoys, and others send complaints about teaching and theology — the modern-day analogue of medieval denunciations, though the official term is not "denunciation" but "delation," as if to suggest referral for a medical procedure. I have sometimes found myself conflating the CDF with the CDC — the Centers for Disease Control. There is a certain parallel.

The Inquisition, plainly, is not what it was. And yet in some ways it is as robust as ever. The historian Edward Peters has noted that the long decline of the actual Inquisition over the centuries was paralleled by the rise of a metaphorical Inquisition that lives on in folklore and popular culture, in works of art and literature, in comedy and polemic. Partly this was a response to, even a mythologizing of, a receding past — a coming to terms with what the Church had done, as perceived through many lenses. Partly it was a response to an evolving present. The world may have been rushing toward whatever we mean by "modernity," but the methods and mind-set of the Inquisition were clearly not confined to the Church. They had taken on lives of their own and could be found in the institutions of the secular world. Arthur Koestler set his inquisitorial novel, *Darkness at Noon,* in a simulacrum of Stalin's Russia, at the height of the purges in the 1930s. In the late 1940s, Justice Robert H. Jackson, the chief American prosecutor at Nuremberg, cited the Inquisition in his summation at the close of the trial of major Nazi war criminals. In the 1950s, Arthur Miller evoked the witch hunts of colonial Massachusetts in his play *The Crucible,* a parable of the McCarthy era. Other writers — Aldous Huxley, Ray Bradbury, George Orwell — looked ahead to imagined societies, just over the horizon, where inquisitions of some kind had won control. To conduct surveillance, to impose belief, to censor, to manipulate, to punish people who think differently from those in power: in the modern world the inquisitorial dynamic was more in evidence than ever, and enabled by ever more powerful instruments.

Dostoyevsky's tale "The Grand Inquisitor," in *The Brothers Karamazov,* is as much a secular parable as a theological one — it is about the corruption of any faith. Dostoyevsky wrestled with religious questions all his life. He also suffered censorship and imprisonment at the hands of the czarist state. On one occasion he endured the trauma of what turned out to be a mock execution. In "The Grand Inquisitor," Jesus returns to the living world — to Seville, "in the most horrible time of the Inquisition" — and is brought before the leading cleric for interrogation. Jesus himself never speaks, but the Grand Inquisitor delivers a scathing indictment, condemning Jesus for the gift of moral freedom, which mankind can neither comprehend nor wisely use. But no matter. The Church understands full well the implication — understands that moral freedom leads only to trouble — and so has taken steps to curb it. The Grand Inquisitor tells Jesus, "We have corrected your deed. . . . And mankind rejoiced that they were once more led like sheep." And he asks, "Why have you come to hinder us now?"

In the end, Jesus makes no answer, save to kiss the old man on the lips. The Grand Inquisitor sets him free, but with this injunction: "Go, and do not come again."

Into the Archives

The speed limit for motor vehicles inside Vatican City is 20 miles an hour. The forward motion of the curial bureaucracy is slower, as you'd expect with gerontocrats at the wheel. The Holy See takes its time. In 1979, the historian Carlo Ginzburg wrote a letter to Karol Wojtyla, who had recently been installed as Pope John Paul II. Ginzburg, who is Jewish, had firsthand experience of hatred and persecution. His father, Leone, was an anti-fascist agitator who was beaten to death by the Nazis, and young Carlo spent the war in hiding with his non-Jewish maternal grandmother, under the name Carlo Tanzi. In his letter, Ginzburg petitioned the pope to open the Archivio to scholars. Ginzburg no longer has a copy of what he sent — it is probably under seal in the archives somewhere — but he remembers that it began like this: *"Chi le scrivo e uno storico ebreo, ateo, che ha lavorato per molti anni sui documenti dell'Inquisizione"* — "The writer of the present letter is a Jewish historian, an atheist, who has been working for many years on inquisitorial papers."

He heard nothing for nearly twenty years, until, in 1998, he received a letter from Ratzinger inviting him to the opening of the Archivio. Ah, bad luck: he had a conflict, Ginzburg wrote back. Then came a phone call from a monsignor at the Vatican. Ginzburg again demurred. "That's a pity," said the monsignor, "because your letter played a role in the opening of the Sant'Uffizio archive." "Which letter?" was Ginzburg's reaction. The monsignor said, "Your letter to the pope." "What a memory!" Ginzburg replied. He found a way to change his plans.

The Archivio was not opened fully — scholars could examine documents only up to the death of Pope Leo XIII, in 1903. ("Naturally," said a Vatican official, without elaboration.) But it was a start. "We know all the sins of the Church," Cardinal Ratzinger said in making the announcement, "and I hope more will not be added to them."

In the academic and religious worlds, the partial opening of the Archivio was a very big deal. It was marked in Rome by two conclaves of Inquisition scholars. Ratzinger was present at the first of them, and the pope himself welcomed participants at the second. The ravages of Parkinson's disease hampered John Paul's speech, and those who heard him didn't quite know what he had said until a transcript was made available the next day. Among other things, John Paul asked the historians not to "overstep the boundaries of their discipline and give an ethical verdict" on the Church's behavior. Two years later, on Ash Wednesday 2000, the pope led a penitential procession through the streets of Rome to apologize for errors and misdeeds of the past — including, prominently, the Inquisition. Pointedly, the apology referred to deeds done by followers of the Church rather than by the Church itself.

The man who today presides over the Archivio is Monsignor Alejandro Cifres Giménez, fifty-one, a diminutive Spaniard from Valencia (the city where, as it happens, the Spanish Inquisition's last execution took place). Cifres is mild-mannered, genial, and competent. He sometimes displays a dry sense of humor. When I asked him whether the magazine I work for was being considered for papal condemnation, he said, "Not yet." He listens to country-and-western music, has a CD player in his car, and once revealed that among his favorite movies is *Happy, Texas,* a comedy about convicts on the lam who disguise themselves as gay beauty-pageant coaches, which would probably have earned two thumbs down from the Papal Index. Cifres is not a historian. He is by training a theologian, and also a certified archivist and paleographer. He was brought to the Archivio to be an administrator, his superiors recognizing that the superannuated clerics who had long overseen the Inquisition's documents were not what an open archive demanded. Cifres obeyed the orders of his bishop and came to work at the Congregation, and directly for Josef Ratzinger. It was Cifres who made the call to Ginzburg.

The first time I met him, he led the way down a hall to his office near the stacks. I dawdled a little, to read the writing on the document boxes. The Archivio consists essentially of two parts. One is the historical archive, the Stanza Storica, which contains the old files of the Congregations of the Inquisition, the Holy Office, and the Index. But the Congregation is also a living administrative entity — it does Church business and generates paperwork every day, which becomes part of the active archive. A lot of that paperwork — about theological issues, about problems with the clergy — is highly sensitive. Theologians are still called to Rome, and are disciplined or silenced, sometimes after procedures akin to trials. Walking down the hall, I paused at a few shelves of modern files. Msgr. Cifres came back, took me by the elbow, and led me along. When I asked him what the files pertained to, he replied, "How do you say? Defrockings?" On that visit, I didn't see as many defrocking files as I had imagined there would be, given the immensity of the pedophilia scandals. The shelves are surely groaning now.

Sitting behind his desk, in Roman collar and black, short-sleeved clerical shirt, Cifres tried to convey a sense of how complicated his position is. To begin with, money is tight. In earlier times, the Inquisition could rely on a certain amount of revenue from confiscations (though not nearly as much, historians say, as has sometimes been alleged). Confiscation, happily, is no longer an option. Cifres had created a Friends of the Inquisition Archives program — Tabularii Amicorum Consociato, to give it the official name — to raise money from private donations. He also charges a modest fee for use of the Archivio. He did not mention plans for a gift shop.

The filing system also presents challenges. There is a logic to it, but it is not a familiar logic. Nothing is classified according to any modern category, much less arranged alphabetically. What you need to know in order to find something is the bureaucratic structure and mental map of the Vatican itself — less technocratic Dewey decimal system than intricate "memory palace" of Matteo Ricci. Documents dealing with defrockings are in the Sacerdotal section. Documents dealing with apparitions, revelations, and other extraordinary phenomena are in the Disciplinary section. Documents dealing with censorship are in the Doctrinal section. A huge category under the Doctrinal rubric is called simply *Dubia* ("Doubts") — documents relating to intimate questions of faith as relayed by priests and bishops from around the world. Doubt occupies an oddly exalted status in Catholic theology. It's a state of mind experienced by everyone, but also an essential tool of philosophical inquiry: "doubting well" is a step toward truth, as Aristotle (and Aquinas) maintained. Theologians love to slice and dice. What kind of doubt have we here? Is it positive or negative? Speculative or practical? Simple or methodical? Real or fictitious? Distinguished careers have been built on a bedrock of doubt.

In practice, certainty has been more highly prized by the Church. Until 1920, a placard over the doorway to the Vatican Archives threatened excommunication for anyone entering without permission. The Vatican is committed, it now says, to free inquiry in the archives. Access to the historical files has gradually been expanded — scholars can now study materials dating up to the death of Pope Pius XI, in 1939. But you can't escape the reminders of censorship and other controversies. Wandering among the shelves in sections where the archival materials remain off-limits, I noticed rows of fat document boxes labeled "Küng," "Boff," "Lefebvre," "Greene." The urge to reach out and pull one down was almost irresistible. Hans Küng and Leonardo Boff are prominent Catholic theologians whose work has frequently been targeted by the Vatican. Marcel Lefebvre, a breakaway right-wing archbishop, was excommunicated in 1988 by Pope John Paul II. Graham Greene's work came under intense Vatican scrutiny in the 1940s and 1950s.

One day, among the stacks, I came across two polished wooden boxes, resembling old library card-catalogue drawers, with hinged wooden tops. The boxes rested one above the other on a wooden rack of Victorian vintage. The lower box was labeled "A–K," the upper one "L–Z." Inside each box, well-worn index cards ran its length, their upper edges velvety from use. I took one of the boxes down and flipped quickly through the cards, seeing citations for works by Sade, Sartre, Spinoza, and Swift, among hundreds of others.

"What's this?" I asked Msgr. Cifres, showing him the box. He took it from me, closed the top, and put it back on the rack. "That," he said, "is the Index of Forbidden Books — the very last one." I thought of the whispered horror from decades ago — the Papal Index! — and found it hard to imagine that it all came down to soiled cards in a shoebox. There is no longer a Congregation of the Index, once so closely associated with the Inquisition, and the much-feared Papal Index was discontinued in 1966. Its open coffin had rested briefly in my hands.

The Index was not, however, completely repudiated; the very document that abolished the Index also reaffirmed its "moral value." The CDF still looks closely at books and periodicals, and sometimes issues a *monitum,* or warning. The absence of an official Index does not mean the absence of things you should not read. Some will remember that although the Vatican has never taken an official position on the Harry Potter books, and certainly has not issued a *monitum,* Cardinal Ratzinger in 2003 raised an eyebrow in a private letter at the "subtle seductions" of the series. Ratzinger's comments came even before the release of *Harry Potter and the Order of the Phoenix,* the fifth volume, which introduced the character Dolores Umbridge, the High Inquisitor of Hogwarts. Umbridge is a skilled practitioner of thought control:

> Very well, Potter, I take your word for it this time, but be warned: The might of the Ministry stands behind me. All channels of communication in and out of this school are being monitored. A Floo Network Regulator is keeping watch over every fire in Hogwarts — except my own, of course. My Inquisitorial Squad is opening and reading all owl post entering and leaving the castle.

The Birth of the Modern

The opening of the Archivio at the Vatican is one more development in what has, during the past several decades, become a golden age of Inquisition scholarship. Until the appearance of Henry Charles Lea's magisterial *History of the Inquisition of the Middle Ages,* in the late nineteenth century, most writing about the Inquisition had consisted of bitter polemics by one side or another. Even Lea's work, though in many ways unrivaled, exudes an undisguised animus against the Catholic Church. Inquisition history will never be totally "decanonized" — that is, uncoupled from sectarian agendas — but it has come a long way. In recent decades, using materials newly available in repositories outside the Vatican, and now including those of the Holy See itself, historians throughout Europe and the Americas have produced hundreds of studies that, seen as a whole, sharply revise some traditional views of the Inquisition.

To begin with, the notion of "the Inquisition" as a monolithic force with a directed intelligence — "an eye that never slumbered," as the historian William H. Prescott once phrased it — is no longer tenable. Rather, it was an enterprise that varied in virulence and competence from place to place and era to era. "The Inquisition" remains a convenient shorthand term, and I'll continue to use it, but it should be understood as a collective noun. There were many inquisitions.

Another finding of modern research is that insofar as their procedures were concerned, Inquisition tribunals often proved more scrupulous and consistent than the various secular courts of the time. It probably used torture with less abandon than secular authorities did. Of course, the bar here is low, and in any case scrupulosity and consistency are no obstacle to cruelty or injustice. Nor is legality. What the writer Michael Kinsley observed of modern Washington applies just as comfortably to the Inquisition: "The real scandal isn't what's illegal; it's what's legal." Still, the Inquisition did adhere to certain standards and did allow accused persons certain rights.

Contemporary scholarship has also revised the casualty figures. Some older estimates of the number of people put to death by the Inquisition range to upwards of a million; the true figure may be closer to several tens of thousands — perhaps 2 percent of those who came before the Inquisition's tribunals for any reason. That said, arguments over body count quickly become pointless and distasteful. The former commandant of Auschwitz, Rudolf Hoess, presented with a copy of his confession, in which it was stated that he had "personally arranged the gassing of three million persons," took a fountain pen from a lawyer, crossed out "three million," wrote in "two million," and then signed the document. Whatever the number killed may be, the Inquisition levied penalties of some sort on hundreds of thousands of people, and the fear and shame instilled by any individual case, even a minor one, rippled outward to affect a wide social circle. This didactic effect, of course, was no small part of the purpose. Little wonder that the Inquisition has left such a deep psychological imprint.

But from between the lines the new scholarship has some larger lessons to offer. The Inquisition can be seen as something greater and more insidious than a sustained effort pursued over centuries by a single religious institution. The conspiracy-theory view of history—that the ills of the world have been spawned by the Masons, the Illuminati, the Trilateral Commission, Opus Dei, Skull and Bones, or Goldman Sachs—represents the easy way out. If only the source of evil were so simple to identify, so easy to confront. Shift perspective slightly—turn the object in the light—and you can see that the Inquisition was enabled by some of the broader forces that brought the modern world into existence, and that make inquisitions of various kinds a recurring and inescapable feature of modern life. Inquisitions advance hand-in-hand with civilization itself.

Why was there suddenly an Inquisition? Intolerance, hatred, and suspicion of "the other," often based on religious and ethnic differences, had always been with us. Throughout history, these realities had led to persecution and violence. But the ability to sustain a persecution—to give it staying power by giving it an institutional life—did not appear until the Middle Ages. Until then, the tools to stoke and manage those omnipresent embers of hatred did not exist. Once these capabilities do exist, inquisitions become a fact of life—standard operating procedure. They are not confined to religion; they are political as well. The targets can be large or small. An inquisition impulse can quietly take root in the very systems of government and civil society that order our lives.

The tools are these: There needs to be a system of law, and the means to administer it with a certain amount of uniformity. There needs to be a well-defined process for conducting interrogations and extracting information. Procedures must exist for record-keeping, and for retrieving information after records have been compiled and stored. An administrative mechanism—a bureaucracy—is required, along with a cadre of trained people to staff it. There must be an ability to send messages across significant distances—and also some capacity to restrict the communications of others. And there must be a source of power, to ensure enforcement.

The source of power can vary. From the outset, the religious aims of the Inquisition were enmeshed with the might of secular rulers.

The relationship was sometimes symbiotic and always complicated, and it changed over time. With the Medieval Inquisition, the Church sought to leverage secular power to achieve its ends (though the secular authorities had their own purposes in mind). The Spanish Inquisition threw this arrangement into reverse: the crown made the Inquisition an official component of the Spanish state. During the Roman Inquisition, the tribunal was controlled directly by the papacy, and within its own territories church and state were the exact same thing. (Outside the Papal States, the Inquisition operated on terms laid down by local governments.) The twentieth century would bring a new evolutionary stage: inquisitions that lay fully in the hands of the state and required no religious dimension at all.

Their Inquisition — and Ours

There's one more factor in the making of an Inquisition: the conviction that one is absolutely right. Cardinal Alfredo Ottaviani, the prefect of the Holy Office through most of the 1960s, adopted as his motto the Latin phrase *Semper idem* — "Always the same." The inquisitors — like their masters and their theological associates — shared an outlook of moral certainty. They believed that they enjoyed personal access to an unchanging truth. They accepted without doubt that God paid close attention to the affairs of human beings, and was active in the Inquisition's cause. This outlook was as unquestioned as modern-day belief in the laws of gravity or genetics. To be sure, as time went on, many inquisitors were functionaries and careerists — but the premise of the institution itself remained unchanged.

In a world of moral certainty, the unthinkable becomes permissible. The sanctity of private conscience was no longer deemed inviolate, and techniques for ensnaring the innocent in scenarios of scripted guilt became increasingly sophisticated and systemic. The title of an influential study of the Medieval Inquisition — *The Formation of a Persecuting Society* — gets across part of what occurred. One twentieth-century historian concludes, "The medieval inquisitors had perfected techniques by which the very fabric of reality could be altered." A Franciscan inquisitor once confided to King Philip IV of France, in the early fourteenth century, that if Saints Peter and Paul had appeared before his tribunal, he had no doubt that the techniques he employed would be able to secure their convictions. A Church apologist of the early 1400s, writing approvingly about the inquisitors, stated: "We persecuted the seeds of evil not only in men's deeds, but in their thoughts."

It all sounds very medieval, but it's not *merely* medieval. Scholars may debate whether there truly is such a thing as a "totalitarian" state, and what its essential characteristics are, but the desire to control the thoughts of others — joined to the conviction that history itself will ultimately render an approving judgment — underlies much of the sad narrative of the past one hundred years. Some phenomena loom with menace because they seem so alien. The Inquisition does so because it seems so familiar.

Looking at the Inquisition, one sees the West crossing a threshold from one kind of world into another. Persecution acquired a modern platform — the advantages afforded by a growing web of standardized law, communications, administrative oversight, and controlled mechanisms of force. It was run not merely by warriors but by an educated elite; not merely by thugs but by skilled professionals. And in its higher dimensions it was animated not by greed or hope of gain or love of power, though these were never absent, but by the fervent conviction that all must subscribe to some ultimate truth.

Every subsequent outbreak of persecution, whether political or religious, has been abetted by these same forces. They ensure that the basic trajectory of repression will always look remarkably the same. They suggest why persecution is so difficult to stop. And they help explain why the Inquisition template has translated so easily from the religious sphere into the world of secular governments and secular ideologies, where for more than a century it has been primarily lodged.

I began to explore the Inquisition as one who happens to be both a Catholic and an American. I'm no less aware of the sins and failures of church and country than I am of the capacity of church and country to inspire and do good. I am also aware that for all the fine recent scholarship, most of the writing about the Inquisition over the centuries has been less than neutral. Studies of the Inquisition have grown out of the agendas and concerns — whether acknowledged or not — of those doing the writing. To this, and without the inducement of strappado or rack, I plead guilty. I ventured into the world of the Inquisition and its offspring in the 1990s, motivated at first by the Vatican's attempts to silence or censor a significant number of prominent theologians, some of whom I had come to know. There was also a broader context. Many friends and colleagues were experts on the former Soviet Union, and had engaged in long-running debates over the inherent nature and internal mechanisms of that repressive regime. At the same time, America's political and legal culture seemed to be turning increasingly prosecutorial, increasingly poisonous — this at the end of a century that had seen Red Scares in the 1920s, the internment of Japanese Americans in the 1940s, full-blown McCarthyism in the 1950s, and the government's pursuit of "subversives" and activists of various stripes in the 1960s. After 9/11, the specter of religious warfare came once again to the fore. So did debates over interrogation and torture, and over domestic surveillance in the name of national security. The accelerating inroads of the Internet, meanwhile, gave rise to fundamental questions about censorship, disinformation, and the meaning of truth.

The advent of the Inquisition offers a lens. Through it lies the world we inhabit now, one in which privacy and freedom of conscience are pitted against forces that would contain them. This is a central contest of the modern era and of the centuries that lie ahead. The issues posed by the Inquisition enfold the world we call our own.

2

A STAKE IN THE GROUND

The Medieval Inquisition

> The heretics have lain concealed for a long time,
> scuttling about in hiding like crabs.
>
> —POPE GREGORY IX, 1231

> You, so and so, of such a place, as is stated
> in your confession, did this and this.
>
> —BERNARD GUI, MANUAL FOR INQUISITORS, C. 1323

The Head of the Dragon

THE ROADS OF southwestern France, in the shadow of the Pyrenees, wind among deep valleys and steep gorges. They climb and descend along hairpin turns. Timeless rivers and the ancient paths of shepherds define the best routes still. Silhouetted against the sky, moldering piles of stone crown serrated crags, the remnants of medieval castles—Quéribus, Termes, Aguilar, Puilaurens, Lastours. They occupy the sites of the fortified *castra* where heretics once took refuge, and whose protection from the Inquisition and its allies proved all too temporary.

The most dramatic of these promontories comes into view on the road south from Fougax-et-Barrineuf, soon after it veers off to follow the Ruisseau de St. Nicholas. A sugarloaf singularity looms ahead, the slopes rocky and sheer until gentled slightly at the base by erosion. This kind of geologic formation is known as a pog, from the local word for "peak," and this particular one is referred to by people in the area simply as "le pog." The summit, 4,000 feet above sea level, is capped by a pentagonal fortress, which from below appears inaccessible. But a difficult track picks its way upward through the brambles and the rubble. From the top the view opens out to high mountains in the south, and the valley of the Aude in the north. It was an April afternoon when I made the climb with a friend, and on the surrounding foothills the grass was freshly green. Snow survived in the shelter of swales. The sound of wind was strong and constant — the kind of sound used in documentaries to evoke a sense of mystery and antiquity.

The promontory is Montségur, and in 1244 it became a focal point in the clash between two unyielding systems of religious belief. One was the Christian heresy known as Catharism, which had put down deep roots in this corner of Europe. The Cathars were dualists, believing that a God who was good could not be responsible for the manifest evil in the world, which must therefore have a separate source of creation. In one form or another this outlook is among the oldest and most durable heresies in Christendom, arising as it does from a conundrum central to any belief system that posits a beneficent deity. Earthquake, famine, tsunami, disease — headlines daily nurture the dualist in every heart. Augustine, a Church father in the waning days of Rome, had spent the first part of his life as a dualist and the second part making up for the first. Manicheans, Gnostics, Paulicians, Bogomils — dualistic thinking unites them all.

Very little survives of Cathar thinking from Cathar pens — their documents were systematically destroyed by their enemies. But like other dualists, the Cathars believed that the earthly world had been brought to life by the forces of darkness, and that only the world of the spirit was reliably pure. (Their name may come from the Greek *cathari,* meaning "pure ones," though another derivation, put about by foes, involves the Latin *cattus,* for "cat," whose hind parts the Cathars were alleged to kiss.) The most zealous adherents, who had received a sacrament called the *consolamentum,* and were known as *perfecti* or *parfaits,* were ascetic vegetarians who abstained from sexual relations. Ordinary Cathars, known as *credentes,* or "believers," could live their lives as other people did, saving the *consolamentum* for the deathbed. The Cathars saw licentious and authoritarian local priests as hypocrites; they regarded the Catholic Church as the Great Beast, the Whore of Babylon.

The Church, of course, was the other system involved in this clash of belief. It is far more of a global institution today than it was in the thirteenth century, when the sway of the "universal" Church was confined to Western Europe. It was hemmed in by the sea to the north and west, by Islam to the south, and by Orthodox Christianity to the east. Catharism, also known as the Albigensian heresy (the name comes from the town of Albi, where many heretics could be found), posed a grave internal threat, and indeed represented one of the most serious threats of any kind since the days of persecution by the pagan emperors of Rome. A succession of popes, beginning in the late twelfth century, had determined to root it out. They tried persuasion, sending priests among the heretics to gather the wayward sheep. When that failed, they took up arms — but even brute force had its limitations. Ultimately, the Cathar heresy led the Church to establish a regime of interrogation and punishment that would come to be known as the Inquisition.

This was a clash in which the contending parties, heretic and orthodox, shared certain mental underpinnings. They believed without question in the reality of their God. They believed in sin, believed in hell, believed in redemption. And with God on one's side, there was no basis for compromise.

Montségur saw little compromise. In the spring of 1243, several hundred Cathars — *perfecti* and ordinary believers — took refuge in the fortress, which had been a stronghold since Roman times and probably much earlier. The name Montségur means "safe mountain." The Cathars had been routed from one place after another, and chose the summit for a last stand. The forces of the Church, in the form of an army provided by the king of France, who had his own motives for intervening, put the fortress under siege. For ten months, the Cathars held out, a community of armed men and their families in this Masada of heretics, a dense village of huts clustered tightly against the ramparts. They were sustained by rumors that the Holy Roman Emperor, the pope's bitter enemy, would come to the rescue. He never did.

The hopelessness of their situation became plain only after the king's forces scaled a bluff and erected catapults. Spend some time exploring the mountainside, and you may come across rounded stone projectiles the size of cannonballs in the woods. During the last days, it is said, some of the defenders slipped away with a considerable treasure, to sustain Cathar activities elsewhere. If they did, the treasure has never been found, though the romantic quest continues to animate casual enthusiasts and the occasional novelist. (Inevitably, Nazis figure in the stories.)

Some intimate details are known of life at Montségur as the end approached, because priests of the Inquisition questioned the survivors at length and then wrote everything down. The inquisitors were mainly interested in heresy, and in rolling up Cathar networks farther afield, not in writing an enduring work of social history. Even so, a gripping picture emerges. The Church authorities offered lenient terms to those who would abjure their beliefs. The Cathar *perfecti* refused to do so: as they saw it, the salvation of their souls was at stake. On condition that their followers be spared, the *perfecti* and those closest to them agreed to surrender themselves to execution after a two-week truce. They spent the two weeks in prayer and fasting, and gave away their meager possessions. Specific moments, recorded by the inquisitors, are haunting in their banality. One *perfectus* made a gift to a friend of oil, salt, pepper, wax, and some green cloth. When the truce was over, the Cathars climbed down from the fortress to a slanting field on the slopes. Many had newly accepted the *consolamentum*. More than two hundred people were burned on the spot, mounting ladders to share a single pyre. As the fires smoldered, a message was sent to the pope: "We have crushed the head of the dragon."

A stone marker indicates where the pyre stood. For more than three quarters of a millennium the field has been known in Occitan, the local language, as the *prat dels crematz*—the "field of the burned."

"Let God Sort Them Out"

Travel around Languedoc and the Pyrenees today, and you might think the Cathars had actually won. As in any self-respecting region of Europe, there is a secessionist movement afoot, though its gains are cultural (and gastronomic) rather than political. The flag of Languedoc—the cross of Toulouse, in gold, against a red background—flies everywhere, and the better bookstores display a prominent selection of works relating somehow to the Cathars (and including *The Da Vinci Code*). The Cathar moment in local history has echoes of Camelot and Brigadoon, with a dash of Thermopylae and the Alamo. On the roadways, tasteful signs in brown announce that you are entering Pays Cathare—"Cathar Country"—and hikers can tramp along a rugged 150-mile Cathar Trail. Occitan, closely related to neighboring Catalan, was the language of the troubadors and of courtly love. The name Occitan, like the name Languedoc, derives from *oc*, the Occitan word for "yes." The language is now enjoying a mild resurgence: street names in the region are sometimes given in French and Occitan, and activists are busily inventing homegrown

Occitan terminology for the twenty-first century — *Oeb* site instead of Web site, for instance. Toulouse, the high-tech capital of France and the headquarters of Airbus, uses both Occitan and French recorded messages in its metro system. In gift shops, the Cathar religion is presented as a form of New Age spirituality against a sound track of mournful wind instruments.

The sheer brutality of the Cathar suppression can be hard to summon. The Albigensian Crusade was launched by Pope Innocent III in 1208. Innocent was perhaps the most strong-willed and powerful pope of the Middle Ages, claiming for the holder of his office a status "lower than God but higher than man." He was not a sentimentalist or a happy warrior: his chief surviving work is a glum, or perhaps realistic, treatise titled *On the Misery of the Human Condition*. Innocent greatly strengthened the papal administration and asserted the supremacy of the pope above secular rulers, at one point excommunicating King John of England and placing the entire country under interdict. He also launched an ill-fated crusade to recover Jerusalem from the Muslims.

The crusade against the Cathars went better. The proximate cause was the murder of a papal legate, Pierre de Castelnau, perhaps on the orders of Count Raymond of Toulouse, long known as sympathetic to the heretics. Raymond was an indifferent warrior but a nimble diplomat who shuttled between excommunication and a state of grace throughout his life. To save his skin he would change sides and lead a campaign against the Cathars — and then change sides again.

Heretical movements within Christendom had been emerging with new virulence for half a century or more, and in southern France and northern Italy groups like the Cathars and Waldensians enjoyed growing popular support, along with the quiet or open protection of the local nobility. The Church attempted to cope with the situation by preaching intensively in the affected areas. It was a tough sell. In 1178, a papal legate in Toulouse reported that a large crowd had taunted him and made obscene gestures: *"Digit demonstrarent,"* he complained — "They gave the finger." Several years later, Pope Lucius III issued the decree *Ad abolendam* ("For the purpose of abolishing . . ."), which provided a taxonomy of heretical sects and, to close the tautological circle, made it clear that refusing to submit to papal authority was itself a form of heresy.

The Albigensian Crusade set out to crush the Cathars, and up to a point it succeeded. The pope's own legions were mainly angelic, but he harnessed the forces of local magnates (who saw which way the wind was blowing) and then of the kings of France (who saw an opportunity to extend their control over the south). The crusade was waged over twenty years, punctuated regularly by wholesale massacres. "Forward, then, most valiant soldiers of Christ!" a papal legate urged the warriors at the outset. "Go to meet the forerunners of Antichrist and strike down the ministers of the Old Serpent!"

Modernity, as the geographer David Harvey once noted, is not a time — it's a place. I came across his remark in the twenty-first century, reading a book in the cocoon of an aircraft cruising above the Syrian Desert; pockets of the Middle Ages probably survived only a few miles below. For most people in the developed world, memories of outright religious warfare, once a gruesome fact of life, have long been buried. The past decade, with its ominous references to a "clash of civilizations" between Islam and the West, has revived them. Jihadist violence affords a fresh taste of what religious warfare can be like. In terms of pungency and sensibility, the rhetoric of Islamist groups might have been drawn directly from a thousand years ago. Ayman al-Zawahiri, now the leader of Al Qaeda, sounded not unlike that papal legate when he pronounced an anathema against his enemies in 2009:

O Allah, annihilate the Americans and Jews and the hypocrites and apostates who help them. O Allah, take revenge on our behalf from them. O Allah, make their end one of loss and destruction. O Allah, destroy their riches and harden their hearts . . . O Allah, annihilate the secularist politicians of hypocrisy who rush madly to earn the Crusaders' pleasure . . .

Not surprisingly, apostates and secularists have often risen to the bait. Some have couched their responses in religious terms. President George W. Bush, in a public statement soon after the 9/11 attacks, used the word "crusade" to characterize the task ahead, though he later regretted the terminology. One journalist in Iraq described how, in 2004, members of the 1st Infantry Division painted the words "Jesus Killed Mohammed," in Arabic, on the front of a Bradley Fighting Vehicle. Another journalist that same year recounted a prayer session held by the American troops of Bravo Company on the eve of the battle of Fallujah:

Then a chaplain, Navy Lieutenant Wayne Hall, of Oklahoma City, blessed Bravo: "Today is Palm Sunday," he began. "The day of Jesus's triumphal entry into Jerusalem, where he broke the bounds of Hell. Tonight commences your triumphal entry into Fallujah, a place in the bounds of Hell. This is a spiritual battle, and you Marines are the tools of mercy." As Hall invoked the Holy Spirit, the Marines all dropped to one knee and bowed their heads, removing their bush or field caps as they did so.

A few months earlier, an army lieutenant general, William G. "Jerry" Boykin, a distinguished thirty-year veteran, attracted unwelcome attention when, in the course of a speech, he made reference to a Muslim warlord he had faced in Somalia. Boykin said: "I knew that my God was bigger than his. I knew that my God was a real God and his was an idol." In 2007, General Ricardo Sanchez, who was for a time the commander of U.S. forces in Iraq, ended a speech to a gathering of military reporters with these words, drawn from Psalm

144: "Praise be to the Lord my rock, who trains my fingers for battle and my hands for war."

Around U.S. military installations — on bumper stickers, on T-shirts — you'll frequently come across this injunction: "Kill them all. Let God sort them out." It's an expression of humor and braggadocio, not a capsule version of army doctrine or the rules of engagement. As it happens, the words on those T-shirts and bumper stickers, or something like them, were first attributed to a papal legate named Arnaud Amaury near the outset of the Albigensian Crusade. The context was the siege of Béziers, in 1209, when a force of crusaders under the command of Simon de Montfort broke through into the city and massacred all the inhabitants, Cathar and Catholic alike: God would know his own, Amaury is said to have explained. The crusaders consisted largely of opportunists from the north of France, drawn by a promise of lands confiscated from heretics. Simon de Montfort would by the time of his death be the largest landholder in Languedoc. In his case, opportunism was yoked to religious zealotry and merciless technique. To persuade the inhabitants of the fortress of Cabaret to submit to his will, he took a hundred men from the nearby town of Bram, gouged out their eyes, and cut off their noses and lips. He left a single man with a single eye, who led the mutilated party to the fortress, arms to shoulders, single file. The village of Bram would not enter history again until World War II, when it became the site of an internment camp for Jews.

The Albigensian Crusade lasted until 1229. The crusaders took Béziers, Carcassonne, dozens of other cities and towns, and ultimately Toulouse before suffering reverses and rebellions. The long version of the story is a tortuous saga of betrayal, greed, religious fervor, and wanton bloodletting. The fortunes of crusader and Cathar shifted continually. When the French king finally intervened, Cathar military resistance came to an end.

But the Cathar heresy had not been fully rooted out. It flourished underground. Clerical investigators continued to roam southern

France, where they worked at the sufferance of local bishops, and popes encouraged secular rulers to become heretic hunters in their own right. Both efforts proved politically complicated. Neither brought conclusive results.

Finally, in 1231, Pope Gregory IX issued two documents that effectively created what we know as the Inquisition, though it was for a long time far more decentralized than the word "the" suggests. Henceforth, Rome would pick specially trained clerics to serve as inquisitors — primarily members of the Dominican Order, but also Franciscans and others. The inquisitors ventured into suspect regions, papal writ in hand, examining presumed heretics by the hundreds or thousands. Unlike local bishops, whose diligence was often compromised by close ties with the community, the inquisitors were beholden to no one save the pope. They subjected countless numbers to harsh punishments and condemned many to death by burning at the stake.

The inquisitorial process had a long history. It grew out of developments in ancient Roman law, when procedures governing how aggrieved private parties might adjudicate an alleged wrong were replaced by a more formal public process firmly in the hands of the state. The new process was called an *inquisitio,* and the magistrate who conducted it, the *inquisitor,* served in essence as detective, prosecutor, and judge rolled into one. When Theodosius officially made the Roman Empire a Christian state, in the fourth century, any deviance from orthodox Christian teaching became a crime — indeed, became tantamount to treason, which carried the death penalty. After the fall of Rome, which led to a chaotic hodgepodge of legal regimes in Europe, the *inquisitio* process survived in the internal tribunals of the Church. It would prove to be a powerful tool. In its earliest form, the accused was not told the identities of those who had testified against him and had no right to defense counsel. The proceedings were conducted out of public view, though careful records were kept. The *inquisitio* did not need to wait for someone to file a complaint (though denunciations were frequent); it could bring charges on its own, on the basis of general suspicion. This capability was central and gave inquisitors considerable power that was, in essence, preemptive — power to intervene before a transgression had been definitively discerned, based on a supposition that something harmful might ensue.

Traveling light, with a secretary or two and perhaps a small armed escort, the thirteenth-century inquisitor would arrive at his destination. He would preach a sermon, urging heretics to abjure their beliefs, and would declare a period of grace during which they could repent with relative ease. At the same time, he would begin hearing accusations against specific individuals. When the period of grace expired, he would set about conducting trials. The process was labor-intensive and time-consuming, but it enabled the examination of large numbers of people. In the fifteen months after the fall of Montségur, inquisitors in the Lauragais region of southern France questioned 5,471 men and women. The period of grace was of course a trap, perhaps an inadvertent one. Its lenient terms, coupled with its "sell-by" date, encouraged people to come forward quickly and own up to something — anything — if only to put the matter behind them. It also encouraged them to turn in their neighbors — an inducement that, in every age and place, feeds on tainted motives. In a sense, the period of grace ended up *creating* heresy.

Self-Fulfilling Prophecy

The phrase "take for granted" is a sly one — it conceals the barriers to understanding that the phrase itself erects. In our own age, we take many things for granted, and have no clear idea — never pause to think — about the moment when any of them made the transition from "can't even imagine" to part of the woodwork. We take for granted that micro-organisms cause disease, that our planet is billions of years old, and that we can send pictures through the air. The medieval world, where the Inquisition was conceived, is remote. To begin with, it was physically fragmented. At the time when the Cathars were active, someone in southern France might have referred to a stranger as "French," meaning from the north. More than that: every valley was its own little country. In Emmanuel Le Roy Ladurie's book *Montaillou*, about the Inquisition in Languedoc, there is a passage, drawn from a clerical interrogation, in which a man named Arnaud Sicre recalls meeting a woman who said she was from a town called Saverdun — but he knows from her accent that she must be from somewhere around Montaillou. Fine: most of us can identify people from Chicago or Boston, Minneapolis or New York, by their accents. But the man's remark struck home as I drove around Languedoc one spring and realized that Montaillou and Saverdun are only about twenty-five miles apart.

In medieval Europe, the main usable roads were the Roman roads built a thousand years earlier. It's symptomatic of the poor state of communications that medieval words for some distances were often based not on actual length but on the time it took to cover them. A "league" is the amount of distance that could be covered in an hour. The word "journey" comes from the French *journée* — the amount of distance that could be covered in a day. Politically, the continent was fractured among kings and counts and dukes, bishops and abbots, cities and towns, all with overlapping rights and obligations. No organizational chart is possible. The legal system differed from place to place and was a strange mixture everywhere — bits of Roman law tossed in with ancient customs, feudal mandates, Church prerogatives, and perhaps the newfangled procedures of a distant king. For a historian today, disentangling the power relationships in just one locale — Toulouse, say, or Foix, or Carcassonne — may be the work of a lifetime. Literacy was available to very few; as a proportion of the population, those who could read and write were perhaps equivalent in number to those who can create computer code today. As for religion, everyone was nominally Catholic, but "orthodoxy" was not well defined, parish priests had minimal schooling, and the folkways of yesteryear were very much alive. Peasants everywhere consulted soothsayers. In secret places, young women took part in fertility rites of forgotten origin. Magic and superstition were deeply rooted. A man named Arnaud Gélis, a church sexton in Languedoc, told an interrogator about his beliefs regarding the dead: "When you are walking, do not throw your arms and legs about carelessly, but keep your elbows well in, or you might knock a ghost over. Do not forget that we walk unwittingly among a multitude of ghosts." Ideas like that had filled the heads of ordinary people for centuries, and for centuries, with sporadic exceptions, no one in authority had done very much about it.

And yet change is slowly coming. Roads radiate afresh from towns and cities into a distant beyond; isolated areas once reachable only by track or footpath may now be touched by a *via nova*, a "new road." Along pilgrimage routes, monastic houses repair the ancient bridges and build new ones. In 1300, a Jubilee year for the Church, some two million pilgrims will converge on Rome. Trade expands rapidly throughout the continent. Meanwhile, universities in places like Paris and Bologna start bringing order to philosophy, theology, and the law. Although there will never be anything like uniformity, a new way of doing official business begins to gather momentum at royal courts and in the Church. All this has a bearing on how dissent is perceived and handled.

Why the apparent surge in heretical activity in the twelfth and thirteenth centuries? One can point to many factors: the corruption of the Church, economic stresses of various kinds, the role of charismatic preachers, a pervasive sense of injustice. Individuals, as one historian notes, are also showing "feelings of alienation" and "expanded curiosity about the human condition." The truth is that popular belief had always diverged widely and without discipline from the pure strains of belief and practice as defined by Church councils. What had undeniably changed was the Church itself.

By the standards of the time, it is a modernizing institution, increasingly centralized under a Roman pope whose claims to both spiritual and temporal authority over all of Christendom are to be taken seriously — and to be seriously defended. The papal chanceries become busier and busier; under Innocent III, secretaries begin making copies of every letter for the official files. Clerics sent out from Rome on specific missions now carry the stamp of papal authority with them, superseding the writ of local bishops. At the same time, the conceptual structure of "orthodoxy," together with laws to codify it, has been laid out with unprecedented clarity — the work of scholastics and canon lawyers in the great university centers.

In law, the chief intellectual milestone is the so-called *Decretum*, compiled around 1140 by a canon lawyer in Bologna named Gratian. Gratian is believed by some to have been a member of the Benedictine Order, but most speculations about his life have been shown to be unreliable. The documentary trail is meager. The record of a trial in Venice, held at the Basilica of San Marco in 1143, refers to the presence of a consulting legal expert named Gratianus, and circumstantial evidence suggests that this could well be Gratian the canon lawyer. If so, it's the only "live" sighting of the man himself in the documents.

Gratian's achievement was momentous. The official name of his great work is the *Concordia discordantium canonum* — the "Concordance of Discordant Canons" — and the title aptly captures the challenge Gratian faced. Over the course of a millennium, the Church had accrued for its use a massive stockpile of theological opinions, conciliar decrees, papal pronouncements, biblical injunctions, and legal rulings — massive, and often contradictory. From this clay Gratian molded a coherent code of canon law. It was a revolutionary accomplishment, and would be built on for centuries to come. Gratian's work remained in use by the Church until 1917.

Large swaths of Gratian are devoted to heresy — what it is, how it should be dealt with — and over time the Church's elaborations became more detailed. That the Church had an obligation to prosecute heretics no one doubted — there was biblical sanction in the parable of the wedding banquet, from the Gospel of Luke. In that story, invited guests fail to appear at the appointed hour, so the master sends forth his servant with the command "Go out into the highways and hedges and compel them to come in, that my house may be filled." Augustine had interpreted "compel them to come in" as an injunction to deal with heresy by brute force, if necessary: "Let the heretics be drawn from the hedges, be extracted from the thorns." At the Council of Tarragona, in 1242, the varieties of heretical behavior were sorted out with zoological precision, as if by a naturalist. Apart from the basic category of *hereticus* there were three kinds of *suspectus* and also *celatores* (people who failed to report heretics), *receptatores* (people who received heretics into their homes), and other types of transgressors.

In a less sophisticated and more decentralized world, before the hardening of canon law, heresy and deviance could subsist almost unnoticed, as a kind of "local option." But now, questionable beliefs could be examined against codified standards. Casual remarks could be sorted into pre-existing categories of nonconformity. Groups that might once have represented short-lived eruptions were endowed with a sense of coherence, importance, and menace. To some degree, heresy in its consequential new form was brought into existence by having a definition placed on the table in such a way — here's how heretics behave, here's what they say — that even laypeople could recognize the signs. Daniel Patrick Moynihan coined a memorable phrase — "defining deviancy down" — to encapsulate how standards of what is acceptable are gradually eroded. He might also have noted that deviancy can be defined "up" — that the notion of what is acceptable can become *more* restrictive.

A self-fulfilling dynamic of this kind, set in motion from above, is not unfamiliar. The anticommunist efforts in the United States during the 1950s bore some of the same hallmarks. The Soviet Union certainly posed a security threat, but the Red Scare fostered national paranoia. Popular fears got out of hand, and the government clamped down hard on people deemed subversive. A pamphlet prepared by the U.S. Army in 1955 conceded that "there is no foolproof way of detecting a Communist." It noted that the typical revolutionary was no longer "bearded" and "coarse," and warned people to be on the lookout for anyone using the terms "vanguard," "hootenanny," "chauvinism," "progressive," "hooliganism," and "ruling class." The pamphlet observed that "such hobbies as 'folk dancing' and 'folk music' have been traditionally allied with the Communist movement in the United States."

In our own time, the war on terror has had similar consequences — some of them darkly comic but symptomatic of how the psychological process works. In the summer of 2009, a Pomona College student named Nicholas George was detained and interrogated at Philadelphia International Airport because he was found to be carrying Arabic flash cards for a language course. Here is a press account published after George filed a lawsuit:

> Authorities detained him in the screening area for 30 minutes before he was questioned by a TSA supervisor, the lawsuit states. At one point, the supervisor asked George if he knew who committed the 9/11 terrorist attacks, according to the lawsuit. George answered, "Osama bin Laden." "Do you know what language he spoke?" the supervisor asked, according to the document. "Arabic," George answered. The supervisor then held up the flashcards and said, "Do you see why these cards are suspicious?"

Search Engines

To be effective, any organization must have the capacity to manage information. That capacity is especially urgent for an organization whose purpose is to monitor, to discipline, to control. It is no accident that regimes notable for sustained activities of this kind are also regimes that have created a long paper trail. The Berlin Document Center, which preserves what survives of the bureaucratic product of the Third Reich, contains some 75 million pages of records. The Nazis employed the first generation of IBM punch-card systems in order to count and classify the German population.

Together with the new coherence of canon law there came a revolution in record-keeping as Church chancery clerks developed the art of paperwork — composing in the same legible script, making copies of documents, depositing them in archives, and inventing techniques for retrieving information that had been written down and stored away. They were creating a rudimentary form of something so fundamental to life today — bureaucracy — that we rarely give it a moment's thought.

The digital era has revolutionized data collection and data retrieval. As the historian James B. Given points out, the late medieval world experienced an information revolution of its own. Haphazard approaches to organizational management were wrestled into something recognizably modern. Inquisitors developed standardized systems for logging cases and preserving the history and outcome of every trial. Church councils discussed the proper way to fill out forms and the importance of making duplicates. To give some idea of the scale and speed of the change: in a typical year — say, 1200 — Pope Innocent III would have sent out some three hundred official Church letters; the annual total for Boniface VIII, a century later, was 50,000. No one became more adept at maintaining vast quantities of records — and, just as important, knowing where to find them — than the notaries of the Inquisition. Their new capability extended the reach of the Inquisition and made it durable.

This revolution was in fact a technological one. It may seem odd to think of the way information is organized on paper as a technology, but consider a household item we take for granted — the desk dictionary. It is a codex — a bound volume with pages — rather than a scroll, making it much easier to browse. The words in the dictionary are arranged alphabetically, and the architecture of the typography — catchwords, boldface, italics, capital letters, numbers — presents information in accordance with a clearly defined hierarchy. Getting all this to the point where we don't even think about it was the work of centuries, going back to Roman times, when the basic shift from scroll to codex occurred.

In the Middle Ages, the courts of England and France — the most developed secular governments — were great compilers of archives. Scholars sifting through them today are grateful for their abundance. But the archives were not all that useful to people at the time, because it was hard to find anything — the equivalent of putting your hands on an old report card or love letter among hundreds of boxes in the attic. England's King Edward I was certain that documents existed to prove his claim to the overlordship of Scotland. On two occasions — in 1291 and 1300 — he ordered a search for them in the royal archives, but to no avail.

The medieval inquisitors were more practical and more inventive. Conducting countless interrogations and working constantly, they needed records from the past that they could access quickly. Had some defendant come before the Inquisition previously — even ten or twenty years earlier? Had any immediate family members been identified as heretics — or anyone in the extended family? What about other people in the defendant's village? All that aside, how had inquisitors dealt with similar cases on other occasions? And regarding the issue in question, what was the nature of the Church's teaching over the years? Had it hardened? Softened? Information on all these matters was essential, and the inquisitors designed record-keeping procedures to meet their needs. They created, in effect, the equivalent in parchment of search engines.

On the manuscript page, trial transcripts were abstracted into boxed synopses in the margin, for quick scanning. Cases were grouped by location — a sensible approach in a time when people were not as mobile as they are now, and tended to pass their beliefs down through the generations. The compilation of comprehensive indexes allowed for easy cross-referencing. Had a defendant given different testimony to someone else in another place, perhaps decades earlier? If he had, he might well be found out. A man named Guillaume Bonet the elder, of Villeneuve-la-Comptal, swore to inquisitors in 1246, not long after the fall of Montségur, that he had never participated in the Cathar ceremony known as the *melioramentum*. As it happened, this same Guillaume, during an earlier interrogation by someone else, had admitted to joining in the ceremony; a check of the records made the connection. Guillaume Bonet was caught in a lie. James Given writes, "With tedious frequency one finds at the end of a deponent's statement the notation that his deposition does not agree with the testimony" that he had given on a different occasion.

The Grand Inquisitor

Flawed and patchwork though it was, the secretarial machinery of the Church represented a degree of bureaucratic infrastructure that hadn't been seen in Europe since antiquity. Operating this modern machinery required the service of professionals. Today we would call them lawyers or technocrats or information-technology specialists. Those who served the Inquisition were clerics of various kinds, perhaps schooled in canon law, certainly able to read and write — indeed, to write in a common language, Latin, using official styles of calligraphy and abbreviation that their brethren everywhere could easily read. They were trained to the task with the help of instruction manuals that covered everything from definitions of heresy to conditions of confinement. These manuals offered primers, with sample dialogue, on how to conduct interrogations. A cadre of technicians was essential. Without them, no form of inquisitorial activity could sustain itself for very long.

Umberto Eco, in his novel *The Name of the Rose*, summons to life a dark and compelling character: Bernard Gui, a bishop and papal inquisitor. In the movie, he is played with serpentine menace by F. Murray Abraham. The year is 1327, and Gui has come to a Benedictine abbey in Italy where, as it happens, a murder has just been committed. It falls to Gui to convene a tribunal and examine the suspects. "Bernard Gui took his place at the center of the great walnut table in the chapter hall," Eco writes. "Beside him a Dominican performed the function of notary, and two prelates of the papal legation sat flanking him, as judges."

Eco continues, describing the inquisitor's bearing as the tribunal gets under way:

> He did not speak: while all were now expecting him to begin the interrogation, he kept his hands on the papers he had before him, pretending to arrange them, but absently. His gaze was really fixed on the accused, and it was a gaze in which hypocritical indulgence (as if to say: Never fear, you are in the hands of a fraternal assembly that can only want your good) mixed with icy irony (as if to say: You do not yet know what your good is and I will shortly tell you) and merciless severity (as if to say: But in any case I am your judge here, and you are in my power).

Bernard Gui is a historical figure, though few details of his life are known — Eco had a free hand to embellish. A few facts are certain. Gui was born near Limoges, in 1260 or 1261, professed vows as a Dominican about twenty years later, and rose rapidly as prior at a succession of abbeys. In 1307 he was indeed made an inquisitor by Pope Clement V, with responsibility for the Cathar-strewn area around Toulouse. He did not ignore the Jews, however, and ordered copies of the Talmud to be burned in public. Over a period of fifteen years, Gui pronounced some 633 men and women guilty of heresy. We have the disposition of these cases because Gui wrote everything down — the record survives in his *Liber Sententiarum,* his "Book of Sentences," which now resides in the British Library.

It is a folio-sized volume, bound in red leather. The writing is tiny and heavily abbreviated, and there are no artistic flourishes. The book is the product of an orderly mind. It begins with a list of the towns and cities Gui visited, and the people sentenced in each place. Then come the details of one case after another. Much of the book consists of model sermons to be delivered, carefully modulated according to transgression and punishment. Some of the accused were given relatively mild punishments — for example, ordered to wear a large yellow cross on their tunics (evoking the yellow badge that medieval Jews were often forced to wear, and that a later age revived). In these instances, Gui's text is interrupted by the insertion of a little cross. Other people might be ordered to make a pilgrimage or even a crusade. Still others were sentenced to prison in perpetuity, which in practice usually meant several years. A considerable number, already deceased, had their remains exhumed, their bones incinerated, their homes destroyed. Gui sent more than forty of the living to the stake.

Gui was a detail man. Inquisition records can be shockingly mundane. An itemized accounting of expenses for the burning of four heretics in 1323 survives from Carcassonne:

For large wood	55 sols 6 deniers.
For vine-branches	21 sols 3 deniers.
For straw	2 sols 6 deniers.
For four stakes	10 sols 9 deniers.
For ropes to tie the convicts	4 sols 7 deniers.
For the executioner, each 20 sols	80 sols.
In all	8 livres 14 sols 7 deniers.

The Church handled the matter of executions with philosophical elegance. It was inappropriate for ecclesiastical officials to sully their hands with capital punishment, so a process was engineered to allow the inquisitor to have it both ways: he would formally "relax," or render, the condemned prisoner to the secular authorities, who would carry out the sentence. This sort of moral delicacy has a modern analogue, and it's not just a linguistic one, in what has come to be called extraordinary rendition, whereby a nation whose conscience recoils at the idea of extracting information by means of torture sends prisoners to be interrogated in countries without such scruples. During the past decade, according to one estimate, the United States has handled 150 suspected terrorists this way. There is the case, for instance, of a Canadian citizen, Maher Arar, who was arrested in New York in 2002 because his name appeared on a terrorist watch list. Arar was shackled, trundled aboard an executive jet, and flown by a "special removal unit" to Jordan. He was then driven to Syria, where he was relaxed to the local authorities and interrogated and tortured for months. He was eventually released without charge.

Extraordinary rendition typically occurs in the shadows, involving "ghost prisoners" and "black sites." For the Inquisition, the relaxation of the prisoner to the secular arm occurred in the open, in the course of a ceremonial occasion known as a *sermo generalis*. The *sermo generalis* was held most often on a Sunday, when a great platform would be erected at a central place in a church. A throng would gather there — the ecclesiastical authorities, the secular magistrates, the public at large — and the various sentences would be read out by the inquisitor. The recitation of capital crimes came last, and then power over the prisoners passed from the spiritual to the temporal arm. To emphasize that the Church's hands were clean, the inquisitor would read a pro forma prayer, expressing hope that the condemned might somehow be spared — though there was in fact no hope of that. Those destined for the stake would be led outdoors, where a pyre had been built for the purpose in a public square. In terms of people burned at the stake, Gui's most productive day was April 5, 1310, when, after a *sermo generalis* in Toulouse, he condemned seventeen people to death.

Although little is known about Bernard Gui the person, Eco's characterization gets at something authentic. He was methodical, learned, clever, patient, and relentless — all this can be inferred from the documentary record. Among other things, Gui was a prodigious writer — in his spare time he compiled a history of the bishops of Toulouse, a history of the kings of Gaul, a collection of lives of the saints, a biography of Thomas Aquinas, several theological treatises, and a history of the world up to his own time. More to the point, he wrote a lengthy manual for inquisitors called *Practica officii inquisitionis heretice pravitatis,* or "Conduct of the Inquisition into Heretical Depravity." The manual covered the nature and types of heresy an inquisitor might encounter but also provided advice on everything from conducting an interrogation to pronouncing a sentence of death.

Gui's manual would be followed by others. Their proliferation seems to have been rooted in something ostensibly far less ominous. In 1215, a special gathering of Church bishops, the Fourth Lateran Council, reinforced the duty of all Christians to go to confession at least once a year. Out of this decree grew a modest confession industry, including manuals instructing priests on how to hear a confession properly — how to classify sins and probe the sinner's conscience. It was but a short step from these to manuals involving confessions of a graver kind — from people accused of heresy.

The notion of a "slippery slope" — the idea that one particular step will set the precedent for a second step, ever onward in an unfortunate downhill cascade — is as commonplace as it is controversial. Much has been written about the subject in journals of philosophy, social science, and the law. Legalizing assisted suicide will lead to legalized euthanasia. Legalizing marijuana will lead to the abuse of more-dangerous drugs. The use of surveillance cameras to stop crime will lead to the use of surveillance cameras to monitor personal behavior.

One English essayist recalls the suggestion by his rector at Eton that not wearing cuff links would lead to heroin addiction. Sometimes the examples are silly, but the phenomenon can be very real. In many ways the Inquisition is a cautionary example of the slippery slope at work: how seemingly minor developments in theory and practice open the door to further developments — and on and on.

Bernard Gui would not have put it this way, but his aim in the *Practica* was to create something like a science of interrogation. It depended on an elite who knew the rules, knew the methods, knew the pitfalls. Gui's order, the Dominicans, provided a core group of operatives. Like the Franciscans, who came into existence at roughly the same time, the Dominicans represented a startling new way of doing Church business. Rather than living in settled monastic communities, which were often rich and complacent, they traveled far and wide as individuals or in small groups, recognizable in their white habits, and depending on donations to meet basic needs. Their authority came directly from the pope. In a largely static society — the typical peasant might spend an entire lifetime within a tight radius around his birthplace — the radical character of these aggressively itinerant agents, wielding transcendent power, proved highly advantageous. The Dominicans preached everywhere, to whatever audiences they could find. And they possessed a common body of knowledge. Dominicans received intensive instruction in moral theology and canon law and, as part of their normal training, very practical guidance on how to ask the hard questions. One thirteenth-century training manual for the order offers succinct commentaries under headings such as "In how many ways is one said to be a heretic?" "How should heretics be examined?" "What are the penalties for heresy, according to the law?"

Innocent III had given the founding of the Dominican Order his provisional approval in 1215, the year before he died, recognizing the role these traveling preachers might play among the Cathars. When the Church needed vigorous investigators — even before the Inquisition was formally established — it was natural to outsource most of the work to this order. As one historian concludes, "The Dominicans were not so much asked to prepare themselves for a new challenge; they were called upon because they were already seen to be in a position to meet it." The name of the order gave rise all too easily to a Latin pun: its members came to be known as *Domini canes*, "the hounds of God."

Bernard Gui's outlook, as reflected in his manual for inquisitors, was sophisticated. "It must be noted," he wrote, "that just as all diseases are not treated by one single medicament, but that each disease has its own remedy, so one cannot use the same methods of interrogation, enquiry, and examination with heretics of differing sects, but must employ distinct and appropriate techniques." Gui was well aware that interrogation is a transaction between two people — a high-stakes game — and that the person being interrogated, like the person asking the questions, brings an attitude and a method to the process. The accused may be wily and disputatious. Or he may seem humble and accommodating. He may feign insanity. "It must be noted," Gui warned, "that as the heretics cannot defend themselves against the truth of the faith by strength, reason, or authorities, they quickly resort to sophistries, deceit, and verbal trickery to avoid detection. This double-speak is a clear sign by which heretics can be recognized."

Gui's was not the Inquisition's first interrogation manual, but it was one of the most influential. At a time when "publishing" was a laborious process, it was copied and recopied repeatedly and disseminated across Europe. Nor was it the last interrogation manual. A generation after Gui, another Dominican, Nicholas Eymerich, produced the *Directorium inquisitorum,* which built on the work of his predecessor and achieved even greater renown.

Torture was an integral part of the inquisitorial process, though it was reserved for difficult cases and was technically subject to certain restrictions. Eymerich and others granted wide latitude to inquisitors. For instance, although the accused was supposed to be subjected to a single "cycle" of torture, if he failed to confess or retracted a confession the inquisitors could decide that the cycle had not proceeded sufficiently: the accused, to use the term of art, had not yet been "decently" tortured. The cycle could therefore resume. Half a millennium later, the interrogators of Khalid Sheikh Mohammed, the mastermind of 9/11, employed similar reasoning to expand their options. Like Gui, Eymerich became a figure in later works of fiction. His inquisitor's manual turns up, for instance, in the library of the doomed mansion in Edgar Allan Poe's short story "The Fall of the House of Usher."

Eymerich's methods, and perhaps his personality, frequently landed him in political trouble, and his career was one of frenetic activity interrupted by sudden bouts of exile. But it was never a torpid exile. During one of these periods, he wrote his *Directorium*.

Tricks of the Trade

In modern times, the techniques of interrogation have been refined in theory by batteries of psychologists, criminologists, and intelligence experts, and in practice by soldiers, policemen, and spies. In some quarters, the word "interrogation," with its inescapable undertones, has been replaced by the sanitized "eduction," from "educe," meaning "to lead out." In 2006, the Intelligence Science Board, a government advisory group, published a thorough overview of current and historical interrogation practices under the anodyne title *Educing Information*. It contains papers with titles such as "Mechanical Detection of Deception: A Short Review" and "Options for Scientific Research on Eduction Practices." In passing, it mentions the works of Bernard Gui and Nicholas Eymerich. Place the medieval techniques alongside those laid out in modern handbooks, such as *Human In-*

telligence Collector Operations, the U. S. army interrogation manual, and the inquisitors' practices seem very up-to-date.

The inquisitors became astute psychologists. Like Gui, Eymerich was well aware that those being interrogated would employ a range of stratagems to deflect questions and disarm the interrogator. In his manual, he lays out ten ways in which heretics seek to "hide their errors." They include "equivocation," "redirecting the question," "feigned astonishment," "twisting the meaning of words," "changing the subject," "feigning illness," and "feigning stupidity." For its part, the army interrogation manual provides a "Source and Information Reliability Matrix" to assess the same kinds of behavior. It warns interrogators to be wary of subjects who show signs of "reporting information that is self-serving," who give "repeated answers with exact wording and details," and who demonstrate a "failure to answer the question asked."

But the well-prepared inquisitor had ruses of his own. To confront an unforthcoming prisoner, he might sit with a large stack of documents in front of him, which he would appear to consult as he asked questions or listened to answers, periodically looking up from the pages as if they contradicted the testimony and saying, "It is clear to me that you are hiding the truth." The army manual suggests a technique called the "file and dossier approach," a variant on what it terms the "we know all" approach:

> The HUMINT [human intelligence] collector prepares a dossier containing all available information concerning the source or his organization. The information is carefully arranged within a file to give the illusion that it contains more data than actually there. . . .
> It is also effective if the HUMINT collector is reviewing the dossier when the source enters the room.

Another technique suggested by Eymerich is to suddenly shift gears, approaching the person being interrogated in a seeming spirit of mercy and compassion, speaking "sweetly" and solicitously, perhaps making arrangements to provide something to eat and drink. The army manual puts it this way:

> At the point when the interrogator senses the source is vulnerable, the second HUMINT collector appears. [He] scolds the first HUMINT collector for his uncaring behavior and orders him from the room. The second HUMINT collector then apologizes to soothe the source, perhaps offering him a beverage and a cigarette.

Kindness may prove ineffective. Another way to break the impasse, Eymerich writes, is to "multiply the questions and the interrogations," observing that asking many different questions, quickly and repeatedly, will create confusion, elicit contradiction, and furnish information for deeper questioning. The Army recommends what it calls "rapid-fire interrogation":

> The HUMINT collectors ask a series of questions in such a manner that the source does not have time to answer a question completely before the next one is asked. This confuses the source, and he will tend to contradict himself as he has little time to formulate his answers.

Eymerich and the army describe many other techniques. You can try to persuade the prisoner that resistance is pointless, because others have already spilled the beans. You can take the line that you know the prisoner is but a small fish, and if only you had the names of the bigger fish, the small one might swim free. You can play on the prisoner's feelings of utter hopelessness, reminding him that only cooperation with the interrogator offers a path to something better. Eymerich writes a script, telling the inquisitor he should say that he is obliged to stop the questioning because he must go on a long trip — that he wishes the questioning were at an end, but it must be interrupted until he returns. He does not know how long that will be, perhaps weeks or months, and until that time the prisoner will have to remain in the dungeons . . . unless, perhaps, we can successfully conclude the questioning now? The army manual refers to this as the "emotional-futility" approach:

> In the emotional-futility approach, the HUMINT collector convinces the source that resistance to questioning is futile. This engenders a feeling of hopelessness and helplessness on the part of the source. Again as with the other emotional approaches, the HUMINT collector gives the source a "way out" of the helpless situation.

Who Needs God?

In the background, always, lies the possibility of physical persuasion. Few words summon the Dark Ages to mind as quickly as "torture" does, but the uncomfortable truth is that the emergence of torture as an acceptable instrument reveals glimmerings of a modern way of thinking: the truth can be ascertained without God's help. To be sure, the use of torture goes far back into prehistory. Cave paintings from 12,000 years ago suggest that torture techniques developed very early. "Torture him, how?" asks the judge in Aristophanes' *The Frogs*, who goes on to mention stretching on the rack, putting bricks on the chest, hanging by the thumbs, and other well-known techniques. Torture has been used as a ritual act, a means of deterrence, a tool of coercion, and a form of vengeance. Frequently it has been done simply to slake something fundamental in certain natures. An unidentified member of a Mexican drug cartel spoke about this to CNN:

ANDERSON COOPER: Torture is common?
DRUG CARTEL MEMBER: Yes it is.
COOPER: Why? Just to get information?

CARTEL MEMBER: To — not to get information. Just the pleasure of
doing it.

Torture had been used in ancient Rome as part of the *inquisitio*
process. But as a legitimate tool of jurisprudence it was actually little
known in the darkest part of the Middle Ages. The reason is that in
the early medieval view, when mortals stood humbly before an all-
knowing God, the capacity of human beings to discover the truth
was seen to be limited. Thus the reliance not on judges or juries
but on *iudicium Dei* — divine judgment — to determine guilt or innocence. This could, and usually did, take the form of swearing a
solemn oath before God, perhaps joined by friends and associates
who swore the same oath, that one was innocent of the alleged crime.
With the fate of one's immortal soul in the balance — as everyone at
the time would have believed — such an oath was no small thing. If
the case was of sufficient gravity, an accused person might endure
trial by ordeal: he would be submerged in water, or made to walk on
red-hot coals, or to plunge an arm into boiling water. If he suffered
no harm, or if the wounds healed sufficiently within a certain period
of time, then it was deemed to be the judgment of God that the accused was innocent.

This regime was common in Europe from the sixth through the
twelfth centuries. It conformed naturally to the prevailing mental
outlook, and it suited an age in which the institutions of government
as we understand them were few and overburdened. Trial by ordeal
was unquestionably primitive, even barbaric. But it was expeditious,
and ensured that the quest for truth had a clear and definitive end
point.

The twelfth-century revolution in legal practice — exemplified
by the work of Gratian but manifest everywhere, from ecclesiastical
tribunals to secular ones — took the pursuit of justice out of God's
hands and put it into those of human beings. Edward Peters, who has

written extensively about this subject, offered a brief *tour d'horizon* one morning in his office at the University of Pennsylvania. Peters at the time was the Henry Charles Lea Professor of History, and his dark-paneled office atop the university library opened through double doors into the Lea Library, a Victorian Gothic wonder transplanted from Lea's Philadelphia mansion in the 1920s. It is the room in which Lea wrote his many volumes on the Medieval and Spanish Inquisitions, works still unsurpassed in breadth and ambition.

Underlying the medieval legal revolution, Peters explained, was one big idea: when it came to discovering guilt or innocence — and, more broadly, discovering something akin to truth — there was no need to send the decision up the chain of command to God. These matters were well within human capacity.

But that didn't quite settle the issue, Peters went on. When God is the judge, no other standard of proof is needed. But when human beings make themselves the judges, the question of proof comes very much to the fore. What constitutes acceptable evidence? How does one decide between conflicting testimony? In the absence of a voluntary confession — the most unassailable form of evidence, the "queen of proofs" — what means of questioning can properly be employed to induce one? Are there ways in which the interrogation might be aggressively enhanced? And in the end, how does one know that the full truth has been exposed, that there isn't a bit more to be discovered some little way beyond, perhaps accessible with some additional effort — one more slight turn of the screw? Of course, that turn of the screw is unpleasant — certainly a last resort — and possible to justify only in terms of the greater good. So do you see, Peters asked, how torture comes into the picture?

It was widely used in secular courts, and then crossed into the spiritual realm. In 1252, Pope Innocent IV issued the papal bull *Ad extirpanda,* which authorized the use of torture in the work of the Inquisition. Churchmen could be present but were not to participate — some representative of secular authority would do the job. In theory, torture was somewhat controlled. It was not supposed to cause grave injury or put life in jeopardy. A physician was typically present. Confessions made during a torture session were not admissible — they had to be repeated later, after an interval. And torture could be used only once. The Church laid down more rules governing torture than civil magistrates did. But inquisitors pushed the boundaries. For instance, what did "once" mean? Perhaps it should be interpreted, as Eymerich urged, to mean once for each charge. As for clerics participating in torture — surely it would be permissible if inquisitors absolved one another (as they came to do).

When one pope insisted that torture should have the explicit authorization of a local bishop, Bernard Gui proposed a looser standard: that it should be allowed after "mature and careful deliberation." Gui did not prevail on this point, but torture would prove difficult to contain. The potential fruits always seem so tantalizing, and the rules so easy to bend.

Amoral brutes certainly commit torture, but in their hands it doesn't become part of an integrated system. Torture becomes systematic in the hands of a different sort of person — one who is determined to use the powers of reason, and who believes in the rightness of his cause. This is what Michael Ignatieff means when he calls torture chambers "intensely moral places." Those who wish to justify torture don't do so by *avoiding* moral thinking; rather, they override the obvious immorality of the specific act by the presumptive morality of the larger endeavor. If the endeavor is deemed important enough, there is little that can't be justified. There are no lengths to which one may not go. In Arthur Koestler's *Darkness at Noon,* the protagonist Rubashov ultimately acquiesces in his own condemnation and execution — even uttering a false confession at his show trial — on the grounds that he must bow to the historical inevitability of the revolutionary process. Wasn't this, after all, the same exculpatory logic he had used when dispatching others?

It is a logic without limits. Thomas More points out the dangers in a celebrated exchange in Robert Bolt's *A Man for All Seasons,* when he asks his son-in-law, William Roper, if he'd be willing to cut a swath through the laws in order to ensnare the devil. "I'd cut down every law in England to do that," Roper says. Thomas More replies, "Oh? And when the last law was down, and the Devil turned round on you — where would you hide, Roper, the laws all being flat?"

Just Tell Us Everything

Not knowing where to stop: that turns out to be a central problem of any inquisition. Bureaucracy is not merely passive — it is an inertial force, sustaining action just as mindlessly as it does inaction. Bureaucracies are composed of individuals who have their own interests, their own will, but interests and will are also shaped by the institution. Like a nervous system, a bureaucracy can flex muscles in the absence of overt instruction. It can persist even when by its own lights there is no longer reason to do so. That aside, what, in the end, is the truth one is looking for? And assuming it is ascertainable, at what point is it in fact ascertained? How does one know? The quest has no clear destination.

Montaillou is a village in what is now the south of France. In the late thirteenth century it occupied a more nebulous position. It was part of the Comte de Foix, which had once been independent but now owed allegiance to the king of France, and served as a frontier bulwark against the kingdom of Aragon. The 250 or so people of Montaillou spoke not French but Occitan. And they were heretics. By 1300 the Cathars and their faith had been exterminated almost everywhere, but Montaillou remained untouched, a last redoubt.

Today the village seems as remote as it ever was, in a soft green valley on a road to nowhere. It may in fact be *more* remote than it used to be: this region of France, below the sharply etched defiles that drain the Pyrenees, is losing its people. The landscape of Montaillou has not greatly changed since the fourteenth century, though only a few silent houses stand there now, together with the village church. A ruined castle occupies a rise. If you know the history, and if there's a low, late-afternoon sun to bring out the shadows, you can make sense of the indentations here and there in the rolling grass — where the village square used to be, where the women did the washing, where the tracks to Ax and Prades ran, where the outlying fields were cultivated. The place brings on a sensation of deep loneliness. It was once so thick with events, and now is occupied mainly by the wind.

It holds surprises, though. Stroll around the Gothic church in Montaillou — Notre Dame de Carnesses — and you will see gravestones, some of them quite new, for people who bear the surname Clergue. The sight comes as something of a shock. The Clergues were already living in Montaillou seven hundred years ago, attending this very church. They were the most prominent family in town — part Ambersons, part Corleones, part Simpsons, on a *sou*-sized stage — and their quarrels and ambitions were inescapable. Some of them were central to the drama that played out in Montaillou when an inquisitor set his eyes on the village.

The inquisitor was Jacques Fournier, the bishop of Pamiers. His aim was to clean out the last pockets of Cathars from this backwater of his diocese. In 1318, Fournier proceeded to interrogate everyone in Montaillou; its adult population had been arrested and taken to Carcassonne. Over a period of years he probed into the smallest intimacies of their personal lives — not only their beliefs but also their tastes and habits, whom they liked and disliked, their sexual practices, the village gossip. He wanted detail: names, dates, numbers, locations, relationships. To exert control you must nail people down: identify them, count them, keep track of them, put them in context. He was five hundred years ahead of his time.

It was a celebrated investigation. The fearsome Bernard Gui showed up to watch. Fournier's scribes made transcriptions that were close to verbatim. And then serendipity intervened. Fournier was elected pope, taking the name Benedict XII, and he took his records with him to Avignon, where the papacy then resided. In the ensuing centuries, war, revolution, and simple neglect would consume many other Inquisition archives. Old parchments were scraped clean by secretaries so that they could be reused. Some were sold as scrap to butchers and grocers, for use as wrapping paper. But because Fournier became pope, his records survived. They are now in the Vatican Library.

The Fournier Register is the most intimate record that exists of ordinary life in medieval times. The great French historian Emmanuel Le Roy Ladurie wove these Inquisition documents, these searingly personal transcriptions, into a vivid portrait of the village in his book *Montaillou,* a classic work of social history. He told me once that, as a boy, he had often come across wiretap transcripts in the office of his father, who had been an official of the Vichy government during World War II before joining the Resistance. It was mentioned without irony, and Le Roy Ladurie drew no connection between this fact and his own scholarly interests, or between Fournier and his father. When I ventured a parallel, he gave a Gallic shrug, which could have meant "There you have it" or "Think what you wish."

Montaillou became a best-seller both in France and in the United States — one of those rare scholarly works that strike a deep chord. Of course, there was plenty of sex in the book, but Le Roy Ladurie is also a vigorous writer, and his intellectual pedigree is distinguished. He did come in for a certain amount of criticism — should these Inquisition transcripts be taken at face value? — and surely some element of jealousy was involved. The notoriously cranky medievalist Norman Cantor described Le Roy Ladurie as a "rock star" and compared his youthful looks to those of David Bowie. But the fact that

Inquisition documents had opened up a new world—something quite unintended by their compilers—was beyond dispute.

In the years since *Montaillou* was published, in 1975, the records of the Inquisition have been pressed into service in other parts of the world by historians not much interested in the Inquisition per se. For instance, the only written record of the early Spanish history of New Mexico consists of Inquisition documents that were preserved at the tribunal's headquarters in Mexico City. (Everything else was destroyed during the Pueblo Revolt, in 1680.) India, Brazil, Angola, Congo, the Philippines—Inquisition documents illuminate hidden history in all these places, simply because the inquisitors were in the business of writing things down and filing them away.

I have read *Montaillou* perhaps half a dozen times. It is enthralling in what can only be called its voyeuristic detail. One looks on as women pick lice from the hair of their lovers, and as the fingernails of the dead are clipped for household charms. A girl recalls a night of passion: "With Pierre Clergue I liked it. And so it could not displease God. It was not a sin." That same Pierre Clergue, a libidinous priest, reveals himself to be a pithily nihilistic philosopher: "Since everything is forbidden," he observes, "everything is allowed."

But beyond all this is what we glimpse between the lines: an inquisitorial process that, once set in motion, did not quite know how to end. All the machinery had been brought to bear: the mandate of heaven, the structure of law, the notaries and scribes with their parchments and quills, the magistrates with their pikes and prisons and pyres, the methods of persuasion that can always take an interrogation one more step, the frightened people who may not know exactly what is being sought but have information—endless reams of information—about one another.

Kenneth Starr, the special prosecutor who investigated President Bill Clinton and the circumstances surrounding the Monica Lewinsky scandal, is never going to be pope. If he failed to recognize the name Torquemada, as he indicated, he is unlikely to know the name Fournier. But Starr's record of his own investigation, published as *The Starr Report,* may one day achieve the same status as source material for social history — of fin de siècle Washington, D.C. — that the documents behind *Montaillou* now enjoy.

Starr, a former federal judge, was a Washington lawyer when the Justice Department named him an independent counsel to look into certain business dealings during the Clinton administration. The investigation eventually broadened to include the question of whether the president had perjured himself when explaining his relationship with an intern, Monica Lewinsky. Although in theory the Justice Department could have halted his inquiry at any time, political realities made such a move impossible, and Starr was able to proceed unfettered, with subpoena power, an unlimited budget, a substantial staff, and no apparent boundaries on the scope of his curiosity. And so the investigation wore on, venturing into astonishing levels of detail. *The Starr Report* is in essence a work of microhistory. The suggested comparison of Kenneth Starr to Tomás de Torquemada was never quite right. The real comparison is of Kenneth Starr to Jacques Fournier.

A parallel reading of *The Starr Report* and the Fournier Register is instructive. There is the same attention to mundane social interaction:

Fournier Register: In Lent, toward vespers, I took two sides of salted pork to the house of Guillaume Benet of Montaillou, to have them smoked. There I found Guillemette Benet warming herself by the fire, together with another woman; I put the salted meat in the kitchen and left.

Starr Report: Ms. Lewinsky called Ms. Currie at home and told her that she wanted to drop off a gift for the President. Ms. Currie invited Ms. Lewinsky to her home, and Ms. Lewinsky gave her the package. The package contained a book called *The Presidents of the United States* and a love note inspired by the movie *Titanic.*

Starr and Fournier took pains to document the precise geography and chronology of illicit relations:

Fournier: Straight away I made love with her in the antechamber of the *ostal,* and subsequently I possessed her often. But never at night. Always in the daylight. We used to wait until the girls and the servant were out of the house. And then we used to commit the carnal sin.

Starr: At the White House, according to Ms. Lewinsky, she told Secret Service Officer Muskett that she needed to deliver papers to the President. Officer Muskett admitted her to the Oval Office, and she and the President proceeded to the private study. . . . About 20 to 25 minutes later, according to Officer Muskett, the telephone outside the Oval Office rang. The operator said that the President had an important call but he was not picking up.

In both texts the magistrates linger over the use of unusual sexual aids:

Fournier: When Pierre Clergue wanted to know me carnally, he used to wear this herb wrapped in a piece of linen, about an inch long and wide, or about the size of the first joint of my little finger. And he had a long cord which he used to put round my neck while we made love.

Starr: She also showed him an email describing the effect of chewing Altoid mints before performing oral sex. Ms. Lewinsky was chewing Altoids at the time, but the President replied that he did not have enough time for oral sex. They kissed, and the President rushed off to a State Dinner with President Zedillo.

On it goes. The inquisitorial dynamic is one that tends toward perpetual motion. Its only check is exhaustion.

An End, and a Beginning

Whether because of sheer exhaustion or sheer effectiveness, the efforts of Jacques Fournier in Montaillou constituted the last important chapter of the Inquisition in southern France. One name that crops up repeatedly in the interrogations preserved by the Fournier Register is that of Guillaume Bélibaste, a wily and eccentric character who is known to history as the last Cathar *parfait*. It has been said that Bélibaste was more truly an *imparfait* — the evidence is overwhelming that he failed to live scrupulously according to Cathar standards of diet and celibacy. But a Cathar *parfait* is what he claimed to be, and as such he was denounced to the Inquisition by a spy. Bélibaste was condemned to death in 1321, becoming the last *parfait* to be burned at the stake.

There were victims elsewhere. Papal inquisitors flared into activity on occasion as circumstances demanded — in Spain, in Italy, in Germany, and in other parts of France. Not long before Fournier set about his work in Montaillou, a brutal campaign was waged by the French king, Philip the Fair, against the Knights Templar, whose destruction he sought for political reasons. The Templars were a powerful quasi-religious military order whose origins lay in the Crusades and whose prime was long since past. The pope's cooperation was needed to suppress the order; because the papacy at the time was lodged at Avignon, under watchful French eyes, it was duly obtained (though later rescinded). In October 1307, some fifteen thousand members of the order, of all ranks, were arrested throughout France in a well-coordinated operation. Several dozen leaders were burned at the stake in 1310, and the final few in 1314, bringing the Templars to an end but giving rise to countless conspiracy theories.

Papal inquisitors were involved at two stages. The first began after the arrests, when the Templars were interrogated and in many cases tortured. Inquisitors also visited England at one point to gather evidence. They did not have much luck. A special request to the king that torture be permitted in this instance — that the interrogation be allowed to proceed "according to ecclesiastical constitutions," as the inquisitors euphemistically put it — was eventually granted, but it seems that the inquisitors had some difficulty finding torturers of sufficient caliber. English monarchs were always leery of the Inquisition, and the institution never took hold on English soil.

But the English showed no compunction about using inquisitorial methods for their own ends — to mount a case against Joan of Arc. The charismatic young warrior was captured on the battlefield at Compiègne, in 1430, and after a period of months was put on trial for heresy. The ecclesiastical proceedings against Joan survive in immense detail, and to a great extent they mimic the proceedings of an Inquisition tribunal. She was never tortured, but there were sharp departures from established practice, and nothing could conceal the fact that the trial's conclusions were preordained. Joan of Arc was burned at the stake on May 30, 1431.

As for Raymond VI of Toulouse, that wily lord at the center of so much conflict in Languedoc: against all odds, he died peacefully in his bed. Some saw his opportunism in a good light, and Raymond has achieved immortality of a sort. He is depicted on the walls of the Minnesota Supreme Court, in a century-old mural called *The Adjustment of Conflicting Interests*. He is joined on those walls by Moses, Confucius, and Socrates.

3

QUEEN OF TORMENTS

The Spanish Inquisition

The most ardent defenders of justice here consider it
is better for an innocent man to be condemned than
for the Inquisition to suffer disgrace.

— A PAPAL ENVOY IN SPAIN, 1565

"I wish to interrogate him!" repeated Umbridge
angrily. . . . "I wish you to provide me with a potion
that will force him to tell me the truth!"

— J. K. ROWLING, 2003

Death in the Afternoon

THE GREAT SPECTACLE known as the *sermo generalis,* a
public ritual of punishment and humiliation, came to be
known by another name when the Inquisition took hold in
Spain and Portugal — it was called the auto-da-fé, or "act of faith."
The ritual is depicted in a thousand woodcuts and as many satires.
In Voltaire's *Candide,* an auto-da-fé is held to ward off earthquakes.
In Leonard Bernstein's version of the story, the chorus sings, "It's a
lovely day for drinking / and for watching people fry."

The Spanish Inquisition endured for 350 years. Its first auto-da-fé was held in Seville on February 6, 1481. The event was a shadow of what such occasions became a century or two later, when hundreds of penitents would be led in procession through crowded streets, their sentences pronounced and carried out before an audience of magnates, prelates, and many thousands of onlookers. The king himself might attend. The choreography of the ritual was meant to evoke the Day of Judgment, when all who have ever lived must face the final justice of God. The prisoners parading into the plaza would be followed by carts bearing the exhumed bodies of people convicted posthumously: not even the dead could escape punishment. The living prisoners wore the so-called *sanbenito,* a gown adorned with a cross, and those condemned to die at the stake also wore the *coroza,* a tall conical hat like a dunce cap. Goya captured the image vividly during the Inquisition's final decades.

But the scene in Seville in 1481, though similar in its essentials, was more muted. The Inquisition was new and the city was beset by plague. Six men and women had been condemned to death. They were all prominent *conversos* — people who had converted from Judaism to Christianity, or whose ancestors had, almost always under some form of explicit or implied duress. They had been accused and convicted of "judaizing" — reverting to their former faith — and of conspiracy against the crown. Their most dogged pursuer was a man named Alonso de Hojeda, a Dominican friar who had pressed ardently for the establishment of an inquisition in Spain. The *converso* problem was getting worse and worse, he claimed; *conversos* were judaizing in droves — if, indeed, their conversions had been authentic to begin with. Because *conversos* had become influential in finance, in the professions, in government service, and even in the Church, the threat had to be taken seriously. Hojeda produced a report, and saw his desire for an inquisition fulfilled.

Hojeda himself preached the sermon in the cathedral on that February day. When the service was over, the condemned were relaxed to the secular arm — *relajado al brazo secular.* As in previous inquisitions, the religious authorities would not taint themselves with the grim business of capital punishment. The *relajados* were led beyond the walls of the city to the *quemadero,* or place of burning, on the Campo de Tablada, and bound to the stake. Wood and straw were piled high, and the pyre was lit. Alonso de Hojeda did not have long to savor the moment. He himself was soon carried off by plague.

A heroic equestrian statue of El Cid stands at the *quemadero* today. There is no indication at the site that this was once an execution ground. In the short story "The Surveyor," by Henry Roth, an American tourist named Aaron Stigman uses old maps and surveying tools to locate the precise location of the *quemadero,* and lays a wreath at a certain spot among the flower beds that surround the statue. The act arouses the curiosity of the police. He and his wife are taken in for questioning but released when an understanding lawyer, also Jewish, intuits what Stigman was doing, and why.

These days the words "burned at the stake" are thrown around as a rhetorical flourish, the reality lost in a fog of metaphor. "They'd have me burned at the stake," the right-wing provocateur Ann Coulter writes of her left-wing enemies, "if Cambridge weren't a 'smoke-free zone.'" Burning at the stake was the Inquisition's preferred method of execution, in part because it enjoyed the positive reinforcement of scripture, specifically a verse from the Gospel of John (15:6): "If a man not abide in me, he is cast forth as a branch, and is withered; and men gather them, and cast them into the fire, and they are burned."

The forensic literature devoted to the mechanism of death at the stake is not large. One amateur investigator has made a specialty of Joan of Arc, arguing that her end may have been relatively painless, brought on by heat stroke. It's a theory. By chance or design, some of those burned were luckier than others. If particular mercy was to be shown, the condemned might be strangled before the pyre was lit. If the prisoner was to burn alive, the end could be quick or slow. In a typical execution, the condemned did not always surmount a woodpile, as many illustrations would have it, but often stood within a cylinder of combustible material piled high all around. When a large group of people — dozens or scores — were bound together as one, and the surrounding fire was large and relatively distant, some might die from smoke inhalation — carbon monoxide poisoning. Given the alternative, this, too, might count as a blessing. The intense heat would take some people before any lick of flame: the simple act of breathing, often reflexively in gulps, could sear the trachea, causing edema and asphyxiation. Asphyxiation might also occur because combustion had exhausted the available oxygen at the core of the blaze.

On the other hand, if the fire burned slowly, the victim would experience the fullest possible torment, the flames causing catastrophic damage to nerves and tissue. In these instances, death occurred when loss of blood and fluids brought on hypovolemic shock and pulmonary failure. Michael Servetus, a Spaniard who first described the functioning of the pulmonary system, endured a lingering death at the stake. His execution, in 1553, came at the hands not of the Inquisition but of John Calvin, though the technique employed was a common one — the use of green wood, which burned at a moderate pace and thereby extracted the maximum suffering. Sometimes the authorities allowed a bag of gunpowder — *saccus pulverarius* — to be hung around the waist or neck of the condemned, bringing sudden and definitive closure when the fire reached a certain point.

The six men and women who died on February 6, 1481, were followed a few days later by three more, and then, over the course of the next two decades, by several thousand. The Inquisition came to Spain quickly and with particular virulence. Like earlier inquisitions, the Spanish one claimed jurisdiction over people who were ostensibly Christians. As noted, its primary targets were converted Jews and Muslims whose sincerity as converts was questioned. Later, after the Reformation, it turned some attention to Protestants, though there were never very many in Spain, and to a variety of specific transgressions, such as the solicitation of sex by clergy in the confessional.

Jews had lived on the peninsula since the days of the Roman Empire, and perhaps even earlier. By the end of the Middle Ages, the Jews of Iberia, constituting perhaps 2 percent of the population, were an educated and wealthy class. But a program of persecution and forcible conversion had undermined the Jewish community's identity, and Jews who had accepted Christianity—New Christians—were regarded by many Old Christians with suspicion as judaizers or "crypto-Jews" who secretly held fast to their faith. Another term used for them was *marranos,* sometimes said to derive from a Spanish word for swine, though the etymology is not certain. Muslims had likewise been in Spain for many centuries—indeed, had ruled Iberia after overrunning the Visigothic kingdoms there. But as the Christian reconquest advanced, the Muslims, too, were subjected to persecution and forcible conversion. And like the Jewish *conversos,* the converted Muslims, known as *moriscos,* came to be regarded with suspicion.

The pogroms and conversions had begun long before any centralized, official inquisition was put into place. When the Spanish Inquisition was formally established, in 1478, it built on the previous inquisitions in other places. It used the same interrogation methods that the Medieval Inquisition had, and the same manuals, at least at first. It relied on the same established codes of canon law. It employed the same kinds of record-keeping; indeed, the record-keeping was even better. The records are so voluminous that scholars in recent years have been able to compile a vast computerized database—names, dates, charges, trials, punishments. But the Spanish Inquisition also went down new paths. For one thing, as time went on, it attempted to be more systematic about censorship than the Medieval Inquisition had ever been, drawing up lists of books to be kept out of Spain or destroyed if they found their way in. Many other books were expurgated, as censors wielding inkpots took aim at offensive passages.

The Folger Shakespeare Library, in Washington, D.C., preserves a copy of Shakespeare's Second Folio, from 1632, which was originally in the possession of a Jesuit seminary in Spain. The book bears the official stamp of the Inquisition and reveals the hand of a Spanish censor at work on *Henry VIII*. The last pages of the play hold flattering passages about Henry's daughter, the future Queen Elizabeth, Spain's longtime nemesis, and the censor in heavy ink has crossed out such admiring lines as "Her foes shake like a field of beaten corn."

More important, unlike earlier inquisitions, the Spanish Inquisition was bound up not only with religion but with an ideology of ethnicity — the notion of *limpieza de sangre,* or "purity of blood." It was about classes of people rather than just categories of belief. And unlike earlier inquisitions, the Spanish Inquisition was a wholly owned subsidiary of the state. Previous inquisitions had of course had their political uses — and they depended upon, and employed, secular power — but the Spanish Inquisition was created by the monarchy and was under the monarchy's control. In our own age there is no shortage of polities in which religion or ideology is joined to the state in complicit and complicated ways. The Spanish Inquisition represents an early experiment.

"A Very Busy Year"

The city of Granada, in southern Spain, never experienced the Inquisition on the scale witnessed by Toledo or Seville, but Granada played a special role in the story nonetheless. Here, on a rugged spur of the Sierra Nevada, stands the Alhambra, the palace of the last Muslim dynasty to rule in Iberia. Walking up the escarpment, among olive trees and cactus, one can understand how the romantic Orientalism of the nineteenth century got its start. Washington Irving, the American minister to Spain in the 1840s, occupied a room in the palace when he wrote his *Tales of the Alhambra.* Below his window, Moorish gateways breach the ruddy walls.

The flag of Spain today flies over the Alhambra. So does that of the European Union. And so does the flag of Andalusia, the region of Spain where Muslim rule held on the longest, and one that is again home to growing numbers of Muslims, perhaps half a million, for the most part recent arrivals from North Africa. After decades of local opposition, a new Grand Mosque of Granada has been built in the steep hillside quarter known as the Albaicin. It is one of more than 600 mosques now active in Spain. From its promontory, the Grand Mosque offers a view directly onto the Alhambra, across the wide ravine of the Rio Darro. Al Qaeda and other terrorist groups frequently call for the reconquest of Al-Andalus — the ancient Muslim name for Iberia as a whole. Members of the Al Qaeda cell that plotted the 2004 Madrid train bombings, which claimed the lives of some 200 people, were discovered to have kept a safe house in Granada.

As in other parts of Europe, the Muslim presence in Spain has elicited strong reactions. "They have a grander vision, which is an obsession with the demise of Al-Andalus," said a member of Spain's parliament after the train bombings. "We hear this in the sermons of the militant Islamic sheikhs." In 2007, Spanish bishops turned down a request by Muslims that they be allowed to pray within the precincts of what was once Córdoba's Great Mosque, the Mezquita, a sprawling place of worship that Christians took over at the time of the Reconquista, embedding an ornate cathedral in its heart. "Muslims," the bishops decided, "cannot in any way pray in Córdoba cathedral." In 2010, the bishop of Córdoba went further, launching a campaign to remove the word "mosque" from signs throughout the city that indicate the way to the "mosque-cathedral." Seeds from another age continue to sprout.

Muslim warriors invaded Iberia early in the eighth century, scarcely a century after the emergence of Islam, a continent away. Before long, Islamic forces had surged beyond the peninsula and deep into France, until they were turned back by Charles Martel at the Battle of Tours, in 732. Had this battle gone differently, Edward Gibbon observed, "perhaps the interpretation of the Koran would now be taught in the schools of Oxford, and her pulpits might demonstrate to a circumcised people the sanctity and the truth of the revelation of Mohammed." The Muslims retreated across the Pyrenees, firmly entrenching themselves in what is now Spain. They did not disappear entirely from France, however. The Inquisition register of Jacques Fournier records that an itinerant cobbler from Montaillou, Arnaud Sicre, visited a local Muslim soothsayer on Christmas Day, 1318.

In its golden age, Islamic Spain was among the most civilized places on the planet — renowned for its scientists and philosophers, artists and architects, poets and musicians. The Muslim scholars of Spain helped restore the writings of antiquity to the Christian world. In the matter of religion, Islamic sultans generally tolerated and protected Jews and Christians. Though he later emigrated, the Jewish philosopher Maimonides was born in Islamic Córdoba (and wrote largely in Arabic). Scholars today disagree on just how cordial this so-called *convivencia,* or "living together," actually was. The historian Henry Kamen cautions that whatever the degree of tolerance, the arrangement "was always a relationship between unequals."

The *convivencia* idea is under stress even now, but the modern tourist industry understands that it is good for business. In Córdoba and Seville, you'll hear the claim made that the Spanish exclamation *"Ole!"* is a corrupted form of "Allah," though this is not true. Hawkers on street corners sell T-shirts bearing a trio of symbols — the Crescent, the Cross, and the Star of David — above the words "The secret is in the mixture." Exaggerations aside, it is generally true that the Muslim sultans behaved better toward Christians and Jews than their Christian successors would behave toward Jews and Muslims. Among other things, they allowed Christians to pray in the very mosque from which Muslim prayer is now prohibited. Passing a newsstand after leaving the Mezquita one day, I saw a photograph of Josef Ratzinger on the cover of the magazine *El Semanal.* Inside was a quotation from Ratzinger that took up half a page: *"Dios tiene un agudo sentido del humor"*— "God has a sharp sense of humor."

Islamic rule, though fragmented, extended over the bulk of Iberia for centuries, even as Christian warlords, pushing south, chipped away at Muslim territory. It finally came to an end in 1492, when King Ferdinand of Aragon and Queen Isabella of Castile expelled the last sultan and brought all of Spain under a unified Catholic monarchy. The final chapter took place at the Alhambra, in the Hall of the Ambassadors. The room is three stories high, every inch of its walls etched with passages from the Koran. Latticework covers the windows, dappling the interior with sunlight. In this chamber, the sultan capitulated to Ferdinand and Isabella, who promptly moved into his palace. A few months later, at a meeting in the Alhambra, the monarchs told Christopher Columbus to go ahead with the speculative voyage he had been pestering them about (which would be underwritten by a loan from the *converso* financiers Luis de Santangel and Gabriel Sanchez). Not long afterward, in this same room, Ferdinand and Isabella signed the order to expel from Spain all Jews who would not convert to Christianity. I once overheard a guide at the Alhambra capping his account of all this activity with the bright summary "It was a very busy year," which elicited guarded laughter.

The original copy of the Edict of Expulsion is held (with other documents) at the Archivo General, a fortress in Simancas, near Valladolid. The parchment has yellowed, and the ink has browned. It begins: "In our land there is no inconsiderable number of judaizing and wicked Christians who have deviated from our Holy Catholic Faith." It goes on: "We have, therefore, decreed to order all Jews of both sexes to leave the confines of our lands forever." With a calligraphic flourish in their own hands, Ferdinand and Isabella concluded the edict with the words, *"Yo, el Rey,"* and *"Yo, la Reina"* — "I, the King," and "I, the Queen."

Spain was not the first kingdom to expel its Jews. In England, Jews were considered royal property, and it was in England that the anti-Semitic "blood libel" — the false accusation that Jews slaughtered Christian children and used their blood for ritual purposes — seems to have originated. England expelled its Jews in 1290. France followed suit in 1306. But the Jewish population of Spain was by far the largest in Europe. Nor would expulsion stop with the Jews: in 1609, Spain began to expel large numbers of *moriscos.* (Some of them would be shunned as "Christians" in the Muslim countries to which they fled, and a number were executed as a result.) Expulsion was not a policy invented by Spain, and it has never gone out of use. For more than a century, it was the declared policy of the U.S. government with respect to Native Americans, and a very successful one from Washington's point of view. Greece and Turkey, by mutual agreement, expelled Turks and Greeks from their respective countries in the 1920s. As a result of the Partition, in 1947, Hindus by the millions were displaced from Pakistan, and Muslims by the millions from India. The Balkan wars of the 1990s were both sparked and fanned by policies of expulsion on all sides — ethnic cleansing, as it was then called. The reality of expulsion is that it is brutally effective and invariably swift. These qualities never lack for champions.

A number of accounts describe the scene in the Hall of the Ambassadors as the king and queen prepared to promulgate the Edict of Expulsion. The proposition was a simple one: Any Jew who converted to Christianity could stay. (Of course, living in Spain as a *converso* had its perils; there was the Inquisition to contend with.) Those Jews who did not convert would have to leave. The Jewish leaders Isaac Abravanel and Abraham Senor on three occasions sought to dissuade Ferdinand. "Please, O King, what is it that you want from your subjects?" said Abravenal, according to his own account. "Ask us anything: presents of gold and silver and whatever you want from the house of Israel that we can give to your native land." The story is told that Abravanel offered the king 300,000 ducats if he would reverse his decision. Tomás de Torquemada, the powerful inquisitor general, got wind of the offer and angrily confronted Ferdinand and Isabella at the Alhambra, holding a crucifix before them and saying, "Judas Iscariot sold his master for thirty pieces of silver. Your Highness would sell him anew for three hundred thousand."

The exodus from Spain began. Abravenal managed to wring a single concession: the expulsion would be delayed until August 2, which in 1492 coincided with the ninth of Av in the Jewish calendar — a day that marks the destruction of the temple in Jerusalem. Ferdinand and Isabella were unaware of the symbolism.

It is impossible to get an accurate fix on the number of Jews who refused to be baptized and were forced to leave Spain — estimates run to more than 100,000, at the high end, and to as low as 40,000. Certainly the trauma was immense. Most went to Portugal, which accepted them for the time being, though its own ferocious inquisition was not far away, and Jews living there would have to move on once more. Others fled north to the kingdom of Navarre, in the elbow of southwestern Europe, where the Pyrenees meet the Atlantic. The rest found their way primarily to North Africa and Italy. In time, large numbers would settle within the empire of the Ottomans. Many would also venture to Iberia's overseas colonies in Asia and America. One *converso* wrote to a Jewish friend who was embarking: "Do not grieve over your departure, for you have to drink down your death in one gulp, whereas we have to stay behind among these wicked people, receiving death from them every day."

Poisoned Hearts

There had been inquisitions, on the medieval model, in parts of Spain during the previous two centuries. These were intermittent and mainly desultory affairs, and organizationally similar to the inquisitions in southern France and elsewhere in Europe — that is, highly decentralized. The Spanish Inquisition, as brought to life by Ferdinand and Isabella, would be different. There is no simple way to describe the society out of which it grew.

Romantic notions of *convivencia* may touch on something that once was true, but they also hide the bitter reality of divisions within divisions in a land both troubled and poor. Power was dispersed among competing jurisdictions and fractious rulers, even as the frontiers of faith shifted over time. Religious distinctions were deeply important, but distinctions based on class and status cut across them, and religious communities were themselves divided. The occasional tactical expulsion of one group or another — Christians from Muslim territories, Jews and Muslims from Christian territories — created a social regime of displaced loyalties and burning resentments.

"Religious distinctions," "class and status," "tactical expulsions," "burning resentments" — the terms are bloodless in their abstraction, the abstraction further bleached of passion by the remove of half a millennium. Perhaps some perspective on the dynamic at play — how easily animosities can be stirred — may be gained from looking at a happier place: a society that is not poor but rich, one that guarantees religious freedom and individual equality in its Constitution, and one whose national mythology is pretty well summed up in those T-shirts from Córdoba: "The secret is in the mixture."

The United States of America in the twenty-first century is about as different from late-medieval Spain as a country can be. And yet a controversy during the summer of 2010 demonstrated how little effort is required to whip up popular fervor on issues of "otherness." The controversy involved the matter of "birthright citizenship" — that is, whether people are American citizens simply by virtue of being born in the United States, or must be deemed eligible on the basis of other characteristics — for instance, having parents of the right sort, however that may be defined, or seeming to represent the kind of person the country "wants."

Enshrined for more than two centuries in American practice, and for a century and a half in the Fourteenth Amendment, birthright citizenship suddenly found itself under powerful attack. The spark came in the form of charges that undocumented aliens in large numbers were coming to America to bear children, and then using the children as "anchors" to keep themselves legally in the country. The charges were themselves undocumented; under existing law, such children cannot apply for residency permits on behalf of their parents until they are twenty-one. The background, of course, was the unease, heightened by economic recession, over illegal immigration per se and, more broadly, over the nation's changing demographic and cultural character — phenomena that have kindled deep anxiety and occasional violence throughout American history. But birthright citizenship was a new target. Politicians on the right began to stoke the issue. Senator Lindsey Graham of South Carolina called birthright citizenship "a mistake." Other legislators demanded congressional hearings to give the Fourteenth Amendment a second look. Keith Larson, a Charlotte-based radio host, offered an analogy: "If a Catholic mom were to give birth in a synagogue, would the baby automatically be Jewish? It's absurd." Representative Louie Gohmert of Texas highlighted the national-security angle. "There are people coming into this country," he said, "who want to destroy our way of life. I talked to a retired FBI agent who said that one of the things they were looking at were terrorist cells overseas who had figured out how to game our system. And it appeared that they would have young women who became pregnant, would get them into the United States to have a baby."

Within a matter of weeks, birthright citizenship had moved from something that people took for granted to something that, according to opinion polls, nearly half of all Americans had decided they opposed. In January 2011, a group of state legislators unveiled a proposal to create what some described as a two-tiered system of birth certificates, one tier for babies born to citizens and legal immigrants, the other for children of illegal immigrants. Shortly afterward, two U.S. senators proposed a constitutional amendment that would deny birthright citizenship outright to children born to illegal aliens, regardless of the consequences. As one commentator pointed out, "Without the concept of birthright citizenship, it is possible for someone to be born without having citizenship in any country at all."

The point is not to make a facile comparison between incomparable regimes. It is simply to note that dangerous passions — about social contamination, about religious incursion — can be found anywhere. It does not take much to arouse them. Spain in the fourteenth and fifteenth centuries was acutely susceptible. One source of instability was the Black Death, which ravaged Europe beginning in 1348. Within two years, Spain's population had been reduced by a third. Medievalists sometimes joke, if that's the word for it, that the Black Death was good for one thing: it raised the minimum wage. That may have been true in the cities and towns of urbanized Europe, but in agrarian Spain the Black Death meant mainly . . . death. Iberia endured a degree of economic hardship it had not experienced in centuries.

Add to this the religious divisions. As a boy growing up in the 1950s and 1960s, on the eve of the Second Vatican Council, I remember references in Catholic liturgy to the "blindness" of "perfidious Jews." The references were mumbled and formulaic, but ugly and corrosive all the same. Within a few years, the Vatican would revise the liturgy somewhat, and would also formally abjure the charge of "blood guilt"— the charge that the Jewish people were to blame for the Crucifixion. Eventually, the Vatican would offer a guarded, defensive apology for the role that its teachings "may have played" in fostering anti-Semitism. But in fourteenth-century Spain, the anti-Semitic teachings of the Church were in full flower. They were distilled in the person of Ferrand Martínez, a priest in Seville, who identified Jews as the cause of economic misery and spent the 1380s carrying that message from town to town. The king of Castile tried to suppress Martínez, who responded that his work was authorized by a power higher than any earthly monarch. Martínez continued to preach.

In recent years, political writers have made note of a phenomenon they call "epistemic closure." The term refers to the ease with which people can become caught in an information loop that offers a fully satisfying explanation of the way things are and presents no challenges to that perspective. The great practical advantage of free speech and a robust media, it has been said, lies in the way they enable a continual testing of propositions and ideas. But the Internet and social networking, which some tout as mainly a force for good, also allow people to confine themselves to a Möbius strip of the like-minded. Evangelicals and gay activists, Tea Partiers and jihadis, anarchists and Marines—any group can exist within an information membrane of its own devising, unchallenged by outside sources. The consequences for civility and public discourse are becoming all too clear.

Ferrand Martínez, a loud voice in a community of illiterates, had a closed loop to himself, and in 1391 his words incited anti-Jewish riots in Seville, Barcelona, Córdoba, and Valencia. Thousands of Jews were killed. In the aftermath, Jews were confronted by the authorities with a choice: convert to Christianity or suffer the consequences. Those who did not convert were confined to ghettos, forced to wear badges, and barred from traditional professions. Expulsion was not yet contemplated, but 1391 was a prelude. A significant proportion of the Jews of Spain converted at that time, adding a body of *conversos*—regarded with suspicion or hostility by Christians and Jews—to an already unstable situation. As Christians, the *conversos* could seek advancement in fields once closed to them—and they did. But the allegation that *conversos* were unreliable was never far from the surface. In the hands of people like Alfonso de Hojeda, this allegation was a powerful weapon. It was used to provoke paranoia and resentment, and led to frequent outbreaks of violence.

In 1478, Ferdinand and Isabella sent a formal request to Rome for the establishment of an inquisition in Spain. Pope Sixtus IV granted the request and, in a break with precedent, allowed the secular authorities—the monarchs themselves—to have power of appointment and dismissal over the new inquisitors. Sixtus had little choice—he needed Spain's military help against the Turks—and in any case, he had other distractions: the Sistine Chapel, the rebuilding of Rome, and the elevation of his many nephews to the cardinalate. For two years, the Inquisition remained quiescent, but in 1480, Ferdinand and Isabella named the first inquisitors, and within a few months, as Hojeda whipped up anti-*converso* fervor, that first auto-da-fé was held in Seville. The next several years were horrific, and the pope, getting wind of events from afar, succumbed to grave second thoughts. Sixtus expressed his reservations to the king and queen in writing, and soon thereafter issued a bull in which he spelled out his concerns and laid down strict guidelines for how the Spanish Inquisition should proceed. Referring to the confiscations that routinely followed convictions, he declared that the Inquisition in Spain "has for some time been moved not by zeal for the faith and the salvation of souls but by lust for wealth." True and faithful Christians, he went on, had been wrongly sent to their deaths, "setting a pernicious example and causing disgust to many." Henry Charles Lea would call this document "the most extraordinary bull in the history of the Inquisition."

It was also a dead letter. The king and queen resisted. They viewed the Inquisition as a royal prerogative — indeed, as an essential under-pinning of state power. In attempting to bind a patchwork of jurisdictions — each with its own customs, laws, and bureaucracies — into a unified Spanish kingdom, the monarchs had created a number of supercouncils, of which the Inquisition was one. Indeed, it was the only one whose prerogatives pushed royal power to every part of the kingdom. The Inquisition was an essential organ of state. One historian, stepping back, sees its role in surprisingly contemporary terms. Rather than being an "icon of premodern irrationality," the Spanish Inquisition seems "remarkably modern" and an "unheralded ancestor" once you get to know its procedures:

Like state bureaucracies everywhere, the Inquisition was formally organized and regulated by protocols: inquisitors swore to follow universal norms and standards, to be fair and just in decisions, to be impartial in their practices, to work for the greater benefit of the public weal. Of course, like their twenty-first century counter-parts, inquisitors learned to fudge.

In the end, Sixtus stood down, revoking his bull and effectively acquiescing in state control over the Inquisition, with the stipula-tion — never to be honored — that Rome had the right to review certain sentences if presented for appeal. The king and queen ap-pointed Tomás de Torquemada to the position of inquisitor general of all Spain. When Sixtus died, his successors confirmed the existing arrangement, and even strengthened the royal prerogatives.

The Mastermind

The name Tomás de Torquemada is more closely linked to the Span-ish Inquisition than any other — with cause — though at this point it is hard to disentangle fact and fiction. Not much fact survives to start with. Like Cleopatra, King Arthur, or the Marquis de Sade, Torque-mada has achieved a form of meta-existence. He is a character in literature and a metaphor in polemics. He shows up in a poem by Longfellow, a play by Hugo, a rock song by Electric Wizard. Marlon Brando played him in the movies. The web comic *Pibgorn* features a demon who assumes the guise of a game-show host in hell and calls himself Tom Torquemada. If Kenneth Starr drew a blank on the name, he must not have been paying attention.

Torquemada was born in Valladolid, in the Kingdom of Castile, in 1420, and entered the Dominican Order in his teens. Whether he himself had Jewish ancestry is difficult to establish; his uncle, Juan de Torquemada, a powerful cardinal, certainly did. In any case, such an-cestry would hardly have been unusual. Many of the great families of Spain, along with many ordinary ones, had over the years intermar-ried with *converso* families. Torquemada eventually became the prior of the Dominican monastery of Santa Cruz, at Segovia, and it was there that he met the young Isabella, daughter of the king, forging a close personal bond and becoming her confessor. He encouraged her marriage to Ferdinand, which united the kingdoms of Castile and Aragon, and in time became confessor to Ferdinand as well. After the Inquisition was set up under royal control, Torquemada was appointed as one of several inquisitors, and assumed the position of inquisitor general a year later. His habits were ascetic — he wore a hair shirt, shunned finery, ate no meat — but in the course of his tenure, Torquemada amassed a considerable fortune, which he used to embellish his old monastery and to found a new one, St. Thomas Aquinas, in Avila.

"Full of pitiless zeal," writes the historian Henry Charles Lea, "he developed the nascent institution with unwearied assiduity. Rigid and unbending, he would listen to no compromise of what he deemed to be his duty, and in his sphere he personified the union of the spiritual and temporal swords which was the ideal of all true churchmen." With allowances for Victorian high dudgeon, the assessment is not far off the mark. And Torquemada knew that many of his countrymen shared a dim view of him. He typically traveled with a large armed force. Upon his death, in 1498, his body was interred at the monastery of St. Thomas Aquinas. Documentation is elusive, but the story is told that Torquemada's grave was opened by rioters in the 1830s, as the course of the Spanish Inquisition neared its end, and that his remains were exhumed and ritually burned, as if at an auto-da-fé.

By then, the Spanish Inquisition had been in existence for 350 years. Its basic procedures had been set out very early by Torquemada himself, in a work called the *Copilación de las Instrucciones del Oficio de la Santa Inquisición*. Torquemada's manual built on the manuals of Eymerich and others. Inquisitors would come to a town and, following the practice of the Medieval Inquisition, preach a sermon, calling upon people to make a clean breast of their lapses — and, just as important, inviting them to point out lapses by others. Anyone who came forward and was "reconciled" within the period of grace would be treated gently. Anyone who failed to come forward and was later accused would be treated harshly. As had happened before, the very structure of the process encouraged confession and denunciation — not to mention false confession and false denunciation. One historian writes, "The edicts of grace, more than any other factor, served to convince the inquisitors that a heresy problem existed." During the early years in particular, the numbers of people throwing themselves on the Inquisition's mercy were very high. The prisons in Seville were filled. In 1486, some 2,400 people were reconciled in Toledo alone.

Now let's put this group of people aside. They would have been given modest penances and gone on with their lives. For a second group — those who faced the judgment of a full tribunal, proclaiming their innocence or standing their ground — the future looked very different. The Inquisition did not bring a presumed heretic or judaizer to trial unless it was already convinced of the person's guilt. A conviction was virtually guaranteed. And the deck was stacked heavily against the accused. To begin with, the proceedings of the tribunal were secret. The accused did not know, when initially charged, what the specific allegations against him were. He did not know, when presented with evidence, who his denouncers might be. Furthermore, the most persuasive denouncer often turned out to be the denounced person himself, because he confessed. The application of torture in the preliminary stages of an investigation, to determine if a confession might be forthcoming, always loomed as a possibility. In a departure from the Medieval Inquisition, the accused in Spain could be represented by a lawyer, but the gesture was an empty one: the lawyer was given no information. Conviction rates from place to place were uniformly high. During the first half century of the Inquisition in Toledo, for instance, acquittals averaged about two a year. As a practical matter, the main question for a person facing trial was not whether he would be found guilty but what the punishment would be.

The penalties varied. Almost everyone would be made to spend a period of time wearing the *sanbenito*, the penitential gown with its large red or yellow cross. For some, there was flogging; for others, imprisonment as well. For unrepentant or relapsed heretics, the unavoidable penalty was burning at the stake. Short of the stake, the most feared penalty was a sentence to serve as an oarsman on the galley ships of the Mediterranean fleet. Such a sentence, technically, came with a specified duration, which generally proved to be a legal nicety:

> Disease could decimate a fleet in weeks. The galley was an amoebic death trap, a swilling sewer whose stench was so foul you could smell it two miles off — it was customary to sink the hulls at periodic intervals to cleanse them of shit and rats. . . . The oared galley consumed men like fuel. Each dying wretch dumped overboard had to be replaced — and there were never enough.

The use of galleys as punishment was a Spanish innovation, and a direct product of the Inquisition's status as an agency not just of religion but of government. Spain was a maritime power, and would be engaged for centuries in contests against European rivals and the Ottoman Turks. The punishments levied by the Medieval Inquisition had been, at least in theory, penitential ones, designed to bring convicted sinners into a restored union with God. Sentencing prisoners to the galleys served a different purpose altogether — it was designed to bring convicted sinners into battle with enemies. Another example: horse-smuggling was a problem on Spain's northern border, and corrupt local officials did nothing to stop it. The king put the matter into the hands of the Inquisition, which not only brought prosecutions but also contrived to define horse-smuggling as a "crime of faith." Where did the needs of the king leave off and the demands of God begin? In Spain, it became impossible to discern the answer.

Consider the group of people known as *familiares,* an essential adjunct of the Inquisition. The *familiares* were not clerics but laymen, chosen in every locale to provide the Inquisition's administrative substructure — part informer, part functionary. They were thick upon the ground. At one point, Valencia had one *familiar* for every forty-two of his neighbors. There were so many *familiares* that people often complained about them to the king — as well they might, because it was he who determined their number. And in some sense they were already his men: they had been chosen because they were prominent in public life — local mayors, constables, merchants. Their service to the Inquisition gave them secular benefits, such as relief from taxation and the right to bear arms. By law, they both served the Inquisition and represented the local populace in dealings with the crown. The *familiares,* every one of them, straddled church and state.

"Oh Dear God!"

The five stages of dying, posited by Elisabeth Kübler-Ross, run from denial and anger through bargaining, depression, and acceptance. We pass through similar stages when it comes to dealing with historical trauma — and then move on to new stages beyond. One of them might be called sanitation, or perhaps gentrification. Whatever the word, it reflects the fact that eventually history is safely caged and tamed. Any visitor to Antietam or Gettysburg or the Somme has seen how the bloodiest battlefields become landscapes of verdant serenity, primped with tasteful monuments. Romans walk their dogs among the umbrella pines that edge the quiet precincts of the Circus Maximus, where countless Christians went to their deaths.

Sanitation has taken hold in the old Jewish Quarter of Córdoba — still called the Judería, despite the fact that Jews have been largely gone for five hundred years. Wandering through the narrow, winding streets, a few blocks from the Mezquita, one can't help recalling Peter De Vries's remark about how so many places are named for what had to be removed in order to make them what they are.

De Vries had suburban subdivisions in mind (Orchard Hills, Fox Run), but he could have been talking about any U.S. state with an Indian name — or about the Judería of Córdoba. At one time, as many as 10,000 Jews lived here. They supported more than twenty synagogues. Today, the walls of dwellings are freshly whitewashed, flowers bloom in window boxes, and souvenir shops sell small brass menorahs. The sole medieval synagogue that escaped destruction has been restored. Not far away, in a public space, a bronze Maimonides sits contemplatively, a book open in his lap.

And then, right around the corner, you come upon the Galería de la Tortura — the museum of torture. This sort of commercial showcase seems obligatory in cities where religious persecution was once endemic — it's part of the taming process. Someday, when strife has subsided and memories have cooled, there will no doubt be an Abu Ghraib museum, at the prison outside Baghdad, with a waxen figure of the hooded man on the box, electrodes trailing from his fingertips. At the museum in Córdoba, the devices of torture are all on display. But the effect is oddly Disneyfied — a theme-park version of inhumanity. The same is true of exhibits of torture instruments that from time to time go on tour. The names the instruments have been given reinforce the sense of distant fantasy: Brazen Bull, Iron Maiden, Pear of Anguish, Judas Cradle, Saint Elmo's Belt, Cat's Paw, Brodequins, Thummekins, Scavenger's Daughter, Pilliwink, Heretic's Fork, Spanish Tickler, Spanish Donkey, Spanish Spider, Scold's Bridle, Drunkard's Cloak. They could just as easily be the names of pubs, or brands of condoms, or points of ascent on a climber's map.

The failure to shock lies as much in the times as in the curators. These days, the reality of torture is graphically accessible to everyone — in grim color photographs, in macabre videos posted online, in voluminous interrogation transcripts pried from intelligence agencies. The public profile of torture is higher than it has been for many decades, and arguments have been mounted in its defense with more energy than at any other time since the Middle Ages. In the so-called Bybee memo (later modified), the Bush administration argued that interrogators could not be prosecuted for their deeds if they were acting in good faith: "The absence of specific intent negates the charge of torture." (Following Aquinas, the inquisitors, too, cited the cleansing power of good intentions.) The administration also asserted a very narrow definition, arguing that for an action to be deemed torture, it must produce suffering "equivalent in intensity to the pain accompanying serious physical injury, such as organ failure, impairment of bodily function, or even death." To put this standard in perspective: the Bush administration's threshold for when an act of torture *begins* is the point at which the Inquisition stipulated that an act of torture must *stop*.

The legal scholar Alan Dershowitz, though not a proponent of torture, has argued that democratic governments should make provision for the issuance of official "torture warrants" that would sanction the use of torture in extreme cases — his argument being that torture is employed clandestinely in any event, and it would be better to subject it to legal regulation. "The major downside of any warrant procedure," Dershowitz writes, "would be its legitimation of a horrible practice, but in my view it is better to legitimate and control a specific practice that will occur, than to legitimate a general practice of tolerating extra-legal actions, so long as they operate under the table of scrutiny and beneath the radar screen of accountability."

The Spanish Inquisition is not what Dershowitz had in mind, but it, too, sought to legitimate and control a regime of torture, just as the Medieval Inquisition had. Torture might once have been limited to *crimina excepta* — crimes of the utmost gravity — but over time that category was broadened, and the threshold of permissibility was lowered. The phenomenon is sometimes known as torture creep. It comes in various forms. In the aftermath of the killing of Osama bin Laden, in May 2011, a number of commentators asserted that the Al Qaeda leader's hideout had been discovered owing mainly to information gleaned from torture — demonstrating just how worthwhile torture can be. The claim was not true, but the fact that it was made illustrates a moral slide: where once torture was seen as justified only by some "ticking time bomb" scenario, now it was seen as justifiable for obtaining useful intelligence of a lesser kind.

Inquisitors resorted to torture for one main purpose: to elicit statements by the victim, about himself or people he knew, that they could legally regard as "the truth." Torture was not employed officially as punishment, though it would be impossible to rule out such a motivation — in the hearts of many who wield it, torture has always entailed some measure of punishment. Officially, it was a tool of jurisprudence — an essential element in the hierarchy of proof. Because the gravest of crimes brought a penalty of death, it was essential to have an ironclad assurance of guilt — and no assurance was more persuasive than a confession. Crimes against the faith were also crimes of personal conscience, and the testimony of witnesses could be suggestive but not conclusive — which again put a premium on confession.

Darius Rejali, the most prominent modern specialist on torture, has divided certain torture techniques into what he calls the Greater and Lesser Stress Traditions. The Greater Tradition consists of methods that are applied with few limitations and that leave victims with "permanent, visible injuries." The Lesser Tradition comes with certain rules and leaves "fewer telltale marks." When modern democracies resort to torture, as they do, their tendency has been toward the Lesser Tradition — easier to hide, easier to explain away. Authoritarian regimes have no such concerns. The Inquisition straddled both traditions. It operated in an environment in which secular authorities could treat suspects as they pleased. Some of the methods employed could by their nature do irreparable damage. At the same time, the Inquisition's procedures and rituals represented a clear attempt at limitation. The moral may be that the regulation of torture never really works — it just points the practitioners in new directions. As Rejali writes, "When we watch interrogators, interrogators get sneaky."

Before a session began, the person to be interrogated by the Inquisition would be placed within sight of the instruments of torture — *in conspectus tormentorum* — in the hope that this would suffice to compel his testimony. Often it did. A physician was generally in attendance. Records were kept meticulously; the usual practice was for a notary to be present, preparing a minutely detailed account. These remarkable documents survive in large numbers; they are dry, bureaucratic expositions whose default tone of clinical neutrality is punctuated matter-of-factly by quoted screams ("Oh! Oh!"). Henry Charles Lea reproduces one such account at length — the interrogation of a woman in Toledo who had fallen under suspicion because, among other things, she did not eat pork.

> She was told to tell what she had done, for she was tortured because she had not done so, and another turn of the cord was ordered. She cried, "Loosen me, Senores!, and tell me what I have to say: I do not know what I have done, O Lord have mercy on me, a sinner!" . . . More turns were ordered, and as they were given she cried, "Oh! Oh! Loosen me for I don't know what I have to say."

It continues for pages. Statements made during torture were not themselves admissible as evidence — they had to be repeated afterward, freely, not sooner than a day later and in a location away from the torture chamber. It is a mistake to assume that duress is absent when its instruments are out of sight; and those who retracted their confessions knew they might be tortured again. But the practice of allowing a respite and demanding a repetition at least reflected the recognition, well understood by modern interrogators, that people will say anything while being tortured. Nor does torture per se need to be involved to produce such a result — any kind of intense interrogation can lead to a false confession.

In 1975, as Britain attempted to cope with an upsurge of lethal activity by the Irish Republican Army, the so-called Guildford Four and

Birmingham Six were convicted of murder and sentenced to life imprisonment for their alleged role in the bombing of two pubs. Under duress, eight of the ten defendants had confessed to complicity — but all ten were probably innocent. An appeals court overturned their sentences, after a government investigation, and the prisoners won their freedom. A recent study in the *Stanford Law Review* discussed more than forty cases in America since 1976 in which DNA evidence has led to the exoneration and release of individuals who, usually as a consequence of harsh interrogation, had confessed to crimes they had not committed.

The unreliability of torture has yet to deter it. Three main forms were employed by the Spanish Inquisition, each of which came in a number of variants. None were new. All were widely employed by secular jurisdictions of the time, in Spain and elsewhere. All remain in use today, as investigations by governments and human-rights organizations attest.

The first technique was known in Spanish as the *garrucha* ("pulley") and in Italian as the *strappado* (a "pull" or "tug"). It was a form of torture by suspension, and worked through simple gravity. It was widely known as the Queen of Torments. Typically the hands of the person to be interrogated were tied behind his back. Then, by means of a pulley or a rope thrown over a rafter, the body would be hoisted off the ground by the hands, and then be allowed to drop with a jerk. Sometimes weights would be tied to the feet. The strain on the shoulders was immense. Joints could be pulled from their sockets. Muscles could be stretched to the point where elasticity would never return. Damage to the brachial plexus, the nerve fibers running from the spinal cord to the arms, could cause paralysis. The weight of the body hanging from the arms contorted the pleural cavity, making breathing difficult (the typical cause of death in crucifixion, for the same reason).

Under various names — "Palestinian hanging," "reverse hanging" — the *strappado* appears frequently in later history. It is commonplace in our own times. Senator John McCain was subjected to a version of it, called "the ropes," when he was a prisoner of war in a North Vietnamese camp. Leaving aside its use by authoritarian regimes, as documented in many reports, it has been employed in the interrogation of prisoners in U.S. custody. One prominent case is that of Manadel al-Jamadi, who died during interrogation at Abu Ghraib in 2003. His hands had been tied behind his back, and Jamadi had then been hung by the wrists from the bars of a window that was five feet off the ground. Michael Baden, the chief pathologist for the New York State Police, explained the consequences to Jane Mayer, of *The New Yorker:*

> If his hands were pulled up five feet—that's to his neck. That's pretty tough. That would put a lot of tension on his rib muscles, which are needed for breathing. It's not only painful—it can hinder the diaphragm from going up and down, and the rib cage from expanding. The muscles tire, and the breathing function is impaired, so there's less oxygen entering the bloodstream.

The second technique employed by the Inquisition was the rack. In Spanish the word is *potro,* meaning "colt," the reference being to a small platform with four legs. Several things could occur on this platform. The victim might be placed on his back, his legs and arms fastened tautly to winches at each end. Each turn of the winches would stretch him by some additional increment. Ligaments might snap. Bones could be pulled from their sockets. The sounds alone were sometimes enough to encourage compliance in those brought in to watch. Another version of the rack relied not on radical extension but on tight compression. Rope would be wrapped around the body and fastened to the winches, coiling tighter with every turn. The rope sometimes cut through muscle, all the way to the bone.

Here is an account of a suspected heretic who had been placed on the *potro* and was being questioned by inquisitors in the Canary Islands in 1597. The winch had just been given three turns. The suspect would confess after five more. The recording secretary preserved the moment:

> On being given these he said first "Oh God!" and then, "There's no mercy": after the turns he was admonished, and he said "I don't know what to say, oh dear God!" Then three more turns of the cord were ordered to be given, and after two of them he said, "Oh God, oh God, there's no mercy, oh God help me, help me!"

The third technique involved water. *Toca,* meaning "cloth," was the term in Spanish, the reference being to the fabric that plugged a victim's upturned mouth, and upon which water was poured. The effect was to induce the sensation of asphyxiation by drowning. "Waterboarding" is the English term commonly used today, for a similar practice with a similar consequence. The modern term in Spanish is *submarino.* One expert on torture writes,

> Even a small amount of water in the glottis causes violent coughing, initiating a fight-or-flight response, raising the heart and respiratory rate, and triggering desperate efforts to break free. The supply of oxygen available for basic metabolic functions is exhausted within seconds. While this is sometimes called "an illusion of drowning," the reality is that death will follow if the procedure is not stopped in time.

There are collateral consequences as well. A review of contemporary cases by a medical journal noted that the water is "often contaminated with hair, vomit, saliva, mucus, urine, etc." and that most victims suffered "acute respiratory symptoms during the torture and also later." The CIA has acknowledged that one of its detainees, Khalid Sheikh Mohammed, the mastermind of the 9/11 attacks, was waterboarded 183 times in a single month. Defenders of the practice contend that this figure is misleading — that 183 refers to the number of individual "pours," and that they occurred in the context of no more than five "sessions." It is an argument that recalls the hairsplitting semantics of the Inquisition. Faced with statutory limitations on the number of times a person could legally be tortured, Church interrogators defined episodes that were beyond the limit as simply a "continuance" of the earlier, legal sessions.

What, in any event, is a "pour"? In 2008, the journalist Christopher Hitchens put himself in the hands of U.S. Special Forces veterans in order to experience the reality of waterboarding. "You may have read by now," he wrote afterward, "the official lie about this treatment, which is that it 'simulates' the feeling of drowning. This is not the case." He went on:

This was very rapidly brought home to me when, on top of the hood, which still admitted a few flashes of random and worrying strobe light to my vision, three layers of enveloping towel were added. In this pregnant darkness, head downward, I waited for a while until I abruptly felt a slow cascade of water going up my nose. Determined to resist if only for the honor of my navy ancestors who had so often been in peril on the sea, I held my breath for a while and then had to exhale and — as you might expect — inhale in turn. The inhalation brought the damp cloths tight against my nostrils, as if a huge, wet paw had been suddenly and annihilatingly clamped over my face. Unable to determine whether I was breathing in or out, and flooded more with sheer panic than with mere water, I triggered the pre-arranged signal and felt the unbelievable relief of being pulled upright and having the soaking and stifling layers pulled off me. I find I don't want to tell you how little time I lasted.

U.S. forces used various forms of water torture in the Philippines to suppress an insurgency there at the turn of the last century; William Howard Taft, then the governor of the Philippines, and later president of the United States, referred to the technique as the "water cure." Water torture was used by the French in Algeria in the 1950s; a vivid account was left by the French-Algerian journalist Henri Alleg in his book *La Question*. Vice President Dick Cheney, half a century later, called waterboarding "a dunk in the water." Defenders of the practice insist that waterboarding is not torture, on the grounds that the procedure does not cause lasting impairment — which, as it happens, was precisely the Inquisition's standard of performance. The Inquisition, however, understood that the *toca* was torture.

A Clash of Explanations

There is yet another stage in the life cycle of historical trauma — the stage called revisionism. We all live within cocoons of received wisdom on every subject imaginable. A commonly accepted view provides basic mental orientation on such things as the lessons of Vietnam, the virtues of free speech, the dangers of cholesterol. Because the passage of time is what it is, and generations rise and fall, we don't carry around long memories of how the received wisdom used to be different. Typically, we don't even stop to ask ourselves if it was.

With respect to the Spanish Inquisition, persecution of the Jews is today the first thing that comes to mind. That wasn't always so. The enmity between Protestant England and Catholic Spain was long reflected in the writing of history and polemics. Until the nineteenth century, most readers in the English-speaking world would have associated the Spanish Inquisition with a pursuit of Protestants. Eventually, the work of prominent historians began to move the Jews to the center of the story. But only within living memory have revisionist scholars — some but not all of them impelled by the long shadow of the Holocaust; some but not all of them Jews themselves — produced work that has altered the mental map of people outside academe.

Among the most notable of these scholars are Benzion Netanyahu, who lives mainly in Israel, and Henry Kamen, who lives mainly in Barcelona. As individuals, they could hardly be more different. Netanyahu, now age 101, is the patriarch of one of Israel's most prominent political families. His son Benjamin, known as Bibi, is the leader of the Likud Party and has twice been prime minister. "Benzion looms above his son," David Remnick has written, "no less than Joseph Kennedy loomed over his clan, and his views are at the root of Bibi's sense of a menacing world."

Netanyahu came to Palestine from Poland as a child, in 1920. His father, Nathan Mileikowsky, was a prominent early Zionist — he gave one of the eulogies at the funeral of Theodor Herzl — and was active in the Jabotinsky wing of the movement. Nathan adopted the Hebrew name Netanyahu, meaning "God-given." Politically, Benzion was cut from the same Jabotinsky cloth as his father, taking a hard-line view of Greater Israel as a nation that by rights should extend unbroken eastward from the Mediterranean to somewhere beyond the Jordan. Not until he was in his forties did Benzion find real traction as an academic. For reasons that may combine the personal and the political, he found the path difficult in Israel and eventually moved to the United States, in time becoming a professor at Cornell.

As a scholar, Benzion Netanyahu has produced dense and massive tomes that stand like fortresses on the shelf. The best known of them — the one most frequently read, or at least hefted into proximity — is *The Origins of the Inquisition in Fifteenth Century Spain*. The documentation is immense. In starkest outline, Netanyahu's argument is relatively simple: the charge advanced by the Inquisition — that the *conversos* of Spain were in fact unfaithful Christians and secret judaizers — had little basis in reality. He presents the testimony of other Jews at the time, notably rabbis in North Africa, who professed no doubt that most of the *conversos* had indeed abandoned their heritage, and railed against them in withering terms. "The wickedness of these people is greater in our eyes than that of the gentiles," wrote one rabbi, and another applied to the *conversos* a line from the

Book of Proverbs: "When the wicked are lost, it is a cause for rejoicing." But here's Netanyahu's point: if the judaizing charge was false, or largely false, then the enmity toward *conversos* was not really about religion. It was about antagonism toward Jews as a people.

Mainstream scholarship had long accepted the judaizing charge at face value: in other words, had accepted that many converted Jews secretly kept up the old ways, and in their hearts continued to see themselves as Jewish. The short story "The Surveyor" takes this view for granted. ("I knew where the *quemadero* was," the Spanish lawyer says, "because I feel the same way about the people who died there that you do. Because I cannot forget their heroic constancy, as you call it.") This is, after all, what the verbatim record of thousands of Inquisition tribunals would have you believe — it is right there on the page, in the transcripts of interrogations and the testimony of witnesses.

Some *conversos* certainly did maintain their original faith in secret. And others, though sincere Christians, kept up certain cultural practices. But whatever the Inquisition documents might say, Netanyahu argues, there was no significant amount of judaizing in Spain; his heart is not warmed by the "incredible romance" (as one historian put it, years ago) of the conventional account. Beginning in the 1960s, Netanyahu posed a radical challenge — and he did so in trademark style. His work is at once magisterial and merciless, vigilant and aggressive. In conversation, too, he takes no prisoners. Netanyahu's English — American-inflected, with a baritone nasality — is remarkably similar to Bibi's, and suffused with the sharp, dry heat of disdain. He speaks in precise paragraphs, punctuated with courtly impatience: "You will perhaps permit me to say . . ." "I speak now with candor . . ." "You will forgive me for expressing myself with, shall I say, frankness . . ." He brushes aside a question about what motivates his scholarship: "I do not approach this subject with emotion. People always say, 'You write in the shadow of the Holocaust. You have Nazis always on your mind.' But this is not true. I write only as a historian, to find out how it really was. *They* are the ones who are political."

If Netanyahu is right — if relatively few *conversos* in fact returned to the religion of their fathers, or secretly practiced it all along — then how does one explain the Inquisition? Netanyahu offers a number of linked explanations. For one, he argues, many Christians resented the high station that *conversos* frequently attained. Because the *conversos* were now Christian, they could hold public office, which they did with great distinction. Moreover, being Christian, they could no longer be attacked on religious grounds, leaving only the racial argument — impurity of blood. In other words, there was something inherently wrong with Jewishness. Finally, the Spanish crown, especially Ferdinand, saw a political advantage in siding with the Old Christians — and, incidentally, saw an opportunity to strip the New Christians of their wealth.

Henry Kamen agrees with Netanyahu on one big thing: that most of the *conversos* weren't really judaizing. The two disagree on many other points. Kamen is diminutive and soft-spoken, with features that invite speculation about his origins. Despite his surname, he explains, he is not Jewish; colleagues who know his work only from the printed page have been surprised, upon meeting him face-to-face, to find Southeast Asia gazing back. Kamen's father was an Anglo-Burmese engineer for Shell Oil; his mother was half Anglo-Irish and half Nepalese. His earliest memories come from his childhood in Japanese-occupied Burma during World War II, before the family fled to India. Kamen went on to be educated in England and France.

The Inquisition was not Kamen's original research interest, but while pursuing another project, he began spending time in the archives in Madrid — comprehensive, well catalogued, and extending back unbroken to the fifteenth century. He found the gravitational pull irresistible. Kamen was struck by the way Inquisition scholarship has always been politicized. Writers in English (the "Anglo-Saxons," he calls them, a linguistic tic from his studies in Paris) tended to have a Protestant bias, reflected in the *leyenda negra,* the Black Legend, about the dark doings of perfidious Spain. Spanish scholars, or at least the liberals among them, carried different baggage. They couldn't help seeing the Inquisition with vivid memories of the Franco regime — as if all of Spanish history presented a seamless authoritarian weave.

Acutely aware that he himself was making a politically charged argument, Kamen came to view the Inquisition in different terms. Apart from occasional moments of feverish violence — especially during the earliest decades under Torquemada — the Spanish Inquisition, he believes, was moderately restrained by the standards of the day. Violence and intellectual repression penetrated everywhere, to be sure. But those grand autos-da-fé depicted in epic paintings at the Prado were few and far between; a Spaniard might live an entire lifetime and never see one. As an institution, the Inquisition was always understaffed and never particularly wealthy. For many of those in its employ, it was a means more of advancing a career than of enforcing a worldview; people became invested in it. In the end, Kamen argues, the Inquisition was a bureaucracy like any other — often mindless, often operating out of sheer inertia, often heedless of its consequences, often manipulated by other forces. In some ways, that is part of its horror.

Kamen agrees with Netanyahu that in the century leading up to the Inquisition, the rivalry between Old Christians and New Christians could be intense — but it did not occur everywhere in Spain, he points out, and even where it did occur, the intensity was by no means constant. He agrees that a doctrine of blood purity began to take hold in public life in the decades before the Inquisition, but he points to instance after instance in which statutes meant to embody that doctrine — for instance, to prohibit Christians of Jewish ancestry from holding public office — were rejected. "Only *after* the founding of the Inquisition," he writes, "did the trend to discriminate against *conversos* on grounds of blood purity become pronounced." As for

Ferdinand's ulterior motives? The Jews of Spain, Kamen argues, were for the most part poor, like everyone else, and many of the richest ones were allowed to leave with their assets. Financially, the monarchs stood to gain little from the expulsion. Later on, Kamen notes, Ferdinand continued to stand by his *converso* advisors, and they by him.

Where Netanyahu's life calls attention to the power of roots, Kamen's life follows a very different model. Kamen admits to having felt oddly globalized from an early age, a citizen of everywhere and of nowhere. His work is devoid of a national perspective or any hint of national feeling. Emmanuel Le Roy Ladurie is French to the marrow — he writes about Montaillou from within the tradition of generations of French scholarship. When he invokes the "green purgatory of rural society," you have a sense that Gallic ancestry is flowing out the nib of his pen. Kamen writes with distance and dispassion.

Perhaps because he is rootless, Kamen pays special attention to roots everywhere else. Understanding from below — that is his major difference with Netanyahu. It is one thing to seek to understand the Inquisition as an institution. It did what it did, it was occasionally powerful, it was clever at adapting as times changed, it was entwined like a vine with the structures of secular power. But that does not explain the environment that made it possible. "The real problem," Kamen told me, "is the state of mind of the Spanish population at specific periods of its history."

He explained all this one afternoon in Barcelona, as we walked through the old quarter, the Barri Gòtic, which sits atop the old Roman city and in some places still follows its street plan. Bits of Roman walls are embedded in the cathedral. Kamen pointed them out — and then, turning down an alley, paused at the Palau Episcopal, the headquarters of the Inquisition. The first autos-da-fé were held in the courtyard here, where workmen were setting up chairs for an evening concert. The Inquisition did not plant itself deeply in Catalonia, in part because Catalans have always resented interlopers — such as anyone from a faraway capital — and in part because after the pogroms of 1391, most of Barcelona's Jews were already gone.

Kamen kept coming back to a single theme: how something like the Inquisition can take hold. He thinks in terms of organic processes, processes that are slow and perhaps not quite visible even as they unfold. He is skeptical about attributing too much autonomy to the institution itself — as if, in a backward society, a sophisticated machine could just descend from above. The lens needs to be turned in the other direction: something had happened to Spain itself. "All police bodies — *all* police bodies, whether they're the village policeman or the Gestapo or the traffic police — all of them are repressive," Kamen said as we strolled. "They cooperate in exactly the same way. They are created to cause fear. Sometimes they succeed, sometimes they don't; sometimes they overpass the limits, sometimes they don't; and so on. The important question to ask is why these bodies are allowed to exist. If a country such as Spain allowed a repressive body like the Inquisition to exist for four hundred years, it is not because the Inquisition forced itself on the Spanish nation. It is because the Spaniards allowed it to exist."

We wound around to a nearby plaza — a place of execution during the Spanish Civil War — and then to the Plaça Sant Jaume, the seat of Barcelona's government since antiquity. From the Plaça, a dark, narrow street led into the Call, the Jewish Quarter. A few shops sell Hebraica to tourists. As in Córdoba, the Jewish presence in the Call is thin. Even "veneer" is too ambitious a word.

"Netanyahu cannot simply discount all these people who are denouncing other people to the Inquisition," Kamen went on. "For me, the denunciations are the principal problem, not the Inquisition. You have to understand a bit about police systems in Europe in the fourteenth and fifteenth centuries. There *are* no police systems. There are no *police*. There are only one or two people who, if crimes arise, have to deal with the problem. Okay? So how do crimes get denounced? For the most part, in Europe in the fifteenth century, crimes do not get denounced. If there is a rape in your village, how do you deal with it? Well, if you like the guy who did it, you descend on his house and you say, 'Look, we've got to solve this. Do you love my daughter? Are you going to marry her? And you also have to pay some money to make good the wrong.' If you don't like the guy, you kill him. The whole thing gets resolved. You don't go through the courts — there is no legal system. In the same way, if there is a problem of social rejection of certain people, you resolve it in your own way — you attack them, you have riots against them. That is why you have all these riots against the Jews in the Middle Ages.

"But now, suddenly, there exists a state body called the Inquisition — which from your point of view is really just two priests in a city six hours away — and you have the possibility of taking legal action. As a result, bit by bit, these social pressures against the Jews get funneled toward these two people. What is most important here? Is it the existence of these two people? No, it's the existence of social pressures — it's the anti-Semitic nature of society. What exists for me is the common people. It's the people — lots of them — who are denouncing *conversos* to the Inquisition. So my interest is in the background and roots of the Inquisition — what brings it into existence."

Kamen does not have an answer to the question, but it is a crucial one: What turns a society, any society, from one thing into another? What combination of factors — economic distress, ethnic hostility, physical threat, moral fervor, latent envy, political manipulation — can alter the historic character of a people or place? Spain, Kamen notes, was a land where three religions had gotten along tolerably, though without love, for many years. In most regions of Spain, the Medieval Inquisition had never found a friendly reception. More than those of other nations, its rulers and mariners looked outward to the possibilities of a beckoning planet. And then, in a relatively short period of time, something changed. The Inquisition became a dangerous institution — but only because Spain itself had already curdled.

Under Sail

In August 1492, at the port of Palos de la Frontera, on the Atlantic coast of Spain, Christopher Columbus prepared to embark on his voyage west across the ocean. As noted, his expedition had been financed by *conversos*. There were *conversos* among his crew. From his caravel he watched as Jewish refugees on other ships—those who had refused to be baptized—took leave of their country. He described the scene in his log as a "fleet of misery and woe."

As Columbus set sail, the Inquisition in Spain was at a peak of severity. Statistics on most aspects of the Inquisition are contested, but a widely accepted estimate for the number of people put to death in the Spanish Inquisition's first two decades is 2,000, with the total rising to about 12,000 during the full course of its history. The corresponding total for Portugal, whose inquisition began somewhat later, is about 3,000. To put this in perspective, in 1450, the combined population of Spain and Portugal was only about 7 million. The pool of potential victims was smaller, given that only a few specific groups constituted the chief targets of the Inquisition.

But focusing on executions does not convey the extent of the Inquisition's penetration. Francisco Bethencourt, trying to get a handle on the number of people who were drawn, one way or another, into inquisitorial procedures in Iberia over the institution's lifetime—not just those actually hauled before a tribunal but all those who were denounced, along with informers and witnesses—puts the overall number at 1.5 million. Perhaps 300,000 of those people stood trial.

Those are the figures for Iberia. But the Inquisition was not confined to the peninsula. The Medieval Inquisition had been primarily a localized affair. The Spanish, like the Portuguese, traveled vast distances and planted inquisitions all around the world. Columbus helped open the way.

4

THAT SATANIC DEVICE

The Roman Inquisition

It is a fearful thing to fall into the
hands of the living God.

— EPISTLE TO THE HEBREWS, 10:31

I myself hardly ever read a book without feeling
in the mood to give it a good censoring.

— ROBERT BELLARMINE, CARDINAL-INQUISITOR, 1598

The Emergency

THE BASILICA OF Santa Maria sopra Minerva lies a few paces beyond the Pantheon in Rome, facing a small piazza where a modest Egyptian obelisk rises from the back of a marble elephant, in accordance with a design by Bernini. It's hard to miss. On the church's exterior wall, plaques in Latin with pointing fingers indicate how high the Tiber's floodwaters reached on epochal occasions. "Up to here grew the Tiber," reads one of them, from 1530, "and Rome would already have been completely flooded, had the Virgin not performed here her swift action."

Santa Maria sopra Minerva is something of an oddity — the only Gothic church in Rome. Near the altar stands a statue of Christ, sculpted by Michelangelo. Saint Catherine of Siena is buried here. So is the painter Fra Angelico. Like Catherine, he was a Dominican, and Santa Maria was for a long time the order's headquarters in Rome. The Dominican connection points to an Inquisition connection, and in fact there are many. To begin with, the roof above the nave was built and paid for by Cardinal Juan de Torquemada, the uncle of the inquisitor Tomás.

I asked a Dominican priest if I could visit the adjoining cloister. He took out a set of keys, unlocked a wooden door, and led the way. "Only a dozen of us live here now," he said. "There used to be hundreds." The walls and ceilings of the cloister are covered with frescoes. In the open square, cats doze among fallen columns from an ancient building. Palm trees rise high enough above the tiled rooftops to catch a breeze. Here, in 1633, in a second-floor room, Galileo Galilei was made to face an Inquisition tribunal for advancing the view that Earth revolves around the Sun. When the tribunal's work was done, Galileo formally abjured his beliefs. Santa Maria has not invested heavily in publicizing this aspect of its story. The basilica's Web site does not mention it. The literature at the front door is silent. "Pay no attention to 1633," the church might as well be saying. "But look! Over there! The tomb of Fra Angelico! And look — a Michelangelo!"

Galileo is only the most prominent person to have been caught up in what is now called the Roman Inquisition. The successor to the Medieval Inquisition, and separate from the Spanish Inquisition, it was created at a moment of crisis — an existential emergency for the Church. Its purpose was to blunt the rise of Protestantism and to spearhead the Counter-Reformation, and it was run in a coordinated way directly from Rome. Eventually it would expand the range of its targets — to heretics and freethinkers of various kinds, to magic and superstition, to aspects of science and rationalism. Of course, it always had an eye on the Jews.

The Roman Inquisition was established in 1542, by Pope Paul III. Paul himself was more of a humanist than a prosecutor. He was painted by Raphael when young and by Titian when old. He issued a bull confirming that the Indians of North America were human beings. The true architect of the Roman Inquisition was Giovanni Pietro Carafa, who as a cardinal pressed for its creation, and who in 1555 was elevated to the papacy as Pope Paul IV. In many of its procedures, the Roman Inquisition resembled the medieval one, but it was centralized and bureaucratized as never before. Its inquisitors were not itinerant agents but functionaries of an apparat. They answered to a committee of cardinals overseen by an inquisitor general. The Roman Inquisition established permanent offices in cities throughout Italy.

The accomplishments of Paul IV, the sternest of the Inquisition popes, were from his perspective considerable. He created the Index Librorum Prohibitorum — the Index of Forbidden Books. He sent hundreds of convicted heretics to the stake, placing the idea of due process, as one historian writes, "under an almost unbearable strain." He forced the Jews of Rome to wear distinctive clothing and confine themselves to a ghetto. Nor did he neglect the arts. Paul IV discontinued Michelangelo's pension and ordered that the nude figures in *The Last Judgment,* in the Sistine Chapel, be draped in veils and loincloths. The painted garments, the work of Daniele da Volterra — known ever afterward as Il Braghettone, "the breeches-maker" — are still there to be seen. They were unaffected by the restorations of the 1980s and 1990s.

The historian Leopold von Ranke rendered his own last judgment on Paul IV, directing attention to Paul's sense of utter certainty: "From time to time characters like that of Paul re-appear on the theater of the world. Their conceptions of the world and of life are formed from a single point of view; their individual bent of mind is so strong that their opinions are absolutely governed by it." Ranke went on:

He favoured, above all other institutions, the inquisition, which indeed he had himself reestablished. He often let the days pass by which were set apart for the *segnatura* and the consistory; but he never missed the meetings of the congregation of the inquisition, which took place every Thursday. He wished its powers to be exercised in the severest manner.

At Paul's death, in 1559, a Roman mob sacked the original headquarters of the Inquisition, which had been located on the banks of the Tiber, near the Mausoleum of Augustus. They set free more than seventy prisoners and then put the place to the torch, destroying most of the Inquisition's books and files. The mob then moved on, threatening to burn down Santa Maria sopra Minerva. Atop the Campidoglio, the old Roman capitol, they attacked a marble statue of the late pope, dragging its head through the streets and then throwing it into the river.

With the Inquisition's palazzo in ashes, the new pope, Pius V, set about building an even more imposing central headquarters. This work was deemed so urgent that every other task took a lower priority. Rome at the time was still a half-dead city. Islands of Renaissance grandeur rose from among sprawling slums and malarial marshes. Over the centuries, only one of the eleven ancient aqueducts had functioned continuously. The Basilica of St. Peter's was as yet unfinished — the circular drum that now supports the dome was not complete — but the pope pulled away the stonecutters and masons for the Inquisition project. The cannons at Castel Sant'Angelo saluted as the first stone was laid. A diplomat reported to the Holy Roman Emperor that the work was proceeding *gagliardamente* — "spiritedly." An inscription would be placed over the main entrance, declaring that the palazzo had been erected as a "bulwark" in the war against the "adherents of heretical depravity."

The new headquarters was a vast, fortresslike structure, with high barred windows and stout towers on the corners. Prisoners were held in the eastern wing. Slits for muskets bracketed an iron door. A renovation and a calmer ocher façade would one day soften the palazzo's appearance, but not until the 1920s. "In the interior of the building," a nineteenth-century British visitor reported, "is a lofty hall with gloomy frescoes of Dominican saints, and many terrible dungeons and cells, in which the visitor is unable to stand upright, having their vaulted ceilings lined with reeds to deaden sound." An American visitor, a few years later, described a "gloomy and forbidding pile of massive masonry" with "deaf stone ears and voiceless walls." In his own moral taxonomy, this visitor placed the palace within "the Rome of Caligula and Nero and the Borgias."

As for Paul IV, you can find him in Santa Maria sopra Minerva. An imposing statue sits above his remains in a side chapel off the nave. Paul glowers at the world, tiara upon his head, an arm raised imperiously. The funeral monument lies in deep shadow, but a few coins in a meter will buy a moment of illumination. The lights click on with a sharp metallic sound, and with the same sound, seconds later, they are abruptly extinguished.

What Do You Mean by This?

That the story of the Roman Inquisition can be known at all in many of its details is something of a historical accident. The documents that tell the story are lodged in a number of locations. Some can be found here and there in the Vatican's Archivio Segreto. A portion of this archive occupies a complex of elaborately frescoed rooms adjacent to the Vatican Library. The rest spills over onto fifty miles of shelves in the Vatican bunker. These are the day-to-day papers of the popes and the papal bureaucracy, and they run back to the end of the eighth century, dwindling in volume as they recede in time. Henry VIII's request for an annulment of his marriage to Catherine of Aragon can be found in these files, the wax seals of the king's legion of co-petitioners hanging from the document on red ribbons. Papal absolution for the Knights Templar — too late to help their cause — can also be found here, and original works by Galileo.

A second group of documents make up the Inquisition archives per se — minutes of meetings, official correspondence, the personal papers of the inquisitors, and much else. These are preserved at the headquarters of the Congregation for the Doctrine of the Faith, in the Inquisition's old palazzo.

A third group lies outside the Vatican: Inquisition records can be found in the archives of Bologna and Modena, Venice and Naples and other places where intense Inquisition activity took place. The documents in these locations include the records of thousands of trials.

In 1809, Napoleon, whose armies controlled most of continental Europe, and who had effectively annexed the Papal States, gave the order to transport as many documents as possible from the first two groups — that is, everything at the Vatican — to Paris. The pope himself, Pius VII, was already in French custody. The Vatican had not been singled out for special treatment: Napoleon was taking control of archives everywhere, and planned to create a vast pan-European repository in his imperial capital. Over a period of three years, at enormous expense, more than 3,000 chests of papal documents were hauled by wagon across the Alps. Along the way, some disappeared forever, sliding by accident into rivers and canals. At last they arrived at the Palais Soubise, where the French national archives are kept even today. The Palais Soubise holds the records of the trial of Joan of Arc. In the margin of one page is a sketch of Joan, apparently drawn not long after her death.

No sooner had the last of the archives arrived in Paris than Napoleon fell from power; the archives could now be returned. But the French government wouldn't pay for shipment, and the pope was nearly penniless. Gone were the days when a Renaissance pontiff like Sixtus IV could spend a third of the papacy's annual income on a coronation tiara. To reduce the cost of transportation — and perhaps also to get rid of unwelcome evidence pertaining to the Inquisition—the Holy See ordered its commissioners in Paris to destroy many of the documents. Some were shredded and sold as pulp for cardboard. Some were bought by victuallers and other merchants for use as wrapping paper, the individual sheets inadvertently becoming public fodder, brandished by propagandists of anticlerical bent. (A monograph should be written on the role of food vendors in the transmission or destruction of historical evidence.) Some documents were stolen or quietly acquired by private parties, in transactions that remain shrouded. A substantial trove of records somehow made its way to Trinity College, Dublin, where it remains to this day. Smaller caches turned up here and there—at the Royal Library in Belgium, for instance. Until the end of the twentieth century, these stray collections were the only Inquisition records originating in the Vatican itself that scholars could consult.

In the end, only about two thirds of what had gone to Paris made its way back to Rome. Among the documents destroyed were many that concerned the trial and suppression of the Knights Templar, and all the arguments for the defense in the case of Giordano Bruno. The records of the trial of Galileo were lost for decades, inspiring dark theories, but they eventually surfaced in Prague and found their way back to Rome.

For a long time, the archives just sat there. Toward the end of the nineteenth century, Pope Leo XIII agreed to open the Archivio Segreto to a few outside scholars, most notably the historian Ludwig von Pastor. The Inquisition archives, however, would remain sealed for another century. In 1979, Carlo Ginzburg sent his letter to Pope John Paul II, and the Vatican's resistance began to erode. By all accounts, the man who argued most forcefully that the archives should be opened, and eventually saw to it that they were, was Cardinal Ratzinger. In the five years after Ratzinger became pope, more attention was lavished on his sartorial choices—the designer sunglasses, the red Prada shoes—than on his scholarly credentials. Ratzinger is not a liberal, but he is indeed an intellectual, and the values of the academy exercise a gravitational pull on some important part of him. Even before the Inquisition archives were officially opened, in 1998, Ratzinger had begun allowing a handful of scholars to burrow in the stacks, under careful supervision.

One of those scholars was Peter Godman, a New Zealand–born historian who now teaches at the University of Rome, and who for many years divided his time between archival work at the Vatican and a professorship at the University of Tübingen. Tübingen is also the home of the liberal theologian Hans Küng, who for fifty years has played mongoose to the Vatican's cobra (or, depending on one's perspective, the other way around). Küng and Ratzinger were once like-minded colleagues in their role as *periti,* or advisors, at the Second Vatican Council, in the 1960s. In those early days, Küng in fact gave Ratzinger a job at Tübingen. Personally and theologically, the two men drifted apart. In 1979, Ratzinger played a role in stripping Küng of his *missio canonica* — his permission to teach as a Catholic theologian.

Peter Godman looks boyish for his fifty-five years. He has been haunting the Inquisition archives for a decade and a half. He knows the various sixteenth-century secretaries by their handwriting and speaks about the cardinal-inquisitors in the present tense, as if they were about to walk down the hall. He has a particular feeling for Giulio Antonio Santori, the inquisitor general who oversaw the condemnation of Giordano Bruno. Sometimes he uses the word "we" to refer to the blended world of historical Inquisition and modern archive, a locution that I am not sure he notices.

One afternoon, he led the way up the spiral staircase in the reading room and into the tight furrows among the shelves. "You never know what you're going to find," he explained. "In this manuscript here" — he pulled down a volume — "I found the deliberations regarding the censorship of Descartes." (His *Meditations* and his *Metaphysics,* along with some other works, were placed on the Index in 1663.) Godman moved along and pulled down another volume. "In this one are the preparations for the Syllabus of Errors"—a compendium of theologically noxious ideas, issued by Pope Pius IX in 1864. "The collections were formed arbitrarily—there was a system which was invariably chaotic. The system can be geographic. It can be thematic. Here you have things about animal magnetism and hypnotism." His fingers lightly traced the spines.

Godman drew another register off the shelf. "Here's an English case. Grately. Edmund Grately. We had him in prison here, upstairs. He claimed he was an ecumenical, trying to mediate between Roman and Anglican. They thought, of course, that he was a heretic. They found him with a considerable amount of money, and weapons, and also these bizarre writings in English. The inquisitors had the writings translated into Latin—very unusual for them to take the time to do that. Grately, it turned out, was a spy for Elizabeth I. And here—look—here is the sentence: life imprisonment. In practice, that typically means three years. The sentence is written out in the hand of Cardinal Santori—the grand inquisitor himself."

We moved on a little farther. Godman opened one last register, from 1574. He said, "This case is of great interest because the accused—his name was Filippo Mocenigo—was an archbishop, in Cyprus. He was an important figure. What he didn't know was that he'd been on trial for heresy for thirteen years—he had been denounced for remarks he had made about free will while on the journey to the Council of Trent." This was the great reforming council that ushered in the Counter-Reformation and set Catholicism's course for centuries. "Nor did he know," said Godman, "that it would last for another nine. The proceedings go on and on. One of the main charges against him was that he wrote a book that no one's ever heard of, because there was only one copy—and it's here. It's a work of simple and very stupid piety, written in Italian and intended for Mocenigo's sister, who was a nun. It was never published. Two or three inquisitors are on the job." They eventually brought Mocenigo in for questioning: What do you mean by this? What do you mean by that? At one place in the interrogation transcript is Mocenigo's plaintive assessment: "It seems to me that *laboramus in equivocis*" — that is, "we labor in equivocation." And the archbishop's fate? "In the end," said Godman, "he was found innocent. But the book itself was condemned. Which is why it's here. The only copy."

The Gutenberg Challenge

The words "only copy" have a whiff of the medieval about them, a scent of the candle. They recall a time when every book was a unique object made with pen and ink and parchment, in a monastic scriptorium or the secretaries' office at a university — and when every additional copy was indeed literally copied, letter by letter, laboriously and by hand. The Inquisition archive itself has a medieval flavor, in part because up until the modern period, all the record-keeping had to be done by notaries, who were priests. Their handwriting is beautiful to look at, and has aged wonderfully on the page.

But the medieval flavor is misleading. If the Roman Inquisition is about anything, it's about the revolution ushered in by the printing press. The Medieval Inquisition and, in its earliest stages, the Spanish Inquisition were directed chiefly at people — that is, at the physical corpora of sentient beings. They were directed at heretics who inhabited a mainly oral culture. Word of mouth can be a powerful force, especially when growing networks of communication allow ideas to spread from valley to valley and port to port, but the personal physicality involved kept the inquisitorial focus on actual people. In Spain, of course, that focus was even more intense. Certain *classes* of people were the target — not just what they believed or the ideas they spread but who they were: Jews and Moors. The Roman Inquisition went after people too; it put a good number of them to death. But it was just as much about the published word.

Books in the codex form we know them had existed for a millennium, but most people couldn't read, and in any case the making of books was a time-consuming process. Books were also expensive. Someone who had a "big" library had at most a few hundred volumes. Petrarch, who first applied the term "Dark Ages" to what we now think of as the medieval era, was one of the great book collectors of his age. He was in his library when he died, in 1374. Petrarch donated his books to the Republic of Venice — a collection numbering only about two hundred volumes. Seventy years later, Humphrey, Duke of Gloucester, began distributing his library to Oxford; the gift, which became the basis for the university library, numbered only about three hundred volumes. If heresy was thought of as a contagion, the most worrisome means of transmission was certainly not books.

The printing press, developed in the mid fifteenth century, changed all that — very suddenly, and by an order of magnitude. To give some idea, here's a single example from very early in the history of printing: it concerns the Ripoli Press, an establishment in Florence that had added a printing press to its traditional scriptorium. The press was operated by nuns. Albinia de la Mare, one of the foremost authorities on the book trade, did the math: "In 1483, the Ripoli Press charged three florins per *quinterno* for setting up and printing Ficino's translation of Plato's *Dialogues*. A scribe might have charged one florin per *quinterno* for duplicating the same work. The Ripoli Press produced 1,025 copies; the scribe would have turned out one." (A *quinterno* was a unit of paper that, if folded and printed on both sides, yielded sixteen book-sized pages.) It is estimated that scribes copied out some 2.7 million books over the course of the entire fourteenth century; printers produced more than that number in the single year 1550. Thanks to the revolution in typography wrought by the printer and publisher Aldus Manutius, more words could be squeezed onto smaller pages and yet still be read without difficulty; books became easier to carry (and easier to conceal). Any town or city of any ambition had a printing shop. The printer's establishment — which also served as publisher, marketer, and defender of copyright — was as central to the civic space as churches and markets.

There is a celebrated passage by Frances Yates, the biographer of Giordano Bruno, in her book *The Art of Memory:*

> In Victor Hugo's *Notre Dame de Paris* a scholar, deep in meditation in his study . . . gazes at the first printed book which has come to disturb his collection of manuscripts. Then . . . he gazes at the vast cathedral, silhouetted against the starry sky . . . "*Ceci tuera cela,*" he says. The printed book will destroy the building.

It is not clear that people at the time were as prescient as Hugo's scholar, any more than those who saw the first automobile understood that it would hollow out the hearts of great cities, put vast power in the hands of tribal sheikhs, and make the oceans rise. Elizabeth Eisenstein, a distinguished historian of printing and its consequences, notes that even Martin Luther, when he tacked his famous ninety-five theses to the door of the Castle Church in Wittenberg, in 1517 ("if indeed they were ever placed there"), claimed not to have anticipated the furor that his challenge to a debate, when harnessed to the printing press, would ignite. Luther wrote defensively to the pope a few months later, "It is a mystery to me how my theses, more so than my other writings, indeed those of other professors, were spread to so many places. They were meant exclusively for our academic circle here." Yes, how could that possibly have happened? Luther was being somewhat disingenuous, but the rapidity with which his ideas gained circulation could never have been anticipated and certainly took him by surprise.

As Eisenstein points out, Luther's theses were known throughout Europe within a few months, "competing for space with news of the Turkish threat in print shop, bookstall, and country fair." She goes on to note that because of the printing press, gifted preachers who posed a threat to the Church could no longer be effectively dealt with by simple consignment to the flames; religious dissidents "were able to send their messages from beyond the grave, as editions of their collected sermons continued to be published long after their deaths." The writer James Carroll recalls that as a young seminarian in the 1960s, he once had to surrender a copy of Jean-Paul Sartre's *The Age of Reason* because, the rector declared, it was "on the Index." Carroll goes on to say, "What really seemed amazing was that books on the Index were available in paperback."

This was a state of affairs that gravely troubled the Church. The realization did not dawn immediately, when Gutenberg's first printed Bibles made their appearance in the 1450s, but it dawned eventually. Looking back from a vantage point of more than four centuries — and with the explosive reality of another new technology, the Internet, so vividly in the foreground — it may seem that any attempt to exert control was doomed to failure. The way things turn out is often interpreted as the way things *had* to turn out. But the experience of China, where the Internet, along with the media and the educational system, are for the time being under significant control, suggests that attempts at censorship are not completely unworkable even in the digital age.

In 2010, Google became engaged in a battle with the Chinese government on this very issue, when the company announced that it would end the practice of limiting the topics that Chinese users could search for. This put Google into direct collision with Chinese law and practice, and the government threatened retaliation. An uneasy compromise was reached. Google continued to display censored results on its main page but was allowed to include a link to an uncensored version based in Hong Kong; the results of searches on the Hong Kong site can be monitored or suppressed by Chinese filters as information returns to the mainland. Earlier, in the age of print, the experience of the Soviet Union showed that strict controls on information could be maintained for decades on end, even in a modern industrial state. To get around the controls, Russian writers and intellectuals had to revert to medieval methods, creating so-called samizdat, or "self-published" literature, by means of physical copying and hand distribution. Ray Bradbury's *Fahrenheit 451* (the title comes from the temperature at which paper burns) conjures a fictional world in which literature is preserved by a *pre*-medieval method — the oral tradition. In the novel, books are banned but survive in the minds of dissidents who commit entire works to memory.

In the nonfictional United States, controversy erupts with disturbing regularity when activists seek to remove books they deem offensive from schools and libraries. The incidents run into the hundreds every year: the American Library Association has recorded some 4,600 challenges since 2001. The objections are wide-ranging. A school board on Long Island ordered the removal from a reading list of Jodi Picoult's *The Tenth Circle* and James Patterson's *Cradle and All* because of what was seen to be inappropriate sexual content. A school in Alabama ordered the temporary removal of a book called *Diary of a Wimpy Kid* from its library because of concern that it might harm the self-esteem of some students. A book called *And Tango Makes Three*, about two male penguins who adopt an egg, was banned from schools in Charlotte, South Carolina, because of implicitly gay subject matter. A Kentucky statute still in force bans the use in schools of any book of "infidel" character. Within the past several years, *Fahrenheit 451* has been challenged in schools in Stillwater, Minnesota, and Conroe, Texas.

In terms of seriousness, none of these incidents comes close to the fatwa issued by the Ayatollah Khomeini in 1989 against Salman Rushdie and his book *The Satanic Verses*. The fatwa called for the author's execution, and Rushdie was forced into hiding for many years. As the free-speech advocate Nat Hentoff has observed, "The lust to suppress can come from any direction." In the sixteenth century, it came heavily from Rome.

"Absolutely Absurd!"

Attempts at censorship were not new. If the Church wanted biblical precedent for the destruction of forbidden knowledge, it needed to look no further than the Acts of the Apostles, which records the results of a missionary visit by Saint Paul to the city of Ephesus: "And many of those who practiced magic brought their books together and began burning them in the sight of everyone; and they counted up the price of them and found it fifty thousand pieces of silver. So the word of the Lord was growing mightily, and prevailing." As an act of punishment, the philosopher Peter Abelard in 1121 A.D. was made to destroy one of his own works—compelled "with my own hand to cast that memorable book of mine into the flames." Cathar books were burned by the Dominicans during the Albigensian Crusade. Jewish books were repeatedly burned in Spain. In his several Bonfires of the Vanities, in Florence in 1497 and 1498, the reforming zealot Savonarola consigned hundreds of books to the pyre (along with paintings, musical instruments, cosmetics, and mirrors). He himself was cast into the fire a year later. Some 10,000 books were burned by a determined cardinal in Rome on a single day in 1559. But book-burning could never be a systematic approach to the problem—it was too crude, too chancy. Books always seemed to get away. Michael Servetus went to the stake with what was believed to be the last existing copy of his offending book, *The Restitution of Christianity,* chained to his leg. It turned out, however, that three other copies had survived.

If book-burning was not the answer, perhaps preemption was —heading off the threat before it arose. At the Vatican, the task of examining books prior to publication fell to the Master of the Sacred Palace, who was typically a Dominican, and who often held the rank of cardinal. The role had developed gradually over several centuries. When Martin Luther published his ninety-five theses, it was the

Master of the Sacred Palace who was given responsibility for "crisis management." Within his jurisdiction, he examined all books before publication and issued or withheld the official stamp of Church approval, known as an *imprimatur* (Latin for "Let it be printed"), a term that long ago entered English metaphorically as a synonym for "permission." Those concerned about the potential incursion of censorship on the Internet speak of the advent of a "digital imprimatur." Local bishops to this day are expected to affix an imprimatur to certain categories of Catholic books, and can withhold approval if they see fit—or be made to withdraw it. In 1998, the Vatican ordered the bishop of East Anglia, in England, to revoke his imprimatur from the book *Roman Catholic Christianity,* because it was judged to be "not in full conformity with the Catholic faith." The bishop did as he was told. In 2011, a committee of U.S. bishops, citing doctrinal issues, condemned the popular book *Quest for the Living God,* by Sister Elizabeth Johnson. Johnson had not sought an imprimatur in the first place, a fact that the bishops emphasized.

In 1542, with the formal establishment of the Inquisition as an organ of the Holy See, censorship became more pervasive and more deeply institutionalized. The Congregation of the Inquisition took the lead. The first Index of Forbidden Books was issued in 1559, under the Inquisition's auspices; it would be followed by revised and expanded versions. The Index was distributed widely, not just in the Papal States but abroad. In much of Italy, booksellers were expected to be familiar with its contents. In 1572, the censorship effort was placed under its own administrative arm, the Congregation of the Index, which always worked closely with the Inquisition itself. The Master of the Sacred Palace, the Vatican's original censor, served as a member of both congregations.

As time went on, and the prosecutorial efforts of the Inquisition began to wane, the work of the Index continued, and censorship became the main public face the Inquisition presented to the world. In 1907, when the first *Catholic Encyclopedia* was published, the editors were unapologetic about censorship by the Church. It was just something that had to be done, as any fool could see: "As soon as there were books or writing of any kind, the spreading or reading of which was highly detrimental to the public, competent authorities were obliged to take measures against them." The Holy See's powerful secretary of state at the time, Cardinal Rafael Merry del Val, defended this approach: the Church must protect the faithful so that "their lips do not brush up against the tempting cups of poison." The *Catholic Encyclopedia* itself became an object of attempted censorship when, in 1923, the Catholic Daughters of America donated an edition to a public high school in Belleville, New Jersey, and competent authorities took legal steps to remove it (without success).

It will be decades before a truly comprehensive history of the Index of Forbidden Books can be written. The Congregation of the Index existed for more than four hundred years, adding sedimentary layers from its deliberations every day, but scholars have had access to its records for less than a generation. Ever since the Inquisition archives were officially opened (in fact, beginning somewhat before then), a team headed by a priest named Hubert Wolf, a professor of history at Münster University, in Germany, has been engaged in describing, summarizing, and cataloguing the contents of every Vatican dossier relating to the Index. It is the kind of project for which Teutonic scholarship was invented. The endeavor will take years to complete.

The scope of the Inquisition's censorship project is simple enough to lay out in broad brushstrokes. The Church had responded slowly and ineffectually to the challenge of Luther and other critics, and the situation in northern Europe, especially Germany, was profoundly unsettled. There would be wars over religion for a long time to come. Many regions had already been "lost" as the Reformation took hold and Protestant movements found political protection. But (the argument went) it was perhaps possible to stave off Protestant inroads not only in Italy, where the papacy exercised sovereign power over its own ample territories, but also in any domains where papal writ enjoyed some measure of influence. Because it was all too easy for ideas to cross borders, ideas had to be attacked at every stage of their life cycle. The inquisitors knew nothing about the germ theory of disease, but they approached the task as if it were a problem of epidemiology, as indeed it was: an outbreak of freethinking.

The Inquisition's response took many forms. To begin with, inquisitors could discourage certain people from even taking up their pens. They could read manuscripts before publication, insisting on changes or prohibiting printers from publishing certain works at all. They could collect dangerous books after they were published and remove them from circulation, often by burning. Teams of visitors were sent out from Rome to pay stern calls on publishers and to scour the contents of private libraries. Expurgators examined books that had already been published, line by line, marking deletions and alterations that would have to be made if the book was ever published again. Agents traveled to the Frankfurt Book Fair, held twice a year, to keep track of new and shocking titles as they flew off Europe's presses. Inspectors were on hand at major ports and border crossings to search cargo and belongings for contraband. Those who could argue that they had a need to be aware of the contents of certain books — including highly placed officials in the Vatican — had to apply for a license to read them.

It was an ambitious effort. The control of intellect and conscience on such a vast scale had never been attempted before. The poet Ariosto refers in one passage to the printing press as having been invented by a *monachus,* a monk; it's symptomatic of Church attitudes toward this technology that the censors ordered "*monachus*" to be crossed out. That satanic device could hardly have been a monk's doing. "What we need," one sixteenth-century censor wrote privately, "is a halt to printing, so that the Church can catch up with this deluge of publications."

That wasn't possible. Instead, the Church sought to create its own version of what George Orwell, four hundred years later, in his novel *1984*, would call "memory holes" — incineration chutes at the Ministry of Truth where ideas and information could be sent for disposal. The censor's various tools were not wielded with equal fervor at every moment, nor was their application uniform from place to place. The administration of the Inquisition was never a paragon of competence. It was rent by divisions between what today might be called soft-liners and hard-liners, the "wets" and the "dries." Bureaucracies — religious, secular — acquire internal characteristics peculiar to the organism. Each is a living thing, and those inside a bureaucracy exist in relationship to the host. Mental outlooks are shaped accordingly.

Sometimes the results are ludicrous. The bureaucracy itself can become personified: the historian Timothy Garton Ash cites a typewritten memo from the British embassy in Moscow, in the 1940s, that begins, "Dear Department" and ends with the words "yours ever, Chancery." Activities are pursued for no reason other than that they have customarily been pursued: some decades ago, in Milwaukee, the local bishop bestowed his imprimatur on a book consisting of blank calendar pages — perhaps simply because he could, or was expected to. The historian Francisco Bethencourt notes that some two hundred registers a year, detailing searches of thousands of ships for contraband books in one major Portuguese port, survive from a period in the eighteenth century. Virtually no such books were ever found, and yet the searches went on, and the Inquisition's records were faithfully kept. "The maintenance of a structure which produced nothing beyond repetitive and meaningless reports," Bethencourt writes, "is in itself informative with regard to the operating logic of the inquisitorial bureaucratic machine."

In the archives, dossier after dossier yields examples of bureaucratic bungling and administrative idiocy. The archives also offer glimpses of internal resistance, when independent-minded cardinals and other clerics did what they could to deflect the Church's attention or mitigate its wrath. The Jesuit Robert Bellarmine, a cardinal-inquisitor who played a central role in the Galileo controversy, did not question the need for censorship. But he was a more thoughtful and reasonable man than some of his colleagues. A marginal notation in his hand survives in the Archivio — it is his reaction to a particular edict of condemnation issued by the Master of the Sacred Palace. Bellarmine wrote: "This is absolutely absurd!"

The Church's regulatory effort was never a ruthlessly efficient machine. How could it be? There were so many books — more all the time — and the work was labor-intensive. If a book was on the list for expurgation, local inquisitors first had to discover who in the area owned it, collect all the copies, cross out the offending lines, and then return the books to their owners. Think of the manpower required to find every reference to *coitus,* a term that was regarded as obscene; blot it out; and replace it with the more demure *copula.* There was no universal "find and replace" function.

The inquisitorial censors were often myopic, childish, capricious, or daft. Over the years, they would proscribe Descartes, Voltaire, Pascal, and Locke — but not Darwin or Freud. In many books, woodcuts of proscribed writers such as Erasmus and Luther were clumsily blotted out, as if by a schoolboy — and as if that would somehow do the trick. An inquisitor in Padua, with a large stockpile of confiscated books taking up space on his shelves, simply sold them off to secondhand-book dealers. The censors generally could read only Latin and Italian (and sometimes French); books published in German or English tended to escape prohibition until someone had the audacity to publish them in translation. *Uncle Tom's Cabin* came under scrutiny when it was published in Italian, but in the end the book was left alone. (It was a close call, however. The offensive aspect of the book was the positive portrayal of Quakers.) Because they were written in German, the works of Hegel and Kant avoided condemnation for years. *Das Kapital* and *Mein Kampf* escaped completely. Peter Godman, pointing one day to the Teutonic College, which sits inside the

Vatican just a few hundreds yards from the Inquisition's palazzo, and has been filled with Germans since well before the Inquisition, wondered aloud, "Couldn't they have just walked over there and asked for help?"

Certain authorities possessed a hair-trigger sensitivity. Robert Bellarmine came close to having one of his own major works — a defense of Catholicism — condemned by the Index even as he served on its congregation. The pope, Sixtus V, detested his views on papal power in temporal affairs. (Bellarmine thought it was limited.) Because Bellarmine had taken on the Church's critics by name, some censors argued, he was also complicit in spreading their ideas. Only the timely death Sixtus got Bellarmine off the hook.

John Tedeschi was one of the first historians to take a close look at Vatican correspondence relating to the Index of Forbidden Books. Long before the Inquisition archives were opened, Tedeschi found a deposit of documents from Florence in the state archives of Belgium — part of the material taken away by Napoleon and never returned. He traced the growing severity of the Index as works once tolerated, such as those by Boccaccio and Machiavelli, were subjected to harsher restrictions or prohibited altogether. As time went on, the grounds for censorship expanded, moving beyond "heresy," properly understood, to encompass passages that were simply critical of the Church or perhaps merely lascivious. Tedeschi took note, for instance, of the expurgations demanded in a historical work by Philipp Camerarius. The names of Protestant leaders and thinkers must of course be removed. But, Tedeschi writes, there was more:

Also to be excised are Robert Gaguin's insinuation that in France the public good had invariably suffered when clergy became embroiled in affairs of state; a reflection by the historian of the early Church, Eusebius of Caesarea, that the persecutions suffered by Christians under Diocletian were the result of strife and jealousy among bishops; an allegation of papal avarice attributed to a distant patriarch of Constantinople; and the ancient tale that a hairy monster had been born to the mistress of Pope Nicholas III. The four pages that are to be deleted at the end of chapter 58 are an eloquent plea for religious toleration, containing a reminder that men of different faiths have successfully co-existed, as well as Augustine's pronouncement that only God is lord over the consciences of men.

Looked at from one perspective, the Church's regime of censorship was a systemic failure. Much of Europe was simply beyond the Vatican's reach. The Church's moral authority, such as it was, did not apply. Even where the Index was a power to be reckoned with, it was often possible to get books published by shopping for printers in freer locales. This is the same approach that would be taken centuries later in (for instance) the United States. Throughout the mid twentieth century, Catholic writers in America, unable to secure a bishop's imprimatur in one diocese, would seek the services of a friendly bishop in another. Thus, in 1962, New York's Francis Cardinal Spellman denied his imprimatur to a collection of essays from the liberal Catholic magazine *Commonweal*; the editors eventually received approval from the bishop of Pittsburgh. The Catholic publishing house Sheed & Ward long made a practice of publishing its books in Vermont, because it could rely on the good graces of the bishop of Burlington.

So the Inquisition's defenses were porous even where they existed. But that does not mean they did not have a widespread and lasting effect. "Historians are divided . . ." is one of the most common sentiments you'll come across in assessments of the Inquisition. Historians are certainly divided on the full extent of censorship's impact — but not on whether it had one. The writings of Erasmus, to give one important example, largely disappeared from Italy. For about two hundred years, starting in the mid sixteenth century, no new editions of his work were published there. Volumes by Erasmus were widely confiscated, and more or less vanished from collections.

In Spain, whose Inquisition mounted its own censorship effort, paralleling Rome's, a comparison of titles banned by the Index with titles that could subsequently be found in major libraries shows that confiscation and censorship could be damaging indeed.

Vernacular Bibles were a target everywhere. Although the Latin version of the Bible was translated into Italian at a very early stage, and for a long time tolerated, the Inquisition's eventual campaign against the vernacular — to limit the "unmediated" experience of ordinary people, now able to read these fundamental religious texts for themselves — was unrelenting, and on the whole successful. To this day, Catholics have far less direct experience of the biblical text than other Christians do. (The director Dino De Laurentiis, interviewed during the filming of his 1966 epic, *The Bible,* recalled, "Five years ago I had never read the Bible, because in Italy we learn everything about religion from priests.") Some censored books were virtually annihilated. In the mid sixteenth century a tract titled the "Beneficio di Cristo" sold some 40,000 copies in Italian, and went on to appear in French, English, Castilian, and Croat translations. Almost all the books disappeared. A few copies were eventually rediscovered, but not until the nineteenth century.

Works of science were also targeted, to significant effect in many places. Inventories of books confiscated in Spain suggest that Inquisition censors could be surpassingly diligent, removing scientific books regardless of whether they were officially proscribed. Compared with that of other European countries, Spain's political and intellectual development proved to be sluggish. Historians are divided, but the Inquisition may be among the reasons why.

The most pervasive consequence of Inquisition censorship cannot be quantified. "The 'books never written,' and the importance of self-censorship," writes one scholar, remain "major imponderables." The anecdotal evidence, the statistical data from here and there, offer only a meager indication of the "opportunity costs" of the Inquisition, the sheer chilling effect of any regime of intellectual manipulation, no matter how petty and haphazard. Within the Church, intellectual restrictions continue to the present day.

Writing about the limits on intellectual freedom in contemporary China, the journalist James Fallows notes that the country's censorship regime simply cannot be all-pervasive—there isn't the manpower, there isn't the technology—but that it takes a considerable toll nonetheless. The Chinese government, through its Golden Shield Project—often referred to as "the Great Firewall"—has put a variety of obstacles in place to limit what Internet users can get access to, and to slow down their searches. It can monitor sites that are being navigated to and pages that are being viewed, and it can arrange for connections to be automatically severed or for sites to become "temporarily" unavailable. The mechanisms are various, and they change continually. Moreover, people who persist too ambitiously in their searches can be identified and tracked down. These are capabilities that the Master of the Sacred Palace could scarcely have imagined, and might devoutly have wished for. At the same time, anyone in China with a laptop and a little bit of knowledge, money, and time can get around the controls. As Fallows writes, "What the government cares about is making the quest for information just enough of a nuisance that people generally won't bother."

And they don't. References to the Tiananmen Square massacre or to the non-Party-line version of Tibetan history will generally draw a blank from ordinary Chinese. To the Internet restrictions one must add the controls on such things as school and university curricula, and the daily reality that a person's neighbors may be alert to his curiosity—plus the fact that foreign businesses operating in China, mindful of their precarious status, have every incentive to enforce the rules. The result is that in China, official censorship is underpinned by a thick stratum of self-censorship.

So we are back to that—self-censorship. As Peter Godman observes, "Neither confined to the Catholic Church nor restricted to

Italy, that most terrible, because most insidious, of ghosts has never been laid to rest."

Scientist Versus Simpleton

The remains of Galileo Galilei — physicist, astronomer, philosopher, and tactical self-censor — lie entombed in marble at the Church of Santa Croce, in Florence. Or, rather, most of Galileo lies there. In 1737, as his body was being transferred from the place where it had been secretly kept (ecclesiastical authorities for years would not permit its interment in a consecrated church) to the monument in Santa Croce, a group of admirers removed one of Galileo's vertebrae, one of his teeth, and three of his fingers. The vertebra — specifically, the fifth lumbar vertebra — is today preserved at a medical school in Padua. One of the fingers has long been on display in a glass orb at a science museum in Florence that was renovated and in 2010 rechristened the Museo Galileo. The remaining body parts — a thumb, the index finger of the right hand, and an upper left premolar — were missing for more than a hundred years. To general astonishment, they turned up not long ago at auction, and have now joined the finger on display in Florence.

Some visitors to the Museo have professed consternation that the body parts of a man of science should be exhibited as if they were the relics of a saint. Perhaps the response should be that other men of science have at least now been able to have a go at him. An analysis of Galileo's upper left premolar by the surgical dentist Cesare Paoleschi suggests that Galileo suffered from gastric reflux and also that he ground his teeth.

He had plenty of reason to worry, caught up as he was in protracted negotiations with the Inquisition over what he could or could not say on the matter of heliocentrism — the contention, first advanced by Copernicus, and at odds with scripture, that the Sun was stationary and the planet Earth in orbit around it. A vast amount of scholarship has been devoted to the Galileo case, scrutinizing every moment, every fact, every motivation and interpretation. As with the Kennedy assassination or the Alger Hiss prosecution, the documentation and theorizing can seem impenetrable, though the essence of the story is simple: Galileo's views posed a challenge, and the Church set out to contain it. The Vatican would eventually admit, in 1992, that it had erred in the matter; the pope called the episode a "sad misunderstanding that now belongs to the past." Over the centuries, the Galileo affair has been mined by historians and polemicists for its lessons. One lesson has to do with the way dishonesty becomes routine: how a regime of orthodoxy and censorship forces all parties into a game of winks and nods.

Galileo's ordeal must be seen against the backdrop of what had happened to Giordano Bruno. Bruno was born in 1548, not far from Naples, and entered the Dominican Order at the age of seventeen. An iconoclast by nature, he never wore the Dominican habit easily, and eventually shed it altogether. He was renowned at an early age for his capacious recall, which had been trained in a system known as artificial memory; at the age of twenty-one he demonstrated his skills to Pope Pius V, reciting Psalm 86 forward and backward, in Hebrew. But his tastes ran to forbidden literature (he was once disciplined for keeping a book by Erasmus hidden in a privy), and his intellectual interests came to encompass mathematics, cosmology, magic, and the various illicit speculations that the Reformation had unleashed. Bruno embraced the ideas of Copernicus but went further, broaching the concept of a universe without end, with an infinity of stars and planets, and continuously unfolding acts of Creation. Why should there have been only one Adam and Eve — and if there were many, why should they all make the same mistake? Ideas like that make for good science fiction but bad Catholic theology.

Bruno spent most of his life moving from place to place throughout Europe, his peremptory personality and sharp tongue exhausting the patience of one protector after another. Oxford took him in; he repaid the favor by describing the university as a "constellation of the ignorant, pedantic, and obstinate, and a mass of donkey and swine." The Inquisition had its eye on him very early, and at last took him into custody when he returned to Italy, in 1592. The original interrogation and trial transcripts have been lost, but summaries survive, and it is clear that Bruno was willing to recant on some matters. On others he proved adamant. The issues were mainly theological rather than scientific. His interactions with the formidable Robert Bellarmine, one of the judges, proved particularly intense. The two men were intellectual equals and implacable antagonists, each believing that he carried a torch for truth. Positions hardened on both sides. In the end, Bruno was sentenced to death. Bellarmine concurred in the judgment, but was haunted ever afterward by the outcome. How could he have failed to persuade the man?

The Bruno case may have influenced the way he dealt with Galileo sixteen years later. Bellarmine, a Jesuit, was the most brilliant theologian of his age — five feet, three inches tall, but a towering figure. His remains, in a cardinal's red robes, lie in state behind glass under a side altar at Rome's Church of Sant'Ignazio. Bellarmine was intimately familiar with the advanced scientific thinking of his time. He had even viewed celestial objects through that new device, the telescope. Bellarmine was a cardinal-inquisitor, but he had waged his own battles with the Index, which he had the misfortune to head. Its methods taxed his patience, and could be acidic in his reactions. He certainly understood the challenge to scripture if Copernicus was right, but he also understood that there were two ways out of the box: heliocentrism could be condemned, or scripture could be reinterpreted ("with great caution"). Bellarmine and Galileo agreed on one thing: the Copernican theory had not yet been irrefutably proved. Given that fact, Bellarmine would continue to rely primarily on scripture. Galileo, for his part, knew where the evidence pointed. But he was no Bruno. He was a meticulous scientist, not an irascible dreamer. He enjoyed the support of loyal friends and powerful patrons. He was on good terms with popes.

Both men labored within a system whose redlines were clear but also subject to change; indeed, many in the Church wanted the lines drawn tighter. It is possible to see Bellarmine and Galileo as complicit in temporizing—pushing freedom to the nearest boundary and no further. In the famous settlement of 1616, Bellarmine denounced the Copernican system as false but allowed it to be discussed as a hypothesis; Galileo conceded for the record that this was all he had ever meant to do. It was a pragmatic accommodation, the kind made throughout history: minds seek room to maneuver in a dangerous environment. Robust and outspoken opinion is replaced by oblique suggestion or calculated silence, by trimming and feinting. It was the strategy of writers in the Soviet Union. It was the path Thomas More sought to take in his contest with his king. Galileo thought the accommodation a victory.

It would fall apart in 1632, when Galileo published his *Dialogue Concerning the Two Chief World Systems*. By then, Bellarmine was dead, and Galileo crossed a line in his book, perhaps without intending to. The two world systems were the Ptolemaic (the Sun revolves around Earth) and the Copernican (the other way around), and although the dialogue was set up as a discussion of hypotheses, the character arguing the geocentric case was given the name Simplicio, which can be interpreted as "Simpleton." The pope, Urban VIII, took this hard. He had in fact encouraged Galileo to write the book, and to include his own papal views on the matter; now he saw them advanced none too adroitly, in the mouth of a figure who seemed never to get the best of the argument. The *Dialogue* had been provisionally approved by censors in Florence, but the action moved quickly to Rome, where Galileo was made to stand trial. This time there would be no accommodation. As one historian has noted, the trial was not about science but about obedience: "Concern for truth had evolved into concern for authority and power." Old and sick, Galileo abjured any belief in the Copernican system, and lived out the rest of his days under house arrest. The story is told that after submitting to the judgment that Earth is stationary, Galileo muttered under his breath, "And yet it moves!" There is no evidence that he did so. However, the item under glass in the Museo Galileo is without question a middle finger.

The Cheese and the Worms

For obvious reasons, the cases of Galileo and Bruno have been a focus of debate for centuries. But they were in many ways exceptional episodes. Most of those who came to the attention of the Inquisition did not have to defend themselves over the course of many decades. Most did not have a constellation of powerful prelates taking a very personal interest in their cases. The statistics are arguable, but in the two centuries after its establishment, the Roman Inquisition conducted, at a minimum, some 50,000 formal trials. The number of people investigated but never tried runs to several times this figure. Italy's population in 1600 was about 13 million, so the Inquisition's footprint would have been highly visible.

And the number executed? There was a charitable organization in Rome, the Arciconfraternita di San Giovanni Decollato, whose members took it upon themselves to escort the condemned to the stake. In the Roman Inquisition's first two centuries, they performed this service for ninety-seven people. But that's just Rome. Throughout the peninsula, the total number executed by the Inquisition over this same period is around 1,250.

Trials by the Roman Inquisition followed the usual pattern in certain ways, but departed from it in others. The proceedings were secret, and the accused was never told the source of the accusations or the identity of the witnesses against him. (Accounts of reprisals suggest that the accused sometimes discovered their identity anyway.) But the person on trial was made aware of the specific charges — in writing, and in the vernacular — and could hire a lawyer. "Public defenders" were available for the indigent. The position of the lawyer was in some ways awkward. As John Tedeschi writes, "If the lawyer became convinced that his client was indeed guilty and could not be persuaded to abandon his error, he was obliged to discontinue the defense or fall under suspicion himself." Just as inquisitors learned correct procedure from handbooks, so did defense lawyers who practiced before the Inquisition bar. Heresy, they were reminded, was a crime of the intellect, and allowances might be made if a defendant could show a lack of intentionality — it was a slip of tongue, he was drunk, he was sleepwalking.

Because so many Inquisition trial records survive in various archives, it is sometimes possible — depending on how the questioning went, and on the fastidiousness of the recording secretary — to get deep inside the heads of particular defendants. One man who has achieved a measure of immortality is Domenico Scandella, known by the nickname Menocchio, a miller in the small northern Italian town of Montereale. If he were to return to his hometown today, he would most likely be taken aback to find a cultural center named for him (the Centro Studi Storici Menocchio) and to learn that his name also graces a small literary magazine (*I Quaderni del Menocchio*). As Giordano Bruno's case was making its way toward a conclusion, in the late 1590s, so was Menocchio's. Like Bruno, Menocchio was a man who could not stop talking, and although he was burned at the stake for heresy in 1599, his words took on a life of their own.

But not until almost four centuries had elapsed. In the meantime, the transcripts from his trial moldered in the Archivio della Curia Arcivescovile, in Udine, and it was there, in that northern Italian city, that they were discovered by Carlo Ginzburg. Ginzburg is an easy fellow to spot in a crowd, with flaring gray eyebrows and a matching shock of unruly hair — he could be Trotsky's Italian cousin. In the early 1960s, he was at the beginning of his academic career, a lowly *assistente volontario* at the University of Rome, who helped make ends meet by translating books from French and English into Italian. A man with Ginzburg's talents and energy — though not his attitude — would have been a very welcome addition to the staff of the sixteenth-century Congregation of the Index. Of course, the fact that he was Jewish would have posed a problem.

Ginzburg was not consciously aware of the extent to which this part of his background, together with his father's torture and death at the hands of the Nazis in Rome's Regina Coeli prison, had impelled him toward the Inquisition as a subject of study. The realization came only later, as he has admitted. ("How could I have let such an obvious fact escape me?") He began sifting through Inquisition records wherever he could find them, in towns and cities all over Italy. His intention was to study "the persecuted, not the persecutors." One day, quite by accident, in the massive state archives of Venice — he was ordering numbered boxes of documents at random, as if prospecting for ore; playing, as he recalls, "Venetian roulette" — Ginzburg suddenly came across references to trials of people known as *benandanti,* a category of heretic that he had never heard of before, and no one else had heard of either. He was so excited by the discovery that he had to leave the archive and walk up and down outside to restore his composure.

His investigation eventually led to the Inquisition archives in Udine, in the region of Friuli. The archives were closed to outsiders — even the fact of their existence was not widely known — but Ginzburg enlisted the help of a local monsignor who happened to be a historian. The monsignor, who had never met Ginzburg, nonetheless sent a note to the archivist that read: "Dr. Carlo Ginzburg is a serious scholar and a reliable person." He was granted access, grudgingly. The archives in Udine hold the records of some 2,000 Inquisition trials, in hulking wooden cabinets, and Ginzburg worked among them in solitude. "No bureaucracy, no employees," he would remember many years later. "I used to pick up myself the handwritten volumes I needed, since they were stored in the same room where

I was working. I was always perfectly alone. I remember that once I was locked in the archive after closing time; somebody came to rescue me after a couple of hours."

Ginzburg emerged from the archives of Udine with his first major book, *I Benandanti,* translated into English as *The Night Battles.* The word *benandanti* in fact means "good walkers," and it refers to people who engaged in nighttime rituals, probably of very ancient provenance, intended to ensure an abundant harvest. From 1580 to 1634, some 850 people in rural northern Italy were hauled in for interrogation because the Inquisition had heard reports of such activities. Ginzburg writes,

> The *benandanti* spoke, often without being urged to, of the battles for fertility which they fought at night, in the spirit, armed with sprigs of fennel, against witches, male and female, armed with sorghum stalks. All this was incomprehensible to the inquisitors — the very term *"benandante"* was unknown to them and over fifty years they constantly asked what it meant.

The villagers and country people had no idea that they were heretics — what they were doing was simply an immemorial aspect of ordinary life. The inquisitors, for their part, struggled to fit the peasants' behavior into the categories they knew — such as heresy and witchcraft. They were as dismissive of the "mental rubbish of peasant credulity" as many eminent later historians have been. (The phrase comes from H. R. Trevor-Roper, who had little patience for such things.)

To define the problem can be to create the problem. The commodious encyclopedia of witchcraft, the *Malleus Maleficarum,* or *Hammer of Witches,* the work of two Dominican inquisitors, was first published in 1486; the title was clearly chosen for its resonance with another book, the *Malleus Judeorum,* which had appeared earlier in the century. The *Malleus Maleficarum* bore various marks of official approval. During the next 150 years, thanks to the printing press, it was published throughout Europe in some thirty-five separate editions. Its primary purpose was to refute the notion that there was no such thing as witchcraft, and it certainly succeeded in fostering a conviction that witchcraft was widespread. It also created a standard view of what witchcraft was: a pact with the devil, involving magical conclaves and often sexual relations, whose ultimate purpose was the deployment of sorcery to inflict harm on God's good world. Here is a typical chapter heading: "Whether the Relations of an Incubus Devil with a Witch are always accompanied by the Injection of Semen." And the one following: "How, as it were, they Deprive Man of his Virile Member." The last third of the book is devoted to the techniques, including torture, that inquisitors and others should use to discover and prosecute witchcraft. Much of this advice was taken directly from Nicholas Eymerich's medieval inquisitors' manual.

To a modern sensibility, the *Malleus* often reads, as the scholar Anthony Grafton once put it, "like a strange amalgam of Monty Python and *Mein Kampf.*" Nonetheless, the book's taxonomy of beliefs and practices became standard, and influenced other treatises. Witchcraft had been an off-and-on concern of the Church for centuries — sorcery was among the charges brought against the Knights Templar — but it's probably no coincidence that the European "witch craze" made its appearance only after the contents of the *Malleus* became familiar. The witch craze would eventually cross the ocean. The penumbra of the *Malleus* can be glimpsed around the Salem witch trials, which occurred in 1692. Its ideas peek out from behind the writings of Increase Mather, Cotton Mather, and others of the time.

The *benandanti* don't appear in the *Malleus,* and neither do their practices, but Ginzburg shows how decades of repeated questioning by the Inquisition began to shape the way the *benandanti* saw themselves, gradually bending their self-perception toward something the inquisitors could recognize. The Inquisitors were simply asking the kinds of questions that made sense to them — over and over again, until, in time, the answers conformed to the picture they expected. Yes, we gather with Satan in dark of night. Yes, the sex is good. As one historian has concluded: "The study of actual interrogations shows that the dealings with the Devil that suspects were eventually compelled to admit to are actually foisted onto them by the investigators."

It was in the archives at Udine that Ginzburg came upon the case of Domenico Scandella — page after page of Inquisition transcripts. Ginzburg found that the transcripts were rendered almost like a modern screenplay, recording gesture and tone as well as dialogue. He would recount Scandella's story in minute detail in a 1976 book called *The Cheese and the Worms,* one of the most prominent early examples of the genre known as microhistory. What a hundred years ago might have been no more than a glancing reference or intriguing gloss — an unknown individual, a small town, a piece of music, an obscure ritual — becomes the starting point for ingenious narratives. A reduction in scale allows, incongruously, for a widening of perspective.

Menocchio was a man of modest consequence in Montereale. Not only was he a miller, an occupation of some importance, but he had served as mayor of the town. He had fathered eleven children. He played the guitar. And he was literate. He owned a number of books and borrowed others, and according to his testimony in the course of two trials, he had read, among other works, a vernacular Bible, Boccaccio's *Decameron,* and an Italian translation of a book that may have been (according to one witness) the Koran. Montereale lies only about seventy miles from Venice, which at the time was the most cosmopolitan city in Europe — a seafaring republic with a significant population of Jews and Muslims, transients from all over, and a lively intellectual life. The city supported a vast book-making industry — it had at least thirty different publishers in Menocchio's day. In an age before true globalization, Venice was as globalized as a place could be. Menocchio is known to have visited Venice, and to have bought at least one of his books there.

Ginzburg was struck by Menocchio's plucky self-defense and eccentric views. "I have an artful mind," the miller admitted proudly at his first trial for heresy, in 1584. Here is his version of the Creation: "All was chaos, that is, earth, air, water, and fire were mixed together; and out of that bulk a mass formed — just as cheese is made out of milk — and worms appeared in it, and these were the angels." Menocchio, Ginzburg writes, appropriated "remnants of the thinking of others as he might stones and bricks" to construct his own unique cosmology, held together by a mortar of rural folklore.

He had been denounced to the Inquisition by the local parish priest, with whom he had quarreled, and from that moment forward the process unfolded in standard inquisitorial fashion. Menocchio was permitted to hire a lawyer; had he not, one would have been appointed for him. He spent the several months between arrest and sentencing in prison, and during that time he was interrogated — at exhausting length — on at least seven occasions. He was not tortured, perhaps because he spoke freely without any prodding at all. A secretary was present at all times. To judge from the transcripts, Menocchio sometimes seemed to take charge of the proceedings. At one point, he was asked whether he believed that the Church represented the one true religion. He said, "I beg you, sir, listen to me" — you can almost see him leaning forward, loud and insistent, and the inquisitors drawing back, wary but curious — and recounted a story he had read in the *Decameron,* though shaping it to his own purpose:

> There was once a great lord who declared his heir would be the person found to have a certain precious ring of his; and drawing near to his death, he had two other rings similar to the first one made, since he had three sons, and he gave a ring to each son; each one of them thought himself to be the heir and to have the true ring, but because of their similarity it could not be known with

certainty. Likewise, God the father has various children whom he loves, such as Christians, Turks, and Jews, and to each of them he has given the will to live by his own law, and we do not know which is the right one.

In the end, Menocchio formally recanted his views and, as a first-time offender, accepted a relatively modest punishment. Although he was condemned to prison — "where you will remain for the entire duration of your life" — his sentence was commuted after two years, a typical practice. (The reason for such leniency may have been cultural, or even architectural: unlike Spain, Italy had few large prisons.) Menocchio returned to Montereale and resumed his work as a miller, though he had to wear a penitential garment called the *habitello,* emblazoned with a red cross, and for a time was not permitted to venture outside the town.

But Menocchio was not the kind of man who would go quietly. He eventually stopped wearing the *habitello* because it was bad for business: "I was losing many earnings," he would say when arrested again, years later. And he continued to develop his views and speak his mind. "Can't you understand," he would say, "the Inquisitors don't want us to know what they know." A neighbor had once said of Menocchio, "He will argue with anyone." Another man testified, "He said many times, and I heard this from several people, that if he were not afraid of certain persons in this world, he would say things that would astonish." In his interrogation testimony he comes across like one of those vocal autodidacts so common in New York City, with a two-day stubble and the *Daily Worker* in a jacket pocket.

His opinions caught up with him. In 1599, Menocchio found himself standing before a tribunal. This time he was tortured, by means of the *strappado* — "Oh Jesus, oh Jesus, oh poor me, oh poor me" — and yet this time he refused to recant his views. Because he was found to have relapsed — a far more serious matter than a first offense — Menocchio was condemned to death. There is some evidence that the inquisitors in Friuli were reluctant to carry out the sentence, but word of Menocchio's case had reached Rome, which proved insistent. The sentence was confirmed by none other than Cardinal Santori, deeply involved in the Bruno matter, who wrote to the local inquisitor, "Your reverence must not fail to proceed in the case of the peasant of the diocese of Concordia. . . . The jurisdiction of the Holy Office over a case of such importance can in no way be doubted. Therefore, manfully perform everything that is required."

The case was reviewed personally by Pope Clement VIII. Clement was a man who on some matters could be open-minded. He has been credited, for instance, with promoting the introduction of coffee in Europe; it had widely been considered a Muslim beverage, and therefore intolerable for Christian purposes, but the pope relished the taste and is said to have baptized a cup and pronounced it acceptable. He was not so open-minded when it came to Menocchio. Domenico Scandella was burned at the stake in 1599, at the age of sixty-seven.

In Montereale today, you will find in the graveyards tombstones that bear the name Scandella. The small white Church of San Rocco, the parish church that Menocchio attended, still stands at the center of town. Menocchio would have been familiar with the Calderari frescoes inside. The fountain outside the Menocchio cultural center is relatively new: water pours from holes in a very large wheel of cheese, fashioned out of concrete. The water is meant to represent the worms of the miller's imagination. In 1999, on the 400th anniversary of Menocchio's execution, a symposium of scholars was convened at Montereale. Carlo Ginzburg was made an honorary citizen of the town.

"There Must Be Some Mistake"

More than anything else, it was the power of ideas — ideas like "reason" and "freedom of conscience" — that began to limit and then to undermine the Roman Inquisition. One can point to this or that factor—the declining influence of the papacy, the rise of mighty nation-states, the proliferation of new technology, the advance of science—but ultimately the Inquisition was at odds with the spirit of an ascending age. As Francisco Bethencourt has written, "The Inquisition provided the prime example of what European civilization was rejecting."

Bethencourt elaborated on this one afternoon in an office overlooking the Inns of Court. He is a professor now at King's College London, but is Portuguese by birth; he was drawn to the Inquisition as a subject in part by the experience of his native country under authoritarian rule. The point Bethencourt made was a simple one: The Inquisition was a disciplinary institution, operated by an entity—the Church—whose claim to authority was based on values. More than anything else, an organization based on values must beware a challenge made on the very same basis. Ideas have no corporeality. They are slow to take hold. We often discount their significance in our material world. How inefficient they appear to be alongside brute force. But in the long run, they are often the most powerful actors of all. One of those actors was the idea of tolerance. John Locke put it like this in 1689:

Nobody, therefore, in fine, neither single persons nor churches, nay, nor even commonwealths, have any just title to invade the civil rights and worldly goods of each other upon pretence of religion . . . The sum of all we drive at is that every man may enjoy the same rights that are granted to others.

"The Inquisition was extinguished," Bethencourt said, "because it couldn't cope with the profound change of values in Europe throughout the eighteenth century. It started in Protestant countries, mainly in the Netherlands, then in England. It was in these two countries that the issue of tolerance was raised — not for the first time, but as a new value, a new *positive* value. Toleration in the sixteenth century had been a negative value — it was something you 'suffered.' It was something *done* to you under certain circumstances. By the late seventeenth century, tolerance had become a positive value in itself, something that you praised and you were proud of. This idea spread. And the Inquisition collapsed."

It was a development for which there was no cure — the intellectual equivalent of habitat destruction. The Inquisition carried on, as bureaucracies do. It disciplined priests. It condemned heresies. It issued lists of forbidden books. Occasionally it conducted an execution. In terms of authority over life and limb, its writ eventually extended no farther than the shrinking realm of the Papal States in central Italy. The Inquisition was abolished during the Napoleonic Era, when the Papal States were annexed by France, and then reestablished when sovereignty was restored. The emergence of a unified Kingdom of Italy brought an end to the Papal States altogether. Rome was captured by Italian forces in 1870, and Pope Pius IX took refuge in the enclave that would eventually become a sovereign city-state, his temporal powers henceforward restricted to those few acres.

But even in its dying days, the Roman Inquisition could act when it thought it must. In 1858, the city of Bologna was still part of the Papal States, and on a summer night that year, under orders from the Inquisition, the police came to the home of a Jewish couple, Salomone (known as Momolo) and Marianna Mortara, and took away one of their children, Edgardo, who was six years old. Like many Jewish families, the Mortaras had employed a Christian girl as a servant, because Christians were able to perform chores on the Sabbath. While in her care one day, young Edgardo had fallen ill, and the servant, fearing for his life, had taken it upon herself to baptize him.

Edgardo recovered, but in time word of her act began to circulate in Bologna, and then by degrees found its way to the Palazzo del

Sant'Uffizio, in Rome. The rules were clear: Jews were not permitted to raise Christian children. Edgardo was now a Christian — had he not been baptized? And so there came a knock at the door:

> "There must be some mistake," Momolo said. "My son was never baptized. . . . Who says Edgardo was baptized? Who says he has to be taken?"
>
> "I am only acting according to orders," pleaded the Marshal. "I'm just following the Inquisitor's orders."

The boy was brought to Rome. The pleas of the family proved unavailing. On occasion, the Mortaras were permitted to visit Edgardo, but never alone. The case provoked an international outcry — Napoleon III weighed in, along with the Rothschilds and Sir Moses Montefiore — but Pope Pius IX paid no heed. He raised Edgardo as if he were his own son. When Rome fell to the Italian forces, Edgardo was nineteen, and legally free to make his own decisions. By then he had been living in Rome for thirteen years. He chose to remain with the pope, who endowed him with a trust fund.

The historian David Kertzer recounts the story, which was long forgotten, in his book *The Kidnapping of Edgardo Mortara*. Eventually Edgardo became a priest, and made a specialty of preaching to communities of Jews throughout Europe. He died in Belgium in 1940, shortly after the outbreak of World War II. Four years later, when Rome was liberated, Kertzer's father, a rabbi and an army chaplain who had landed with American forces at Anzio, conducted the first Sabbath service to be held in Rome's liberated central synagogue.

Kertzer writes that half a century later, "I sat outside the Chief Rabbi's office there, in the adjacent reading room, poring through the 1858 correspondence between the Secretary of Rome's Jewish community and Momolo Mortara, the desperate father of a boy taken from him and his religion."

5

THE ENDS OF THE EARTH

The Global Inquisition

> Where *is* the stairway to heaven? The Sandia
> Mountains seem to be as close as you can get.
>
> — A BLASPHEMER IN NEW MEXICO, 1729

> This is the man who would like to
> see me burned at the stake.
>
> — TEILHARD DE CHARDIN, 1948

Coming to America

T HE CITY OF SANTA FE, New Mexico, likes to project an image of rich and harmonic diversity. Glance for a moment at the tourist literature, and you will read that this is a place where three cultures thrive — Native American, Hispanic, and Anglo. Up to a point, the public image captures something true. Without a doubt, the ingredients in restaurant kitchens, and in kitchens at home, mingle democratically. Spanish is spoken widely in the city, and even more widely on the outskirts and up in the mountains. Pueblo Indians sell jewelry under the eaves of the Palace of the Governors, and Indian reservations occupy the countryside to the north and west. Anglo money is everywhere. The people who have it tend to be educated and to think of themselves as open-minded, drawn to the city for the very mystique it prizes. The official self-portrait — the "City Different" — is easy to recognize. It lies visibly on the surface.

The things below — sharp divergences in class, ethnicity, outlook, and power — have not disappeared, even as they've changed. Anglos, mostly newcomers, have made up a majority of Santa Fe's population since 1990. The city center, restored to a condition that in reality it never knew, is unaffordable to longtime natives. The old Hispanic community has been altered and divided by an influx of immigrants from Mexico. The plaza, once the city's living heart, is now a tourist zone. At Mass on Sunday, in the cathedral memorialized by Willa Cather, the archbishop sometimes asks how many people are visitors from elsewhere. Often it's a majority.

These days, Americans of every kind are acutely sensitive to historical grievance, and Santa Fe has more than its share. From time to time, events bring that sense of grievance unexpectedly into public view. Several years ago, workers excavating ground for a new parking garage to serve the Santa Fe convention center, which stands a block from the plaza, started turning up human bones. They had stumbled on an ancient burial site. But whose bones were they? The area had been continuously occupied since prehistoric times, so it could well have been an ordinary burying ground for the Indians who inhabited Santa Fe before the conquistadors arrived. It might also have been used by the early colonists. One theory momentarily caused a stir: maybe it was a mass grave for Indians the Spanish had killed.

The notion was not far-fetched. The first Spanish settlers had made their way north from Mexico in the late 1590s. In 1680, Indians throughout the New Mexico territory, acting with great coordination, rose up and expelled the Spanish, who fled south to the safety of El Paso. The Indians destroyed mission churches and burned the invaders' records. They moved into the Palace of the Governors. The Spanish returned in force in 1693 and retook the territory. As the story is commonly told, the reconquest of Santa Fe was accomplished without bloodshed. But in his account of the episode, translated into English in the early 1990s, the leader of the expedition wrote frankly of ordering the execution of seventy Indian prisoners in Santa Fe for the crime of apostasy from the Catholic faith. Their bodies would most likely have been buried somewhere nearby. Had the workers at the convention center just found them?

As it turned out, no. After a brief investigation, archaeologists determined that the bones were those of Indians who had lived around the year 1200. The remains of a few Spaniards were mixed in among them. The city scaled back the size of the garage, out of respect, and construction went on. But an embarrassing question had been raised — all the more embarrassing because every summer for three hundred years the city has commemorated the "peaceful reconquest" with the Fiesta de Santa Fe. A statue of the Virgin Mary that the Spanish carried with them, known as La Conquistadora, is paraded through the streets. Now there sprang up a group called Santa Feans for Truth and Reconciliation to protest the fiesta.

And there have been incidents. The Cross of the Martyrs, near the center of town, honors twenty-one priests, all of them Franciscans, who were killed during the Pueblo Revolt; someone has begun painting it red every year in time for the Indian Market art bazaar. In the plaza, an inscription on an obelisk commemorates the "heroes who have fallen in various battles with savage Indians"; some years ago, a man with a chisel calmly went up to the obelisk and removed the word "savage." It has not been restored.

A friend of my family, Fray Angélico Chávez, a Franciscan priest, served for many years as the official historian of the state of New Mexico. He died in 1996. Chávez was a small man with nut-brown skin and an aquiline nose. He spoke quietly and often slyly. A statue of him stands today outside the library at the Palace of the Governors. Chávez could trace his family back fifteen generations or so, to the original Spanish settlers. In his later years, he would repair in the afternoon to a bar near the plaza, wearing a beret and sipping an old-fashioned under the gaze of provocative but badly painted nude odalisques on the dark-paneled walls. He left the priesthood for a time, returning before his death. His work explored many problematic seams in New Mexico's history, but he was proud of his heritage. He was fond of quoting William Faulkner's observation: "The past is not dead. In fact, it's not even past."

It was Chávez who pointed out to me, during a conversation among the odalisques, that although Americans never think of the Inquisition as something that took root in what is now the United States ("We don't really think of America as having a Spanish history at all," he said), in fact the Spanish Inquisition played a role in the early history of New Mexico. He nodded in the direction of the Palace of the Governors. Right there, in the middle of the city, a governor had been murdered as the result of a dispute with the religious authorities. People had been beheaded in the plaza, where Indians today lay out jewelry on blankets. For historians, he went on, the Inquisition would prove to be a blessing. Virtually the only written records we have from New Mexico before 1680 are Inquisition documents; they were routinely sent for safekeeping to Mexico City, the capital of New Spain, and therefore survived the Pueblo Revolt. Everything else was destroyed. So we should be grateful to the Inquisition for something! Of course, Chávez added, after enjoying his joke, we must not forget that the Inquisition was partly to blame for the uprising in the first place.

Soft Power

Christopher Columbus was a man of worldly ambitions — he harbored dreams of wealth and influence. His contract with the Spanish monarchs stipulated that if his expedition proved successful, he would be knighted, would be made the governor of any new lands, and would be awarded the title Admiral of the Ocean Sea. Also, he was to receive 10 percent of any gold that was found. He haggled mightily over these terms. Columbus owned a copy of the *Book of Marco Polo,* and his highlights, marginal notations, and underlinings — "perfumes," "gold mines," "pearls, precious gems, golden fabric, ivory" — reveal a man with an eye for earthly gain. At the same time, he was deeply religious, even obsessively so. In later life, he compiled the *Book of Prophecies,* a collection of apocalyptic writings. He entertained the idea that his voyages would reveal the site of the Garden of Eden. He came to see his mission, at least in part, as messianic destiny: carrying Christ to a larger world. His very name played into this vision, and in penning his signature he would eventually render Cristoforo as *Christo-ferens,* its Greco-Latin root, meaning "Christ-bearer." In describing his needs to Ferdinand and Isabella, he made specific provision for "parish priests or friars" to set up churches and convert the Indians.

No one knows for sure how to weigh the importance of one motive relative to another in the mind of Columbus. That said, when he set sail in 1492 — scribbling a note in his log about the expulsion of Spanish Jews — he neither considered nor foresaw that his efforts would enable the Inquisition to circumnavigate the world. But that would be one result, and in very short order.

"Globalization" did not become a widely used term until the late twentieth century — popularized by a Harvard Business School professor — but it started to become a reality in the fifteenth, as the age of exploration opened an entire planet to conquest and trade. "The sun never sets on the British Empire," the old saying had it; during the sixteenth and seventeenth centuries, it very nearly didn't set on the Inquisition either. Depending on the time of year, there would have been just a short interval after the sun had set on the Inquisition's outpost in Mexico City before it rose on the outpost in Manila — a few brief moments when the Inquisition was in darkness everywhere.

The Inquisition was able to spread so rapidly for two main reasons.

One of them was simply the revolution in communications — communications understood broadly, as the projection of ideas and power over distance. A disciplinary enterprise like the Inquisition must be able to transmit messages over both short distances (down the hall) and long ones (across the mountains, across the sea). All that secretarial machinery would be of little consequence if words and authority, and the people who embodied them, could travel only with great difficulty, or not at all. The sophisticated communications networks of ancient Rome fell into decay with the end of the empire. It had once been possible for a messenger to make the trip from Rome to Alexandria and back — by land and sea, under perfect conditions — in about three weeks. Such feats were impossible in a medieval world in which roads had crumbled, "law" was local and unpredictable, and the waters were swept by roving marauders. In the early Middle Ages, communication was essentially oral, and neither words nor people traveled very far. Most journeys were made on foot, which in practice meant that one could cover about ten miles a day.

But over time, and very gradually, conditions began to improve. Monasteries and then universities revived the art of making and distributing books. The Carolingian rulers set up a system of *missi domini* — "messengers of the lord" — to bring a semblance of administrative control to their domains. Religious orders created their own networks of messengers. The Cistercian system, probably the best, linked 6,000 establishments throughout Europe. The development of pilgrimage routes — chief among them, the ones that led from all over the continent to the holy sites in Rome — and then of the routes employed by those who joined the Crusades, opened up well-trod pathways with an infrastructure of inns, stables, blacksmiths, and cobblers to support them.

By the fifteenth century, transport by sea could occur over longer distances and with greater safety and accuracy than ever before. For one thing, ships were better. Interactions between northern and southern Europe, and between Europe and the Islamic lands, had led to the development of well-designed, smooth-hulled caravels, with two or three masts and a rudder at the stern — a more robust and reliable vessel than the old clinker ships. The caravels combined lateen-rigged and square-rigged sails — they could make headway running into the wind as well as before the wind. The technology of navigation had advanced. The magnetic compass, floating in a bowl, was now widely in service, providing a general sense of direction, and so were the quadrant and the astrolabe, which allowed navigators to fix a ship's latitude.

The other reason the Inquisition went global was that like anything else based on organizational principles, it was highly portable. The "soft" power of an influential state is the power that derives from culture, religion, technology, and methods of administration, as opposed to simple violence or its threat. Portability is the hallmark of any empire. As different as one city may have been from another in the Roman Empire, its public center bore the unmistakable imprint of Roman rule: the temples of Jupiter, Juno, and Minerva; the imposing basilica; the public latrines. One would have felt, as Edward Gibbon wrote, that imperial authority was being exercised "with the same facility on the banks of the Thames, or of the Nile, as on those of the Tiber." In any British colony during the high noon of empire, you would find a starchy Government House, schoolchildren in tartans, judges in wigs, toasts to the monarch. The Spanish Empire was no different, though its bureaucratic machinery was relatively modest. The institutions of crown and church — strongly linked to Madrid, sometimes to the point of punctilious micromanagement — were transplanted wholesale.

Spain and Portugal changed the places they colonized in many ways. The most successful transplants were language and religion. In time, after centuries, the imperial powers would retreat. The Church itself would lose its tenuous hold on temporal authority. But it would never shed its new, planetary character. The Church became

the world's first truly globalized institution. Its effort to regulate how
people think and behave became global too.

"Mission Creep"

The Inquisition followed the flag, and its targets at first were those
who arrived under that flag, rather than people already living where
the flag was planted. The Inquisition was always a tool for use primarily on Christians, including *conversos* suspected of backsliding; it
did not, for instance, haul Indians into tribunals unless they had previously embraced the faith. There were many *conversos* in the New
World and elsewhere in the empires of Spain and Portugal. Columbus numbered at least five men of Jewish ancestry among the crew
on his first voyage. One of them served as the expedition's physician,
another as its surgeon. A third served as bursar. A fourth, Luis de
Torres, baptized the year Columbus set sail, was brought along as a
translator — he knew Hebrew, Chaldean, and Arabic, and Columbus
believed those languages might come in handy. Life in Iberia was at
best conditional for *conversos,* at worst dangerous, and many chose
to seek opportunities in Asia, Africa, and America. Jews who had not
converted did the same. The new imperial colonies offered hope of
a fresh start, far from the prying eyes and heavy hands of kings and
bishops.

It was a sensible choice, and paid off for large numbers. Many of
them were from Portugal. Their families may have fled from Spain to
that temporarily freer kingdom — only to flee again when the Portuguese commenced their own inquisition. No place in Iberia seemed
reliable in the long run. Portugal sometimes encouraged *converso*
emigration; technically, *conversos* were not allowed to emigrate from
Spain, but the looser reality of a beckoning frontier, and the need for
manpower, made the prohibition largely a dead letter.

The Inquisition took note. As early as 1532, a *converso* family was plucked from Mexico and returned to Spain on orders issued by a faraway tribunal. Before long, clerics in the colonies — mainly members of the Franciscan Order, with their hooded brown habits and belts of knotted cord, but also Dominicans — were given explicit inquisitorial powers. Within the span of a lifetime after Columbus, tribunals of the Inquisition had been put into place in cities around the world — functioning replicas of the tribunals back home. Spain established a tribunal in Mexico City in 1569 and in Lima that same year. An Inquisition office was set up in Manila in 1583 (subject to the jurisdiction of the tribunal in Mexico City) and a full tribunal was established in Cartagena in 1611. Under the Portuguese, the Inquisition was established in Goa in 1560, where its activity was intense. The hand of the Portuguese Inquisition can be seen in places as far-flung as Brazil, Angola, Mozambique, the Cape Verde Islands, and Macau, though its touch in some of these places was light.

"The Holy Office of the Inquisition," writes the historian France V. Scholes, "was the most important ecclesiastical court in the New World." He goes on:

> The jurisdiction of the Inquisition was wide and elastic. Heresy, apostasy, blasphemy, bigamy, the practice of superstition, sorcery and demonology, propositions subversive of the faith, denial of ecclesiastical authority, lack of respect for ecclesiastical persons, institutions, and censures, solicitation in the confessional, evil-sounding words — these were some of the causes for prosecution by the tribunal. No member of the non-aboriginal community was exempt.

Some years ago, the Bancroft Library at the University of California came into possession of sixty-one volumes of manuscript records from the Mexican Inquisition spanning the years 1593 to 1817. Each of the volumes is devoted to the case of a single individual. Some of them run to hundreds of pages. Sewn into the middle of one volume — the case of a man accused of not believing in the Virgin Mary — is the rope he used to hang himself while in prison, in 1597. Looking at the accusations, one gets a vivid sense of the range of transgressions that came before the Inquisition, and of the phenomenon that in our time goes by "mission creep":

"suspicion of being a Lutheran"

"asserting that sexual intercourse with him was not a sin"

"claiming sexual intercourse with saints"

"saying mass and giving penance without being a priest"

"revelations and clairvoyance"

"fraud, superstition, and unlicensed practice of medicine"

"witchcraft"

"seeking sexual intercourse with a woman by telling her that God had ordered it"

"hypocrisy, false visions, revelations, and miracles"

"officiating in the marriage of two dogs"

And, as usual, there was the crime of "practicing Judaism." This accusation would always get the Inquisition's attention, but in terms of numbers, the prosecution of alleged crypto-Jews was concentrated in two great waves of zeal.

The first occurred in the 1590s, in the wake of an influx of *converso* colonists into Mexico, when some two hundred people were investigated for activities that marked them, in the Inquisition's view, as crypto-Jews. The most celebrated among the victims was Luis de Carvajal, the nephew of a prominent conquistador. In 1596, Carvajal was burned at the stake along with his mother, three sisters, and three other convicted judaizers. He left behind a deeply personal and affecting memoir, a testament to his Jewish faith composed between periods of imprisonment. Additional fragments of Carvajal's writing survived in the form of letters he sought to smuggle to his siblings as he awaited execution, written on eggshells or the skins of fruit, or engraved with a pin on an avocado pit. The last entry in his memoir is dated according to the Hebrew calendar: "the fifth month of the year five thousand three hundred and fifty-seven of our creation."

The second wave of prosecution came half a century later, in 1642. A *converso* community was by then a palpable reality in Mexico City — old European patterns had reasserted themselves — and for the most part it was left alone. *Conversos* tended to marry one another. They kept up various rituals. Some observed the Sabbath and specific holy days. Men might be circumcised. (Inquisition surgeons checked.) For certain *conversos*, such behavior was little more than a cultural holdover. For others, Judaism remained the core of identity. The *conversos* tended to cluster in an identifiable neighborhood — it lay between the cathedral and the present-day Church of Santo Domingo, where the Inquisition made its home. The plaza in front of the church was where autos-da-fé were held.

The Inquisition stepped in abruptly. The precipitating event was a geopolitical crisis — what today would be called a national-security threat. For sixty years, Portugal had been annexed to Spain. In 1640, Portugal seceded, and Mexico was gripped by fear of a Portuguese invasion. The ancestors of many *conversos* had come from Portugal; their descendants were even called *portugueses*. Fear of the one became fear of the other — a dynamic of conflation that will seem familiar to modern eyes. Beginning in 1642 and over the next several years, more than 130 suspected crypto-Jews were brought before the tribunal in Mexico City. By one estimate, fewer than 6 percent of this number were completely exonerated of the charges brought against them. The rest were found culpable to some degree. The judicial procedures used were those the Inquisition had developed over time: long periods of incarceration interrupted at irregular intervals by interrogation, with torture employed in about a third of the cases. Personal property would have been seized and sequestered at the outset of the proceedings. In the end, most of those brought before the tribunal confessed to the charges and submitted to "reconciliation"—but in many cases lost their wealth and property anyway, and were expelled from New Spain. A handful of the accused—refusing to be reconciled, or considered to have relapsed—were sent to the stake.

Such was the state of affairs in Mexico City, the capital. But the Inquisition was already moving on.

A Murder in Santa Fe

Roads can be superseded, but they're very hard to erase. Iron Age tracks, like the Pilgrims' Way in southern England, can be found all over Europe, and are still used by hikers. The ancient Silk Road, braiding through Central Asia, remains easy to trace. Interstate 25 is the modern highway that follows the Rio Grande from Santa Fe down through Albuquerque to Las Cruces and El Paso. All along the way, sometimes on the left and sometimes on the right, and especially when the sun is low, you can see notches and deep cuts on successive ridgelines that mark the course of an old road. In the lowlands between, you can make out the ruts left by wheels in the grass. In other places, the road is revealed as a line of sight through the cottonwoods.

This is the Camino Real, the oldest European road in America, which in the course of the sixteenth and early seventeenth centuries gradually pushed its way north from Mexico City. The road followed Indian footpaths. It was the route taken by Juan de Oñate in 1598, a generation before Plymouth Rock, when he and several hundred men, women, and children ventured into what is now New Mexico and settled not far from present-day Santa Fe. The Villa de Santa Fe itself was founded a decade later. For more than two hundred years, until the opening of the Santa Fe Trail, which provided a link to Missouri, the Camino Real would be New Mexico's only significant connection to the rest of the world.

The province was as remote as a space station, and needed massive and regular resupply. A great convoy, or *conducta,* made the journey about once a year in each direction, traveling 1,500 miles at a pace of perhaps twenty miles a day. There would be hundreds of people in each *conducta,* along with trade goods, cattle and pigs on the hoof, and mail. The convoy was heavily armed—attacks by Apaches and other tribes were routine. The documents of government passed in both directions, as did the documents of the Franciscan Order and of the Inquisition.

The documentation is voluminous. The Inquisition records are held at the Archivo General de la Nación, in Mexico City, a massive building that until the 1970s was used as a prison. People called it the Black Palace. Pancho Villa once escaped from it. The prison cells now hold documents, and researchers sit at desks in the hallways outside them. The Inquisition records fill 1,550 folios. They include accounts of depositions and trials, narratives of local events, instructions from the tribunal to distant clerics, the clerics' replies, and humdrum correspondence of every kind. When someone was charged with an offense before the Inquisition, one of the first things interrogators did was to ask him for a *discurso de la vida*—the story of his life—which often yielded a long and rambling narrative, full of incident and revelation. What the Inquisition register of Jacques Fournier accomplished for the village of Montaillou in the fourteenth century, the Inquisition records in Mexico City accomplished for Spain's American possessions two and three centuries later.

The information about New Mexico is surprisingly detailed. In some ways, the role of Emmanuel Le Roy Ladurie was played by France V. Scholes, a student of Frederick Jackson Turner and himself an inspiring teacher to a generation of historians. Scholes was the first American historian to become intimately familiar with the

Inquisition archives in Mexico, and he used them to repopulate the vast empty spaces of early New Mexican history.

Representatives of the Inquisition, known as *comisarios*, rotated through the province regularly, after background checks to confirm their doctrinal fealty and *limpieza de sangre* — their purity of blood. The commissaries took evidence in cases of every kind. We learn of one Indian woman who claimed she had been having an affair with the governor, and of another Indian woman who had been brought from her pueblo to Sante Fe because she possessed certain magical arts, and might save the life of a Spanish soldier. The use of peyote by Indians and colonists alike was remarked. One man reported that some of his belongings had been stolen, and that after eating peyote he had experienced a vision: a man and a woman had appeared to him, and described where his belongings could be found. (And there they were!) We learn about the use of love potions and aphrodisiacs. One woman explained that the way to enchant a man was to wash her private parts with water and then use the water to cook him a meal, or to make him chocolate.

The Inquisition left a double legacy in New Mexico. The first part was immediate, and led to political convulsions that shaped the territory for years to come. The second was demographic, and remains to some extent conjectural.

The immediate consequence was a violent conflict between church and state — between inquisitors and governors or the people standing in for them. Church and state in New Mexico had one large interest in common — the extension of Spanish power — but with respect to day-to-day management, and even ultimate goals, their interests often diverged sharply. The Church wanted to win souls for Christ — to build missions, keep them safe, stamp out Indian folkways, and make the exploitation of Indian labor a Church monopoly. The state needed to support a garrison. It also wanted to lure in enough settlers to develop this poor, dry territory as best it could. It gave away land, tolerated the colonists' abuse of Indians, and even sanctioned slavery and the slave trade.

The clash became especially intense because no buffering institutions stood in the way to absorb the friction. In Europe, neither secular rulers nor the Inquisition could ever act in complete isolation. The apparatus of civil society lay thick upon the ground. Towns and cities enjoyed rights and privileges. Guilds and benevolent societies formed diverse networks of association. Family ties were ancient and complex. Church and state — fractured into subunits and jurisdictions and hierarchies — were hardly monolithic. The power of an institution like the Inquisition was rarely the same in practice as it was on paper.

In New Mexico, the situation was different. The European population living in and around Santa Fe in the earliest decades numbered no more than several hundred. Any internecine conflict immediately achieved the status of a crisis. As Scholes would observe, "The very simplicity of political, social, and economic conditions permitted such issues to assume a greater relative importance than would have been the case if life had been more varied and complex." It was a hothouse environment, where clashes of rights and jurisdiction became intensely personal.

The fact that communication to and from the outside world occurred mainly in rare but regularized bursts must have added a surreal dimension to life in New Mexico. Friars and governors sometimes employed special messengers, though the risk of interception or misadventure was high. That recourse aside, there was only the *conducta*. Imagine the various antagonists in Santa Fe, their animosities building, writing long, furious accounts to their superiors, but having to wait for the next convoy to send them. The warring documents then travel together to Mexico City and are dispersed to their various destinations. Meetings are held. Decisions are made. Sometimes the authorities in Spain must be consulted — the letters undertake another slow journey. Meanwhile, the antagonists stew. Sometimes they fight. At last — six months later? a year? two years? — the responses converge on the next *conducta* bound for Santa Fe. When they arrive, the documents are separated and delivered to the antagonists. The advice and instructions reshape the battle lines. The war continues. Pens scratch busily in the candlelight in anticipation of the next *conducta*.

Church and state never achieved a lasting *convivencia* in Santa Fe. The actors on the scene were to some extent proxies, backed by powerful interests in Mexico City and Madrid. The friars were quick to levy charges of blasphemy, witchcraft, and other transgressions against the governors and their allies, knowing that these would stir the Inquisition's interest. The governors did the same. In 1642, in the aftermath of a particularly ugly and complicated series of church-state altercations, members of the pro-church faction burst in on the former governor, Luis de Rosas, and ran him through with a sword. Rosas was an undiplomatic man with a violent temper. The friars were glad to see him go. But his murder was an affront to civil authority. Competing versions of events made their way to Mexico City. The return trip brought a new governor, who carried secret orders about how to deal with the killers of Rosas. He issued a general pardon to calm things down, and then quietly rounded up the eight men he held responsible. On July 21, 1643, all eight were decapitated in the Santa Fe plaza. The head of a man named Antonio de Baca, the ringleader, was nailed to the gibbet and left there for all to see. A popular guide to Santa Fe, on the lookout for carefully parsed superlatives, refers to the event as "the largest mass beheading of Europeans by Europeans in a continental American town."

The beheadings had a sobering effect, but not for long — the story of the next several decades is one of renewed church-state conflict. Complaints to the Inquisition were again used as a weapon. In the 1660s, the tribunal brought formal charges of heresy and blasphemy against two governors of New Mexico, the wife of one of them, and four soldiers serving in the province. One of the governors had already left the scene. The other six individuals were arrested, bound hand and foot, and hauled off to Mexico City with the *conducta*. In the end, none of the accused went to the stake. One died in prison. The rest suffered penalties ranging from public abjuration to loss of property to permanent exile.

What no one paid much attention to was the effect of all this strife on the Indians. They had lived under Spanish rule since the 1590s, sometimes in servitude and usually with resentment. Some groups were more docile than others; some were overtly hostile. They fought among themselves. But they also took note of the divisions among the Spanish elite. Finally they rose up in a coordinated attack. It occurred within months of the great auto-da-fé held that year in the Plaza Mayor in Madrid, an event celebrated in a monumental painting by Francisco Ricci that hangs in the Prado.

After the reconquest, the old patterns of animosity reasserted themselves, though not with quite the same intensity. The Inquisition remained active in New Mexico, and maintained a quieter presence in Arizona, California, and Texas. The sole trial held in Spanish California involved a man named Ramon Sotilo, in Los Angeles, who was accused of "having expressed views on religion that not even a Protestant would dare hold." On one occasion, the Inquisition's commissary in California confiscated four copies of a game known as El Eusebio. In Santa Fe, cases were opened and closed, reports sent to headquarters, defendants convicted and sentenced. A celebrated episode concerned a man named Miguel de Quintana, the "mad poet" of New Mexico, whose satiric verses brought him into repeated conflict with the Inquisition between 1732 and 1737. Quintana was harassed but not killed, and was eventually exonerated. His work survives because it was confiscated and filed away in the Inquisition archives, along with an immense amount of related correspondence. Fray Angélico

Chávez gave Quintana the epithet "mad," but it was nothing personal: Chávez also suggested that he be made New Mexico's poet laureate.

As time went on, a new threat was recognized: the influx of foreign ideas. The young United States, an empire in embryo that would supplant much of Spain's, was moving inexorably toward the Mississippi and deeper into the continent. The old lifeline south to Mexico City was no longer the only significant path for communications; now there were overland routes to the east. Ships from everywhere sailed up and down the Pacific coast. Books and other influences from the outside world began to make their way in. There is correspondence in the Inquisition files about a California man suspected of owning a book by Voltaire. For the most part, censorship wasn't an issue in California; as one historian observes, Californians weren't known for reading books. In Mexico, a man was denounced — by his mother — for owning a copy of Rousseau's *Social Contract*. Imprisoned by the Inquisition, he escaped and fled to New Orleans.

The issue was not just the pernicious influence of new ideas, although that was a serious concern. There was also a fear that outlanders would pass themselves off as good Catholics — a kind of fifth column, with who knew what agenda. "Particular care was taken to ferret out French and English catechisms that did not have the Holy Office imprimatur," the historian Richard E. Greenleaf writes. "These works were smuggled into New Spain via Louisiana and Texas, and were apparently used by foreigners who wished to appear knowledgeable about Catholic dogma." In 1795, the Inquisition in New Mexico appointed a censor in an explicit but vain attempt to keep printed matter out: the books were too many, the censors too few.

The censors would keep at it until Mexico won its independence from Spain, in 1821, and the Inquisition in North America at last came to an end. Indeed, they kept at it even afterward — the Inquisition's ganglia continued to fire. A decree arrived in California that same year, banning the "*escandalosisimo* dance called the waltz."

Against All Odds

The Inquisition's second legacy in New Mexico, persisting perhaps into our own time, was demographic. As noted, *conversos* by the thousands had made their way to the Spanish and Portuguese colonies. Many lived fully as the Christians they had become. Some lived as Christians but preserved cultural traces of their heritage. And some, whatever the outward appearance, lived secretly as Jews. The numbers in any of these categories are unknowable, and the sporadic flare-up of Inquisition activity made identification with Judaism extremely dangerous. Could it be that small remnant communities of crypto-Jews survived in remote pockets of Hispanic America — and exist even today?

The most comprehensive survey of crypto-Judaism and its tenacity, covering many centuries and many areas of the world, is *Secrecy and Deceit,* by David M. Gitlitz. Considerable evidence indicates that crypto-Judaism in the Americas and elsewhere proved remarkably durable. In 1917, for instance, a small Judaic remnant preserving vestiges of Jewish ritual was identified in an isolated region of Portugal, on the border with Spain. Among other things, the people there still used Hebrew phrases in their prayers. There has been more-tenuous speculation about a survival of Jewish practices among immigrants from the Azores in southeastern Massachusetts and Rhode Island.

The debate is over which examples are "real" and which can be attributed to some other explanation. Certain evocative and seemingly persuasive instances of crypto-Judaism have been called into question. In the late 1940s, the anthropologist Raphael Patai looked closely at the so-called Jewish Indians of Venta Prieta, a small town in Mexico about sixty miles north of Mexico City. Many residents of the town had long believed themselves to be Jewish, preserving customs handed down from generation to generation. Patai suggested, however, that sincere as these people were, their history was different from what they thought: their ancestors a few generations before had been swept up in a Pentecostal movement, Iglesia de Dios, which employed a number of Hebraic rituals, including Hebrew songs and prayers. Whatever the truth about their origins, the self-proclaimed Jews of Venta Prieta got to their desired destination — they eventually converted to Judaism officially (and many emigrated to Israel). The town continues to attract heritage tourists.

During the last few decades of the twentieth century, ethnographers and historians began to take note of certain practices among small groups of Hispanics in rural areas of New Mexico — for instance, the lighting of candles on Friday evening, the observance of Saturday as a day of rest, the shunning of pork, the ritual slaughter of animals, the circumcision of males, the use of the Star of David in folk art and on headstones, the naming of sons Adonay (*Adonai* is Hebrew for "Lord"), and the practice of sweeping debris in a room toward the center rather than out the door (historically, to avoid desecrating a mezuzah on the doorpost). The people involved were often only vaguely aware of what the origin of such practices might be. Stanley M. Hordes, a former state historian of New Mexico, is the scholar who has most prominently made the argument that these rural Hispanics — "the crypto-Jews of New Mexico" — represent a case of true cultural survival. Other historians and ethnographers have pursued the subject and come to the same conclusion.

The most prominent skeptic is the folklorist Judith S. Neulander. She has methodological issues with some of the evidence-gathering and provides alternative explanations for proposed pieces of evidence. The Star of David, for instance, is "a cross-cultural commonplace." Her conclusion parallels Patai's: the ancestors of the "crypto-Jews" of New Mexico were originally Catholics who embraced an aggressive, Hebrew-inflected strain of Pentecostalism. She believes that their descendants, perhaps caught up in the media attention the topic has received, are inventing an "imaginary crypto-Jewish identity" — and that some are doing so because "by negating Mexican national origin," they can achieve "a promotion in social rank or prestige." In a sense, Neulander argues, this amounts to a quest for a form of *limpieza de sangre,* and is tinged with racism.

So the debate has been hot. Stripping away the emotion, the crux of the matter is this: can one establish a firm link between now and then — between suggestive cultural practices in our own time and the reality of events that occurred centuries ago? Neulander is certainly correct in observing that the swirl of cultural influences in the New World, in both the recent and the distant past, is chaotic. People don't necessarily know where family traditions come from. Scholars are not always able to sort things out. And you can't discount the possibility of wishful thinking, among either the people being studied or the experts with their tape recorders and notepads. "Lost tribes" have been turning up for centuries. Hordes and his camp, for their part, have accumulated a wealth of ethnographic and circumstantial evidence. They are also able to show, from Inquisition records, that families known to be of Jewish descent — and individuals suspected of being crypto-Jews — were among the earliest settlers of New Mexico. Genealogical research by Hordes has established connections between these settlers and people in New Mexico who claim crypto-Jewish ancestry.

There is no question that in the course of the fifteenth and sixteenth centuries, people of Jewish blood left Spain and Portugal in significant numbers and made their way to imperial colonies. The documentary evidence is abundant. There is possible genetic evidence as well. DNA testing of the male Y chromosome shows an unusually high incidence of likely connection to the Jewish priestly class, the *cohanim,* among Hispanics of the Southwest. Hispanics in parts of that region also appear to share with Jews an unusually high incidence of a serious skin disease, *pemphigus vulgaris.* And both groups are disproportionately susceptible to a mutation — designated 185delAG — of the BRCA1 gene that markedly increases the risk of developing breast and ovarian cancer.

Judaic culture, as amply documented by Gitlitz, often survived the passage from Iberia, taking root in distant lands. The prevalence of the phenomenon cannot be known — adherence to old practices was secretive, and some of the evidence, such as inquisitorial accusations of "judaizing," cannot be taken at face value. But many Jews held on to elements of their faith, and did so for generations and even centuries.

Crypto-Hindus?

It was not just Jews who tried to maintain their identity. The spread of empire brought the Inquisition into contact with unfamiliar religious outlooks of many kinds. Christians, Jews, and Muslims had been known to one another for centuries. Whatever the hostility, they shared a frame of reference. They were monotheistic, revered common prophetic figures, and regarded the Bible as a sacred text. But in America, Asia, and Africa, Christian conquerors and clerics faced something else entirely. The human sacrifice of the Aztecs had horrified the Spaniards, but this was just the first of many new religious practices they would encounter. In India, the Portuguese came face-to-face with Hinduism and Buddhism as well as Islam. In China, the imperial powers confronted Confucianism. In Africa, they faced a variety of animist religions.

The challenge to conventional thinking was immense, and the response in some quarters was original and admirable. The Jesuits entered China in a spirit of intellectual engagement. They took pains to learn the language, introduced Western science and mathematics, and showed themselves to be shrewd observers and advisors. They also sought to adapt Christianity to Chinese folkways, and translated the works of Confucius into European languages. In the early 1700s, the engraver Bernard Picart and the printer Jean-Frédéric Bernard produced their monumental *Religious Ceremonies of the World*, a foray into what today would be called comparative religion. The illustrated folios documented not only the differences among religions but also their many common elements.

Picart and Bernard wrote from a perspective of tolerant curiosity, in the middle of the Enlightenment. Two centuries earlier, such a perspective was rare — the governing interests were missionary or mercantile. "I seek Christians and spices," the explorer Vasco da Gama declared, and he meant what he said. In the eyes of Catholic missionaries, there was a whole world to convert — and a potentially vast number of new Christians who, once converted, might slide back into their old satanic ways.

In 1510, the Portuguese established a colony at Goa, one of a string of possessions they would control along the western coast of India. They did not relinquish the colony until 1961, when India had been independent for more than a decade. Goa became a thriving mercantile outpost. To this day, it enjoys the highest per capita income in India. Parts of the capital look like the urban neighborhoods of old Iberia. The Portuguese Inquisition arrived in Goa in 1560, and henceforward its tribunal held sway over all Portugal's possessions in Asia and around the Indian Ocean. The Inquisition in Goa had urgent business and great authority — enough authority to displace the viceroy from his palace, forcing him to find other quarters.

The urgent business was twofold. First, many Indians had converted to Christianity during the half century of Portuguese rule, but had often done so to obtain food and jobs. The sincerity of these so-called Rice Christians was highly suspect, and in fact many had quietly reverted to their traditional practices. Although the Portuguese destroyed Hindu temples, the faithful managed to save their idols and carry them to safety in areas beyond Portuguese control — the "flight of the deities," as this process has been called. The idols, just out of reach, were a taunting presence.

The second order of business was not a surprise: the Jews. Many Jews and New Christians had fled the Inquisition in Europe and made their way to places where its authority might prove less likely to reach. In Goa (and other parts of Portuguese India) they soon formed a large and prosperous community. This was intolerable. The New Christians of Portugal apparently got wind of what was coming and sent a substantial payment to Pope Paul IV, in the hope of keeping the Inquisition away from the colonies. Paul took the money but then pleaded that his hands were tied — it was a matter for the Portuguese king to decide.

The Inquisition in Goa got to work quickly, holding its first auto-da-fé within two years. A documentary saga seems to lie at the heart of every inquisition: records lost, records found, records hidden, records kept under seal. In its several centuries of existence, the Inquisition conducted some 16,000 trials in Goa. All the actual transcripts were burned in the nineteenth century, when the Portuguese Inquisition was finally abolished. Indexes and letters survive, however, and provide a general picture. Over the course of its first six decades, the Inquisition held twenty-seven autos-da-fé in Goa and sentenced about 3,800 people to punishments of some kind. Of these, 114 were burned at the stake. Two thirds were New Christians accused of judaizing. The rest were alleged crypto-Hindus or crypto-Muslims.

The Inquisition treated Goa by far the most severely among Portugal's colonies. Brazil was a distant second. The Church's censorship regime there was strict enough that printing presses were kept out of Brazil until the nineteenth century. In other colonies — Angola, Congo, São Tomé, Mozambique — the Inquisition was more relaxed. The secular authorities in Angola at one point even sold the right to collect taxes to a man known to be a Jew (and who was in fact secretly a rabbi). Factional fighting among the Europeans often diminished any zest for persecution. One petty dispute in Angola between civil authorities and the Jesuits — over the slaughter of a few dozen pigs — had to be sorted out by the dowager queen of Portugal and the pope. The Inquisition in these places was not a relentlessly efficient machine. But the Church made converts everywhere. The beginnings of an administrative structure spanned the planet.

The inquisitions in Asia, Africa, and the New World all came to an end when the inquisitions in the mother countries did, unless independence had achieved this result already. Two of the heroes of Mexico's war of independence — the priests Miguel Hidalgo y Costilla and José María Morelos — were excommunicated and condemned by the Inquisition; two hundred years after their executions, the Church has publicly rehabilitated both men. In Spain and Portugal, the death of the Inquisition was long and slow — it was suppressed, revived, and then suppressed again, with finality. Its last decades in Spain were chronicled by Francisco Goya, who had personal experience of being brought before the tribunal. Many of the grim, mordant aquatints known as the Caprichos, from the 1790s, depict the Inquisition literally or allegorically. In 1815, Goya was summoned to answer for his painting *The Nude Maja,* which the Inquisition had confiscated as obscene. Goya refused to say who the woman was, or who had commissioned the painting. Soon after that episode, he completed *Court of the Inquisition,* in which the accused men wear *sanbenitos* and pointed hats, and a man in black directs the questioning. A cross on a gold chain hangs from his neck. He seems unaware that time is running out.

A Second Wind

By 1840, only the Roman Inquisition remained alive. It was already a weakened institution, its temporal sway limited to the Papal States in the central region of the Italian peninsula. Within them, the Inquisition could still act in definitive ways, as the case of Edgardo Mortara had shown. But its days, too, were numbered. On September 20, 1870, the military forces of the Kingdom of Italy trained their cannons on a section of Rome's ancient Aurelian Wall and commenced a barrage that would last for three hours. The process of Italian reunification had been under way for decades, and the Papal States represented the last holdout. Pope Pius IX remained obdurate, but after France withdrew its protection — Napoleon III had just fallen from power — the outcome was never in doubt. Italian forces laid siege to Rome, and for the sake of appearances, the pope deployed Swiss Guards and the multinational Papal Zouaves to defend the walls. They surrendered when Italian artillery opened a breach not far from the Porta Pia. The pope refused to recognize the unified government and withdrew into the walled enclave around St. Peter's, becoming the self-proclaimed "prisoner of the Vatican." A monument on the restored Aurelian Wall, marking the place where the artillery did its damage, states simply, "Through this breach Italy once again entered Rome."

In terms of temporal power, the authority of the Holy See was now restricted to 108 acres. But the moment was a turning point. From that time onward, the Church would seek to put its stamp more firmly — and more globally — on the minds of believers, particularly the intellectual class among them. This class included not only theologians, who typically held posts at Church-related institutions, and were therefore subject to some sort of control, but also the growing ranks of educated Catholics, who kept informed and tried to think for themselves. Modern communications, which helped to create this class and make it significant, provided tools that anyone could employ. They could be used to nourish intellectual freedom or to discourage it.

One possible approach was epitomized by Pope Leo XIII, who succeeded Pius IX in 1878. Leo was the first pope who seems recognizably of our own time. He was thin and ascetic, a skilled linguist, a canny diplomat. He believed in the value of scholarship of a contemporary kind. It was Leo who opened up much of the Vatican archives (but not the Inquisition archives) to independent researchers, and who re-established the Vatican Observatory. Leo was the first pope whose movements are preserved in a motion picture, and the first pope whose voice survives in a recording. His 1891 encyclical *Rerum Novarum,* with its critique of economic inequality and its prescient warning that neither capitalism nor communism offered the answer, made Catholic social teaching a living force. The encyclical joined an ongoing debate in the world outside the Church, and joined it squarely and with distinction. It was headline news in Europe and America — highly atypical for papal pronouncements up to that point. With electronic messaging literally at their fingertips, reporters followed the progress of its drafting and editing. They published leaks. They tracked the reaction and the debate in real time. An account in one British newspaper begins, "The *Standard*'s Rome correspondent telegraphs on Thursday . . ." *Rerum Novarum* was an event, and is widely cited to this day. The *New York Times* in 1895 called Leo "not an individual, but the expression of his century."

Leo was hardly "liberal" in the way secular observers would use that term, and some of the ways in which he was "modern" were oddly antiquarian. Once, years ago, I spent several weeks with a group of Dominican priests outside Rome and in Louvain. Using the most sophisticated techniques available, they were attempting to produce, in scores of volumes, the perfect Latin edition of the works of Thomas Aquinas. It was a task that Leo himself had set in motion a hundred years earlier, and the Dominicans were still at it. The work will not be finished for decades. (One of the scholars involved, Antoine Dondaine, also happened to be the foremost authority on Inquisition manuals.) The editions they had published were superb — each a testament to fastidious scholarship and deep faith. It may seem counterintuitive that this monument to a thirteenth-century theologian would be erected just as physicists were coming to terms with quantum mechanics. Leo would have observed, in his own defense, that Thomism represented a philosophy in which religion and science are not antithetical. A scientist would have replied, But they *are*.

Leo's was one approach to engagement with an evolving world. The other approach prevailed. It was a sensibility that considered the world's Catholics as, in effect, the spiritual subjects of a spiritual monarch. Doctrine was rigid, hierarchy was sacred, and theological speculation was impermissible. In 1864, Pius IX had promulgated his Syllabus of Errors, a list of eighty beliefs that Catholics must condemn. These included the belief that "the Church ought to be separated from the State, and the State from the Church"; the belief that "every man is free to embrace and profess that religion which, guided by the light of reason, he shall consider true"; and the belief that the pope "ought to come to terms with progress, liberalism, and modern civilization." The first Vatican Council, under the same pope, had proclaimed the doctrine of papal infallibility. It was this peremptory action, not the claims of some secular ruler, that provoked Lord Acton's famous remark: "Power tends to corrupt, and absolute power corrupts absolutely." Acton, himself a Catholic, filed trenchant dispatches from the council and tried to rally opposition to infallibility. In his eyes, one historian writes, the doctrine epitomized all the tendencies he hated: "towards power and against freedom, towards persecution and against toleration, towards concealment and against openness."

The Holy See may have been reduced to a few gilded acres, but there were no real limits on what today would be called the papacy's virtual presence. The Congregation of the Inquisition was formally abolished in 1908 — that is to say, its name was retired — but its functions were rolled over into a new Congregation of the Holy Office, which, under a sweeping reorganization in 1917, was given broad new powers to police the faithful. The Congregation of the Index was also abolished — but not the Index of Forbidden Books, which was lodged within the Holy Office. The governing structures of the Church were powerfully centralized — and focused on the papacy — in a way they had not been before. Theologically and politically, the rest of the Church needed to fall into line.

The Holy Office was the point of the lance. As the writer Paul Collins has noted, "The interests of the Inquisition were increasingly focused outward to the universal Church." The conservative and controlling mind-set of this period is perfectly preserved in the form of the *Catholic Encyclopedia,* first published in 1907. In the entry on "inquisition" it observes, "History does not justify the hypothesis that the medieval heretics were prodigies of virtue, deserving our sympathy." It defines "censorship of books" as "a supervision of the press in order to prevent any abuse of it."

The decisive event at the turn of the century was the contest over what would come to be called Modernism — indeed, would come to be called the Modernist heresy. Modernism had no single source or target, and was not really a movement until labeled a deviant phenomenon by the Church — a textbook instance of the power of a name to define a foe into existence. Some of those who would be called Modernists were exponents of the new biblical criticism: the idea, which had gathered momentum and credibility throughout the nineteenth century, that the Bible must be understood as a historical document, its truths conditioned by authors writing in the context of particular times. Other Modernists were attuned to the challenges of science — notably the theory of evolution and its consequences. Still others had social concerns in mind — democracy, nationalism — and speculated about how the Church might respond, adapt, encourage.

From the perspective of a hundred years on, one can see that the Modernists were destined to "win" on all counts in the long run. In the short run, they would lose, being driven from teaching, from the priesthood, or from the Church altogether. George Tyrrell, a Jesuit, was expelled from his order and, when he died, was refused burial in a Catholic cemetery. (A priest who made the sign of the cross over his grave was suspended.) The movement was condemned by Pius X in an encyclical in 1907; the pope hurled the word "anathema" repeatedly, like thunderbolts. In 1910, the Holy Office mandated that all clerics worldwide take a special anti-Modernist oath — "lengthy and ferocious," in the words of the historian Eamon Duffy, "and creating a stifling ethos of unjust and suspicious hyper-orthodoxy." The oath was not abandoned until the 1960s. I knew priests who had to take it, and who described it openly as a charade — gibberish to be mouthed in order to pass through a hoop. A friend of Duffy's, a parish priest in Clapham, remembers being made to take the anti-Modernist oath on four separate occasions as he moved from one stage to the next on his clerical path.

"Let's Not Make a Jonah of Him"

The long, haunting ordeal of Pierre Teilhard de Chardin, one of the premier Catholic theologians of the twentieth century, began a little more than a decade after the advent of the oath. It would continue for thirty-five years, and although vindication of a sort did one day come, it did not come in his lifetime. Teilhard was born in France and in 1911 was ordained a Jesuit priest. The Jesuits have long been regarded as the intellectual elite among Catholic religious orders, and they are typically trained in academic specialties beyond theology. Rather than cloistering themselves away from the secular world, as contemplative orders do, they engage actively in that world. Among traditionalists, they have a reputation for skepticism, epitomized in George Tyrrell's famous prayer: "O God, if there is a God, save my soul, if I have a soul." Teilhard's academic work was initially in geology and paleontology. He spent years on excavations in China, and was involved in the discovery and analysis of Peking Man. His lifelong immersion in paleontology informed his theological speculations about human origins and the future of human evolution. These were dangerous topics.

In the early 1920s, an essay on original sin that Teilhard had circulated privately came to the attention of the Holy Office. To this day, no one is quite sure how it did. Original sin refers to the doctrine that humanity exists in a fallen state — a condition represented by the transgression of Adam and Eve and the expulsion from the Garden of Eden. "There is a twofold and serious difficulty in retaining the former representation of original sin," Teilhard wrote in 1922. "It may be expressed as follows: 'The more we bring the past to life again by means of science, the less we can accommodate either Adam or the earthly paradise.'" Statements like this caused official consternation. Teilhard was summoned to Rome and asked to sign a statement that (in his words) he would "never *say* or write anything against the traditional position of the Church on original sin."

In what was to become a pattern, he submitted obediently, though with frustration, and signed the statement. One factor in his decision was summarized in a letter: "I weighed up the enormous scandal and damage that an act of indiscipline on my part would have caused." In another letter, Teilhard wrote, "Some people feel happy in the visible church; but for my own part I think I shall be happy to die in order to be free of it — and to find our Lord outside of it." Several years later, Teilhard completed a book called *The Divine Milieu*, a work of spirituality that contemplated Christian belief in the context of evolutionary destiny. He circulated the manuscript privately, and then sought permission to publish. Permission was denied. The same fate befell virtually all his subsequent works, including his masterpiece, *The Phenomenon of Man*, which describes human evolution as a path toward greater complexity and collective consciousness. The Holy Office leaned on him hard, forbidding Teilhard to teach, forbidding him to accept a chair at the Collège de France, even forbidding him to reside in Paris, historically a hotbed of theological sedition. Once, in Rome, in the late 1940s, Teilhard looked across a room during a cocktail party and saw a Dominican theologian from the Holy Office — a man who had been aggressively involved in the anti-Modernist campaign, and who had denounced Teilhard publicly only a few years before. Teilhard pointed him out to a friend, saying, "This is the man who would like to see me at the stake." And yet in every instance, Teilhard complied with the wishes of his superiors. Thus, from a letter to the head of the Jesuit Order, in 1947: "The Father Provincial has recently communicated to me your letter concerning me of 22 August. I have no need to say that, with God's help, you may count on me."

By the time of his death, in 1955, Teilhard was recognized world-wide for his scientific achievements. But he had seen none of his greatest theological work appear in print. It would all be published after his death — rapidly — eliciting a stern and public condemnation from the Vatican. Citing "ambiguities and even serious errors," the Holy Office urged priests and teachers "to protect minds, particularly of the youth, against the dangers of the works of Fr. Teilhard de Chardin and his associates." The warning was reiterated in 1981. In 2009, Pope Benedict made a positive reference, in passing, to Teilhard in a sermon, prompting speculation that his status might soon be officially upgraded. At this writing, that had not yet happened.

A less severe but no less characteristic picture of the internal machinations of the Holy Office involves the odd case of Graham Greene, a convert to Catholicism. Greene's novels frequently raised issues of theological ambiguity. They also led to narrative resolutions that provoked thinking people to reflection, and the Holy Office to apoplexy. One novel in particular, *The Power and the Glory*, about a deeply flawed "whisky priest" in Mexico — a fugitive on the run from anticlerical authorities, who will kill him if they can — attracted vehement criticism from conservative Catholics. When he wrote the novel, in 1940, Greene may have been less concerned about threats from the Vatican than about threats from 20th Century Fox. (By one account, he had gone to Mexico, where the idea for the novel germinated, in order to escape a libel action, brought by the studio, for an article he had written about Shirley Temple's performance in *Wee Willie Winkie*.) Because the book was in English — not one of the traditionally civilized or Catholic languages — the Holy Office was slow to take notice. That changed after it was published in France and Germany, and complaints began to arrive in Rome.

The documents in the case — the complaints, the responses, the internal deliberations, the views of consultants, the correspondence between prelates in Rome and London — lie in file boxes in the Inquisition archives. Because they date to the 1940s and 1950s — too recent to be routinely accessible — special permission is needed to examine them. Josef Ratzinger, when he was still the prefect, granted that permission to Peter Godman.

"The German translation has been published and immediately we've received protests. What to do?" That's a handwritten marginal note from 1949 on one of the earliest Holy Office memoranda about *The Power and the Glory*. Given such concerns, the book was put into the hands of two Vatican censors, who duly read it and recorded their observations for the file. They found the book "paradoxical," a work that troubled "the spirit of calm that should prevail in a Christian." They noted the author's "abnormal propensity toward . . . situations in which one kind of sexual immorality or another plays a role." And they did not care for a sardonic remark by one character in the book: "It is good to see a priest with a conscience." The censors considered putting the book on the Index (it had already been banned in Ireland), but in the end recommended that someone in authority, perhaps Cardinal Bernard Griffin, the archbishop of London, give Greene a dressing-down and a warning.

Still, the files reveal some internal resistance to the idea of censure. One high-ranking Vatican official, Giovanni Battista Montini, had read Greene and admired him. He urged that *The Power and the Glory* be given a second look, and recommended Msgr. Giuseppe De Luca for the job. De Luca, a close friend of Montini's, was an intellectual and a bibliophile. (Upon his death, in 1962, he left his personal collection of more than 120,000 volumes to the Vatican Library.) De Luca delivered a long and scathing dissent from the report of the two censors. And he had this to say about the role of writers like Greene:

> To condemn or even to deplore them would be looked askance at in England, and would deal a grievous blow to our prestige: it would demonstrate not only that we are behind the times but also that our judgment is light-weight, undermining significantly the authority of the clergy which is regarded — rightly — as unlettered

bondslaves to puerile literature in bad taste. The crew should not be confused with the pilot: today, great writers are the real pilots of much of mankind, and when the Lord, in His mercy, sends us one, even if he is a nuisance, let's not make a Jonah of him; let's not throw him to the fishes.

De Luca continued in this vein; he was shrewd and worldly, and not a bad critic. But his dissent arrived at the Holy Office too late. Instructions had already gone out to Cardinal Griffin, who called Greene on the carpet in a private meeting — among other things, asking him not to republish *The Power and the Glory* without making revisions. Griffin also preached from the pulpit about the failings of Catholic novelists. The matter was left at that, with no further condemnation. There survives in the record a somewhat toadying letter from Greene to Cardinal Giuseppe Pizzardo, the secretary of the Holy Office. "I wish to emphasize," Greene wrote, "that, throughout my life as a Catholic, I have never ceased to feel deep sentiments of personal attachment to the Vicar of Christ, fostered in particular by admiration for the wisdom with which the Holy Father has constantly guided God's Church."

Dirty Work

Giovanni Battista Montini, the man who came to Graham Greene's defense, was elected to the papacy in 1963, becoming Pope Paul VI. It was he who presided over the Second Vatican Council, which his predecessor, Pope John XXIII, had convened. Those old enough to remember the mid 1960s can easily, if wistfully, recall the spirit of openness and excitement the council generated. The fact that the deliberations were conducted in Latin somehow made its modernizing agenda seem all the more ambitious. When it began, in 1963, librarians at Boston College, a Jesuit institution, still kept books on the

Index in a locked cage in the basement, away from students; by the time it ended, the Index itself had been abolished. The excitement was not confined to religious circles. *The New Yorker* covered its deliberations in a long series — thirteen articles in all — by the pseudonymous Xavier Rynne (in actuality, a Redemptorist priest named F. X. Murphy), who reprised the interpretive role originated by Lord Acton.

It is easy to portray the council as a battle of liberals versus conservatives, which is precisely what Rynne did. If that view is simplistic, there is still a basic truth to it. The strong will of Paul VI kept the council from falling apart, though on issue after issue he himself tended to vacillate, earning the nickname *amletico* — "Hamlet." Paul embodied the ambivalence at the heart of the modern Church. Gathered with him was the cast of characters, many of them young, whose contests and relationships would shape the Church over the next half century. The future John Paul II was present as Karol Wojtyla, the new archbishop of Kraków. Josef Ratzinger was there as a young advisor to Cardinal Josef Frings, of Cologne. Hans Küng, Edward Schillebeeckx, Bernard Häring — they were all participants.

It was at the very end of the council that the Congregation of the Holy Office was renamed the Congregation for the Doctrine of the Faith. The new name could not alter the fundamental nature of the organization. John le Carré built his novel *The Looking-Glass War* around a ramshackle British intelligence agency known as The Department. Its days of glory are past. Its tradecraft is rusty. But on it plods, until the opportunity for extraordinary mischief at last arises. The CDF is in some ways like The Department — always fighting the last Reformation. It attracts the most conservative curial clerics as personnel. Intellectually, it has a reputation for mediocrity, however brilliant its prefect may be. It is bureaucratic and slow. Its procedures build on centuries of Roman habit. To the extent that those procedures are knowable, it is apparent that they are not followed scrupulously: many theologians have found themselves ensnared in processes that seem capricious and opaque.

The instruments available to the CDF are not what they once were. It does not torture, except perhaps in a psychological sense. It does not burn books, or their authors. But it can withhold a license to teach as a Catholic theologian. It can bar people from jobs at certain Catholic institutions, and dismiss people from those same jobs. It can apply pressure through the leadership of religious orders. It can also formally excommunicate, though that is rarely done. The CDF holds the greatest leverage over Catholics in positions of official influence — and in particular, insidiously, over those among them who wish to remain loyal to the Church as an institution. It has no leverage at all over those who simply decide to walk away.

At the time of the Vatican Council, the Holy Office had come under harsh and sustained attack. In a dramatic moment during the second session, in 1963, Cardinal Frings rose to condemn its "methods and behavior" as "a cause of scandal." He went on: "No one should be judged and condemned without being heard, without knowing what he is accused of, and without having the opportunity to amend what he can reasonably be reproached with." The language was supplied by his young advisor, Josef Ratzinger. The Holy Office, Ratzinger himself wrote in 1965, "prejudged every question almost before it had come up for discussion." In 1968, he signed his name to the so-called Nijmegen Declaration, which said in part: "Any form of inquisition, however subtle, not only harms the development of sound theology, it also causes irreparable damage to the credibility of the church as a community in the modern world."

By 1981, Ratzinger had become the prefect of the CDF, under Pope John Paul II. And events had changed him. Before long, he would be known as the Grand Inquisitor. As Garry Wills has observed, "Sixties unrest in the Church soon had the effect on Ratzinger that campus unrest had on American liberals who bolted the Democratic Party and became neoconservatives." A quarter century of "inquisition, however subtle" would ensue. Indeed, it was already under way.

In 1979, the CDF, citing "contempt" for Church doctrine, stripped Hans Küng of his right to teach as a Catholic theologian at the University of Tübingen. Küng had called into question Church teachings on infallibility, celibacy, birth control, and other matters. In 1985, the Franciscan priest Leonardo Boff, a leading proponent of "liberation theology" in Latin America, was silenced — that is, ordered not to publish or to speak publicly — for a year. Boff was also assigned a personal censor to review his writings. Soon thereafter, Charles Curran, who had argued that it was permissible for theologians to dissent on doctrine that had not been declared infallible, was declared to be neither "suitable nor eligible" to teach Catholic theology and was barred from doing so at Catholic University, in Washington, D.C., where he was a professor.

In 1986, the Dominican theologian Edward Schillebeeckx, who held controversial opinions on a variety of subjects, and who had been called to Rome for intensive questioning on three occasions over the course of a decade, was informed that much of his work was "in disagreement with the teaching of the Church." In 1988, Matthew Fox, a Dominican priest with a New Age bent, was silenced for a year. He was eventually expelled from the Dominican Order. In 1997, the Vatican took the extreme step of excommunicating a Sri Lankan priest, Tissa Balasuriya, who had written a book that seemed to depart from established doctrine on original sin and the divinity of Jesus. A year later, he signed a "profession of faith" and produced a careful statement noting that errors and ambiguities had been "perceived in my writings." Balasuriya also agreed to submit future writings to Rome for review before publication. The excommunication was revoked. But the litany of names goes on.

Beyond the individual cases is the overarching attempt to exert a more systemic form of control — for instance, by putting Catholic universities on a tighter leash, a move embodied in the 1990 document *Ex corde Ecclesiae*. Among other things, the CDF demanded that presidents, rectors, and professors of theology and philosophy at Catholic universities take an oath declaring that they adhere "with religious *obsequium*" to whatever the pope and bishops advance as official doctrine at the moment, even if doctrine on some particular issue has no claim to being definitive. In the United States, that demand has been resisted.

The experience of being called to Rome for interrogation — to answer charges that may be vague, brought by accusers who may be unknown, in accordance with procedures that may remain a mystery — leaves a bitter aftertaste. The German theologian Bernard Häring, who was interrogated but never condemned, compared it to what he had endured at the hands of the Nazis. "During the Second World War," he wrote in a memoir, "I stood before a military court four times. Twice it was a case of life and death. At that time I felt honored because I was accused by enemies of God." But to stand accused by the Church he had served all his life? "I would rather stand once again before a court of war of Hitler."

In his book *The Rule of Benedict,* David Gibson offers this vignette from another case:

When Charles Curran met with Ratzinger in Rome in 1986, before he was stripped of his teaching post, he demanded to face his accusers. Ratzinger said, "Your own works have been your 'accusers,' and they alone." Curran told the cardinal, "You are a respected German theologian, and are on a first-name basis with six German moralists whom I could name, and you know as well as I do that they are saying the same things as I am saying." Ratzinger replied, "Well, if you would want to delate these people, we will open a dossier on them." Curran responded, "I'm not here to do your dirty work."

The Pelvic Region

In 2005, the Congregation for the Doctrine of the Faith, acting at the behest of Cardinal Ratzinger, effectively removed Thomas Reese, a political scientist and a Jesuit, from his post as the editor of *America*, a magazine published by the Jesuit Order. Reese had written on Church affairs for years, and continues to do so. His book *Inside the Vatican*, published before he became editor, is regarded as the authoritative modern account of the Holy See's operations. Reese remembers once asking Josef Ratzinger whether, given the CDF's imperfect track record, he ever worried that he might be silencing people who would one day be rehabilitated. Ratzinger replied noncommittally: Well, you pray and do as best you can.

Reese's own firing came after years of confrontation, through intermediaries, with Ratzinger—a delicate proxy war whose conclusion was foreseeable. In a balanced way, *America* had made a point of covering a wide range of controversial Church issues, often involving what Reese calls "the pelvic region"—women's ordination, clerical celibacy, birth control, abortion, homosexuality, stem-cell research—but also extending to freedom of conscience and the governance of the Church. Once, in an editorial, the magazine had referred to the procedures of the Congregation for the Doctrine of the Faith as "inquisitional."

One oddity of Reese's case is that as the affair played out, Reese never had any direct communication with the Vatican. The pressure was forceful, but delicate and indirect. Because of the Jesuit organizational structure, the CDF deals with the order through the superior general, in Rome, who at the time was Peter-Hans Kolvenbach. Kolvenbach would meet periodically with Ratzinger, and Ratzinger would convey his complaints. Kolvenbach would then contact the president of the Jesuit conference in the United States, who would talk to Reese.

At one point, the Vatican went so far as to insist that *America* accept the imposition of a censorship board, and proceeded to appoint the member bishops. Reese consulted with Cardinal Avery Dulles, a fellow Jesuit. "Do you think it would help if I wrote Cardinal Ratzinger?" Dulles asked. Reese remembers saying, in effect, "Yes! Yes! Be my cardinal-protector!" The push for a censorship board lost steam — but not the dissatisfaction at the Palazzo del Sant'Uffizio. "I never could find out who was actually complaining about me," Reese recalls. "They would say, 'Well, bishops are complaining,' but no one would ever tell you *which* bishops were complaining."

Despite the support of his Jesuit superiors, Reese's position eventually became untenable. Looking back, his main regret is that he did not attempt, at some point along the way, to get a direct response from Ratzinger. The question he wanted to ask was: "Can a Catholic publication print articles that are critical of what you say, or not?" By the time Reese was relieved of his position, it was too late anyway. Ratzinger was no longer the prefect of the CDF — he was the pope.

Once, some while ago, I spent an afternoon talking with Hans Küng about his long, troubled history with the Holy Office. He was living on the outskirts of Tübingen, and a large picture window in his house framed the Swabian Alps to the south — the mountains somehow symbolizing, in my mind if not in his, the barrier between him and Rome. He came across as a thoroughly modern sort of man, someone who had always traveled easily among global elites of whatever kind. He is not without a certain self-regard. I remember that, in a stairwell, he kept the framed original of a David Levine caricature of himself. It had run in the *New York Review of Books*. One imagines that he would sooner accept editing from Jason Epstein than from Josef Ratzinger. But he did join Ratzinger for dinner a few years ago, shortly after the cardinal became pope. The two men agreed beforehand that any discussion of doctrinal differences or Küng's possible rehabilitation would be off-limits. They met at Castel Gondolfo, the pope's summer residence, and talked for four hours.

The dinner invitation lay far in the future — and was something not even to be imagined — on that afternoon in Tübingen. Our conversation was about the past, about origins. "Always the first thing to ask about doctrine is, Would Jesus himself understand this?" Küng explained. "Karl Rahner once said that Jesus would not have understood the first Vatican Council on infallibility. But the Church instead asks the question of Grand Inquisitor: Why do you, Jesus, come to disturb us? We have our dogmas about you. We know much better than you. You were not so outspoken. You were not so clear. We have made it much better than you said it."

6

WAR ON ERROR

The Secular Inquisition

Without torture I know we shall not prevail.

— SIR FRANCIS WALSINGHAM, 1575

Politics is not religion, or if it is,
then it is nothing but the Inquisition.

— ALBERT CAMUS, *THE REBEL*, 1958

"If Mr. Lea Is Not Stopped . . ."

THE VAN PELT LIBRARY at the University of Pennsylvania dates back to the 1960s, and like many institutional buildings from that era, it seems designed to make your heart sink. But take the elevator to the sixth floor, and you will find to your relief that the doors open on to the nineteenth century. In 1881, the historian Henry Charles Lea replaced his ample garden with an equally ample library at his home in Philadelphia. After his death, the books and furnishings were given to the university. The walls, thirty feet high, are paneled in eastern black walnut. Dramatic staircases rise to a balcony that girds the room. Marble busts gaze down from the upper reaches. The bookshelves hold 7,000 volumes, and the books are enclosed by doors of glass or mesh, or held back by velvet ropes, as if the rambunctious contents demand restraint.

It is an important room. Lea was the most accomplished American historian of his era, and at his desk in this library he produced three weighty tomes on the Medieval Inquisition and four volumes of equal heft on the Spanish Inquisition. The achievement is all the more remarkable given that Lea had almost nothing to work with: the relevant research materials simply weren't available in America. In 1842, an exasperated president of Brown University had noted that "the means do not exist among us for writing a book, which in Europe would be called learned, on almost any subject whatever."

Lea was seventeen when that statement was made, a quirky and precocious boy with a particular interest in conches. His family was educated and wealthy (the money came from publishing), and Lea was taught almost entirely at home by a private instructor. As his interests turned to history, he confronted the handicap all American scholars faced: few books, no manuscripts. But Lea had money to spend. He wrote to booksellers across Europe, acquiring what he needed. Libraries and monasteries lent him original manuscripts. If manuscripts were for sale, he bought them. If they could not be borrowed or bought, he had them copied. It was a good time to be a book buyer. The French Revolution and the Napoleonic Wars had upended the nobility and the Church; private libraries beyond counting had been dumped on the market. "If Mr. Lea is not stopped," Benjamin Disraeli warned, "all the libraries of Europe will be removed to Philadelphia."

The Inquisition was not Lea's original focus. He worked up to it slowly, starting with medieval French history, then ecclesiastical history, then legal history. In hindsight, it's not hard to see where all this study was leading. The inventories he kept show that he acquired his first books on the Inquisition in 1868, including a very old copy of Nicholas Eymerich's manual for inquisitors. All the while, he was running the family business (his company, Carey & Lea, held the U.S. rights to Poe, Austen, and Dickens, and to Gray's *Anatomy*) and pursuing a multifarious career as a doer of good (public health, civil service reform) in that edifying nineteenth-century way. Eventually, in the 1880s and 1890s, Lea turned to writing the great works on the Inquisition that would secure his reputation, tossing off monographs on clerical celibacy and the *moriscos* of Spain in between. When he died, in 1909, he had just undertaken a major study of witchcraft. He left behind a collection of books and manuscripts relating to the Inquisition that was believed at the time to be unsurpassed anywhere outside the Vatican.

Lea was sometimes criticized as an amateur, but in terms of results he was by any standard a professional. He was not the first to attempt to place the study of the Inquisition on a sound historical footing. In the early seventeenth century, a Venetian named Paolo Sarpi took up his pen — in voluminous letters, in journal articles, and in a pseud-onymously published book on the Council of Trent. Sarpi was not an objective observer. He had been forced to defend himself before the Inquisition more than once. But his perspective has an up-to-date feel about it: he saw the Inquisition's work less as a purely religious undertaking than as an effort driven by political rivalries and personal agendas, as would be true of any program advanced by any state power.

Later in the century, the Protestant pastor and theologian Philipp van Limborch, in the Netherlands, published his massive *Historia Inquisitionis,* which encompassed all the inquisitions — Medieval, Spanish, Portuguese, Roman — and consisted largely of verbatim extracts from Inquisition documents, skillfully arranged and contextualized. Limborch was a close friend of John Locke's and shared his views on religious toleration. Locke's *Letter on Toleration* was dedicated to him. The religious wars of Europe were over, but not religious persecution. Plenty of examples were ready to hand, Catholic and

Protestant alike. John Calvin's Genevan Consistory, an ecclesiastical court, meted out severe discipline in matters of doctrine and morals. Limborch's denomination, the Arminians, had suffered greatly at the hands of the Calvinists. But in the eyes of both Limborch and Locke, the Inquisition stood as the most imposing counterexample to the state of affairs an enlightened polity should embrace.

Then, at the beginning of the nineteenth century, Juan Antonio Llorente published his monumental *Histoire Critique de l'Inquisition d'Espagne,* a study of the Spanish Inquisition that made extensive use of the archives in Madrid. Llorente knew his way around the material: he had been its archivist for years. For a time, he had served as secretary to the Inquisition. Some of his preoccupations seem contemporary: How did the Inquisition's bureaucracy actually work? What happened locally, on the ground, when decisions were sent forth from the tribunal in Madrid? What role did the Inquisition come to play in court politics? What long-term effects did it have on Spain's national life — for instance, on its intellectual vitality and its economic development?

Questions of this kind were new. Today we take for granted a form of storytelling about the past that strives for at least some objectivity, whatever the writer's agenda may be. Even the most controversial subjects can be addressed soberly — indeed, are most persuasively addressed that way. The battle over the Inquisition, in contrast, had been waged mainly by polemicists, their outlooks colored by creed. Protestant Britain harbored deep suspicions of Catholic Spain, with some cause, and thus the Black Legend became a common trope in literature and art throughout the English-speaking world. The cruelties of the Inquisition, the superstitions of Catholicism, the brutal conquest of the Americas, the threat of the Armada — all this was combined into a demonic caricature of Spaniards and their culture (calling forth from Spain, in response, the White Legend, which advanced an angelic caricature with equal fervor). The impact of the

Black Legend has been durable. It's why Hispanic peasants always cross themselves in the movies, and why Latin lovers can never be trusted.

Henry Charles Lea was hardly immune to it, and he harbored the suspicions of his class and time toward Roman Catholicism. He was no admirer of the Church, and saw the Inquisition as the embodiment of forces that stood athwart the advance of civilization. "I have not paused to moralize," Lea wrote, "but I have missed my aim if the events narrated are not so presented as to teach their appropriate lesson." But his work marks the point at which Inquisition history, passing into the hands of true historians, was relaxed to the secular arm.

It wasn't just Inquisition *history* that made the transition. By the time of Lea's death, the Inquisition template, or something like it, had long since passed into hands other than those of the Church. One historian observes that the ground had been well prepared: "The Inquisition, church and state courts, and the legal codes of the Church's Lateran Council (1215), taken together, meant that early modern Europeans inherited a fully fledged apparatus of persecution and an intellectual tradition that justified killing in the name of God."

A set of disciplinary procedures, targeting specified groups, codified in law, organized systematically, enforced by surveillance, exemplified by severity, sustained over time, justified by a vision of the one true path, backed by institutional power: following this definition, inquisitions are not hard to find. Sometimes they retain a religious dimension — for example, the Elizabethan campaign against English Catholics and other dissenters from the established church; or the campaigns against doctrinal foes by Calvin in Geneva and Zwingli in Zurich; or, closer to our own era, the "dirty war" in Argentina in the 1970s and 1980s, waged by conservative, arch-Catholic generals against a shadowy Marxist menace. Sometimes the visionary dimension is secular (think of France after the Revolution, or the fascist and communist regimes of the twentieth century). Sometimes the needs of the state itself become a kind of absolute (as during the Algerian

War in the 1950s, or in Brazil during the period of military governments in the 1960s and 1970s). Add to this an element of fear — the sense of existential threat that lay behind the Red Scare in America after World War II, or, also in the United States, some of the antiterrorism measures enacted during the past decade in the wake of the 9/11 attacks.

Inquisitions may combine all these elements, but they also require an infrastructure. In his book *Prisoner Without a Name, Cell Without a Number,* Jacobo Timerman gives a searing account of his torture and interrogation at the hands of the Argentine military. He begins the book by calmly remarking an irony: that his Jewish family had fled the Spanish-controlled Netherlands for the Ukraine in the sixteenth century, to escape the Inquisition, and had then fled the Ukraine for Argentina in the 1920s, to escape the Soviets. The Jews of his village in the Ukraine had been rounded up and killed by the Nazis in 1942. Now, in the late 1970s, Timerman had come full circle, a captive of people with the same persecutorial zeal that had driven his family from the Netherlands four centuries earlier.

Timerman does not dwell on the institutional apparatus that an inquisition requires. The same tools that sustained the Inquisition sustained the dirty war, during the course of which some 30,000 Argentinians, most of them young, were arrested, tortured, and killed. Language itself was warped. People thrown alive from airplanes into the sea were referred to by the authorities as "fish food"; the term for torture was "intensive therapy." But the structural underpinnings were institutional. "As newspaper accounts of the time declared," one scholar later wrote, "this junta appeared to consist of professional bureaucrats." She described the immense governmental effort involved in compiling lists, building camps, training interrogators.

Transportation, communications, and other institutional conditions have to be arranged. Indoctrination has to be well advanced to ensure loyalty and expertise. In short, coordination and ad vance planning are required, and these things take time and a high degree of organizational experience. . . . This degree of advance organization involves an extensive bureaucratic decision-making and implementation capacity.

This is a dry and clinical dissection. It describes capabilities that the Inquisition possessed in rudimentary form. Over time, the very same capabilities contributed to the power of secular governments, which in turn refined and improved those capabilities. Technology extended their reach. When it comes to inquisitions, a more concise way to describe the modern world would be: fertile soil. Plant an inquisition, and it grows.

Keep Your Faith

"Institutions do what they must to retain power. Isn't it that simple?" The comment came from Eamon Duffy, a historian of the early modern period, whose work has chronicled the difficult and bloody religious transitions in England during the sixteenth century, as a Catholic country was forcibly transformed into a Protestant one. We had been talking about the campaign by Elizabeth I against Catholic priests and their supporters, and the intelligence apparatus Elizabeth put in place to wage it. Duffy's office is in a garret under the eaves of the Pepys Library, in Magdalene College, at Cambridge University. C. S. Lewis taught at Magdalene, as did the theologian Henry Chadwick, and in a more distant time the Protestant martyr Thomas Cranmer, the force behind the Book of Common Prayer, so the place resonates with a certain pedigree. It's hard to imagine a more congenial scholarly space than Duffy's rooms. The doorways are low and uneven, and make you not only stoop but also tilt. A crucifix hangs over one of them. There is a fireplace. Pictures on the walls: Thomas More, Cardinal Newman, William Butler Yeats. A color photograph of Seamus Heaney, a friend, on the mantel. Books everywhere, of course — shelved, stacked, tossed. A bottle of Jameson's in a corner. A teakettle on the hearth. To get to Duffy's garret, you pass through the porter's lodge into a spacious quad and then make for a passageway on the far side. The motto of Magdalene is emblazoned above it: *Garde ta foy.* The popular collegiate translation is "Watch your liver." The correct one is "Keep your faith."

Keeping your faith was a hard thing to do in the period Eamon Duffy writes about. The Reformation had undermined the very meaning of "orthodoxy," and the alignment of secular powers with various religious groups made sectarian disputes murderous. In England, Henry VIII had broken with Rome in 1534, over the issue of his divorce, placing himself at the head of the church and vigorously suppressing anyone who raised an eyebrow. His short-lived son, Edward VI, continued this policy. Henry's daughter Mary, a Catholic, married to the man who would become Philip II of Spain, attempted to lead England back to the fold by force. This is the subject of Duffy's book *Fires of Faith.* Protestants were arrested, and many were burned at the stake. Mary was succeeded by her half-sister Elizabeth, who attempted to steer a moderate course but eventually returned the kingdom to a Protestant path. Mary and Elizabeth were animated in part by expediency: both faced implacable enemies determined to drive them from power. The opposition may have been based on religion, but both monarchs saw it fundamentally as treason. The challenge to Rome had divided Europe in complicated and lethal ways.

"Elizabethan England certainly wasn't a police state, because they didn't have a police force," Duffy said. "But you've got an ideological war going on in Europe, with England very conscious that there's a struggle for the soul. It's a bit like American feeling about Islam now." Once Jesuit priests started arriving — they were being trained and ordained on the continent, and then smuggled back into Britain — popular fears had a sharp focus: "a bogeyman," as Duffy put it. This was something that elements of the government, or powerful individuals with their own agendas, or local folk with scores to settle, could build on. It was also a situation in which unstable people could come to the fore. At the same time, Duffy explained, commitment was growing among large numbers of people to a kind of Protestantism that fed on anti-Catholicism — indeed, that defined itself that way.

"What makes religious persecution so shocking to us, I suppose," Duffy said, "is that cruelty in the pursuit of the things of God seems particularly outrageous. I'm not sure it's any more outrageous than protecting democracy with, you know, waterboarding. Systems find ways of protecting themselves, and ways to justify these things to themselves.

"I feel less shocked by the Inquisition than a lot of people do," he went on, "because you ask yourself, What would they have done? I mean, take Mary's government in the 1550s in England. What should she have done? These people *did* want to depose her, and she *did* think they were murdering souls. What could she have done? And it's not that you're saying, 'I would have done the same in that position,' because we're just not in that position. That was then, and this is now. Of course, these things are outrageous if they're considered in the abstract. But human beings don't live in the abstract. They live in the particular."

Not much is left of "the particular" of Elizabeth I's London, or Mary's, much less the London of their father — not much of the urban landscape, at any rate. It's easy to pretend, in Jerusalem or Carcassonne or Rome, that you've been transported to another era — that you're walking the streets the way they really were in some bygone age. London does not accommodate the imagination that way. The Great Fire swept much of the Tudor city away, and the natural evolution of what was to become an imperial capital took most of the rest. Elizabeth and Henry would recognize only a few nonreligious buildings, such as the Banqueting House of Whitehall Palace, and Hampton Court. By and large, churches have survived most successfully. And street names. The house owned by Sir Francis Walsingham, who ran Queen Elizabeth's intelligence service, stood in Seething Lane, not far from the Tower of London. The house is gone, but you can still walk down Seething Lane. And of course the Tower is there, London's great constant, originally the Roman praetorium, always fortified, a place at the center of so much of England's public history, and also the place where so many personal histories came to an end.

But "not much left" isn't completely accurate — it applies to how the city looks on the outside. From the inside — in the to and fro of government business, the ebb and flow of friendships, the vicissitudes of family fortune, the vagaries of commerce, the pricks of conscience — the remains of sixteenth-century London have been remarkably well preserved in various ways. A good place to start is in the manuscript collections of the British Library. Because many of these handwritten documents originally came from private sources — the papers of Lord Burghley, for instance, who was Queen Elizabeth's chief advisor during most of her reign — the variety gathered up within each leather-bound folio can be astonishing. Imagine throwing an assortment of ordinary papers into a box — canceled checks, report cards, deeds of sale, diary entries, warranties, Christmas letters, road maps. Going through that box decades later brings back to life a former self and another world, in a way few other stimuli can.

That is the sixteenth-century experience on offer at the British Library. Some of it is glorious. Much of it is mundane. Not a little is disturbing. It is an era of religious transition — occurring not organically but by compulsion. The boundary between religious belief and treasonable activity is not always clear, or may not even exist. The state feels itself under siege — from religious enemies inside the realm, and from their powerful allies beyond the Channel. Pope Pius V, in 1570, has issued a bull, *Regnans in Excelsis,* declaring the queen to be a heretic, absolving her subjects from allegiance, and giving papal sanction to attempts to depose her. Englishmen are being trained as priests in foreign seminaries and then smuggled back into Britain. (That censored edition of Shakespeare came from a Spanish seminary for English priests.) Catholic sympathizers seem to be lurking everywhere. Rumors are rife of imminent invasion by Catholic forces.

To meet the threat, the state does what it believes it must. It enacts increasingly harsh penalties on Catholics, and seeks out and confiscates Catholic books and religious articles. It makes support for priests and the old religion tantamount to sedition. It declares treasonous the mere act of being a Jesuit priest or seminarian, even if one has done nothing that could otherwise be construed as treasonous. As one historian writes, "It was now treason to belong to a particular category of person, a remarkable extension of the law." The state also revives attempts at censorship, requiring printers in England to secure a license from the crown. One printer will be executed under Elizabeth, and an unwise pamphleteer will lose his right hand (to a meat cleaver hammered by a croquet mallet). The deposition scene from Shakespeare's *Richard II* will be deleted from a printed version of the play — it is too incendiary.

Under Elizabeth, the government creates a powerful intelligence apparatus whose networks extend throughout England and deep into Scotland, France, Spain, the Netherlands, and Italy. It relies on spies and informers, idealists and opportunists. It keeps a watchful eye on what is being taught in universities. It subjects prisoners to prolonged interrogation under conditions of horrific duress — to extract information as well as confessions. Many are condemned to death — typically drawn and quartered rather than burned at the stake. From 1581 to 1603, some 130 Catholic priests will die in this manner, together with some sixty members of prominent Catholic families.

The manner of execution represents a divergence from the Roman Inquisition, which had been launched by the pope a few decades earlier. But in other respects, the secular inquisition in England shares points of resemblance. For obvious reasons, people rarely drew the connection openly. Edward Peters writes, "To the English, Inquisition was exclusively Spanish or Roman. Nothing that English judges might do to Englishmen of different religious persuasions could imaginably be considered as Inquisition." But the connection was there, and sometimes noticed. Lord Burghley himself commented on one occasion that the inquisitors of Spain "use not so many questions to comprehend and trap their preys" as some English prosecutors did.

High-Value Target

For many years, this apparatus was run by Francis Walsingham, Elizabeth's principal secretary. A portrait of him, by John De Critz the Elder, hangs in the National Portrait Gallery, alongside portraits of several people — such as Mary, Queen of Scots — for whose fate he bore some responsibility. MI6, Britain's modern intelligence agency, looks to Walsingham as "the father of the British Secret Service." His web of informants was extensive, and he harbored no doubts as to the utility of torture for obtaining reliable information; indeed, without torture, he would say, he couldn't do his job. Nor did his jailers employ just the rack and other instruments; the corrosive effects of sleep deprivation, a modern staple, were well understood. One room in the Tower, known as Little Ease, was so low and tight that a prisoner could only crouch, awkwardly and painfully. Sleep was out of the question.

The tenor of the period is captured vividly in the documents. A nobleman's letter of confession to the queen sits alongside his last will and testament, his property carefully itemized. There is an English spy's lengthy account of life among the Jesuit seminarians studying in Rome — dining with this person and that, discussing theology and foreign affairs, and mentioning names that will turn up a few years later in the execution rolls of Tyburn Hill. A single folio page amounts to a cheat sheet for interrogators, listing sample questions to be asked of priests and other Catholics in custody, to determine how danger-

ous they are: for instance, do they believe the "poape" has the power
to depose a British monarch? There are lists of known popish sympathizers, county by county, and the outline of a plan — scrawled by
Walsingham himself — to round up members of prominent Catholic
families and hold them in what amounts to detention camps. On two
sides of a page, the plan is neatly laid out in columns — one for "The
Castels" where the camps would be located, one for the lord who
would serve officially as "The Keper," and one for the counties from
which the detainees for each camp would be drawn.

Interrogation records are plentiful — not always verbatim transcripts, but at a minimum detailed accounts. Looking in a bound
volume for something else one afternoon, I was startled to see, in the
upper left margin of a folio page, "Primo Julij 1587 Rich. Topclyff."
Richard Topcliffe had been trained in the law, but history remembers
him only because he was a brutal interrogator. There, in the margin, in neat brown ink, was his name. Running across the next three
pages was a report on the interrogation of "Christofer Sothworthe,
Preiste."

Southworth had arrived in England only recently, and had practiced his vocation very briefly before being apprehended: "Hee came
over Aboute xprmas Laste and i. taken in Lente of a greate and peril-
ous family." On the folio pages, here and there, a little drawing of a
pointing finger calls attention to some matter of special interest: "Hee
is of Extraordinary authority," the manuscript notes of Southworth
in one place, and then at another takes pains to emphasize the point:
"Hee hathe some Authoritie of A Bisshopp." In other words, Topcliffe
regarded Southworth as what today would be called a high-value
target.

Southworth was from a stubbornly Catholic branch of a prominent family in the troublesome north of England. He left the country
to enter a seminary in Rome, and was ordained in 1583. As the report indicates, Southworth was discovered and arrested soon after
his return. His life was spared. A roster of prisoners from 1595 finds

him in one of those internment "Castels" — Wisbech Castle, an ancient place in the Fens where many other priests were held. He is no. 12 on the list: "Xpofer Southworth sonne to Sr John Southworth a Seminary prieste a man of especiall accoumpte amongest the papists who doe much relie upon him & hath diuers tymes intelligence from beyonde the Seas & dispseth it abroade." He was eventually released, and returned to the north of England, where he played a role in the saga of the so-called Samlesbury Witches. The details are not germane, but the episode was one of many that would occur throughout Europe and in North America as the clash of religious beliefs, and the inquisitorial systems through which it was channeled, produced bizarre accusations and very serious prosecutions. Whether it arose in Salem or Samlesbury, the phenomenon has been much picked over by social historians looking to explain the origins of mass hysteria.

"Systems find ways of protecting themselves," Eamon Duffy had said, "and ways to justify those measures to themselves." The measures, though sometimes rolled back, seem mainly to accrue. In England, the efforts of Mary built on actions by previous monarchs, just as the efforts of Elizabeth built on the actions of Mary. Motivations may change, targets may shift, but the infrastructure builds by increments. Proof of identity, record-keeping, informers, surveillance, denunciation, interrogation: these are the basic instruments. And as medieval kingdoms remade themselves into modern states, the instruments became better and were applied in a more systematic way.

France was a leader. By the mid eighteenth century, the government's undercover police apparatus deployed some 3,000 paid informers in Paris alone, and 10,000 throughout the realm. A lieutenant general of the police in Paris boasted at the time, "When three people are chatting in the street, at least one of them is certain to belong to me." The police controlled the organs of censorship. (Voltaire and Diderot were both imprisoned for committing unfettered thoughts to print.) They routinely opened letters, read them, resealed the envelopes, and sent the letters on their way. The apparatus of surveillance could not stave off the Revolution — but did survive it. France in the 1790s would invent the passport and the identity card (and the words for them we still use), and under Napoleon and his chief prefect, the redoubtable Joseph Fouché, the secret police would become a pervasive force. Six days a week, wherever he was, Napoleon received from Fouché the equivalent of the President's Daily Brief — a digest of news, intelligence, rumor, and gossip. A French nobleman, looking back at the period, referred to the Napoleonic system as "a revolting inquisition."

Revolting, but also influential. The czars modeled their secret-police system, the Okhrana, on that of the French — and after the Russian Revolution, Lenin took it over and made it his own. It evolved into the KGB. Prussia created a considerable undercover network, which was later adopted by a united Germany and then brought to a state of high performance under the Nazis. After the collapse of communism and the breakup of the Soviet Union, the security services temporarily fell on hard times. Russia, in name, was a democracy now, and citizens had rights. Former agents gravitated to the private sector — to the service of criminals and oligarchs. Their skills proved portable; even the organizational charts were replicated. Eventually, under Vladimir Putin, the security operations were rebuilt. The Federal Security Service, or FSB, as it is now called, is more powerful than ever, and there is no Communist Party to answer to. It has perhaps 200,000 employees. It controls the Border Guard. Its network of agents on "active reserve" hold key positions throughout the government. Ties with the Russian Orthodox Church are close. Fingerprint dossiers have been assembled for fully half of Russia's population. A system of "watchdog surveillance" targets individuals not suspected of any crime — Islamists, members of youth groups and "pagan cults," journalists, trade unionists. Cameras with face-recognition software, known as VideoLock, operate at airports and train stations. Once, in the 1990s, before he became Russia's president, Putin was asked by a reporter if he planned to organize a coup d'état against the serving president, Boris Yeltsin. Putin replied, "And why do we need to organize a coup d'état? We are in power now."

One trait all systems of state security share is a passion for establishing identity: counting the population, writing down names, connecting people to locations, and issuing documents to match names and individuals. These are acts of baseline authority. They are essential, of course, for specific tasks, such as raising armies and collecting taxes — foundational functions of the nation-state. But they constitute tools of control in every sphere. Identity as skeleton key: it comes across as a modern thought, even a postmodern one, though it would not have surprised Jacques Fournier, the interrogator of the village of Montaillou. The philosopher Johann Gottlieb Fichte made the point clinically in 1796: "The chief principle of a well-regulated police state is this: That each citizen shall be at all times and places . . . recognized as this or that particular person. No one must remain unknown to the police."

Finkensteinallee No. 63

"Note-taking and record-keeping were prescribed down to the last detail, so that the Holy Office might study all of the records and keep persons in question under surveillance." That is the assessment of a historian of the Inquisition in the New World. He could have made the same observation about the Inquisition in medieval France or Renaissance Rome. Collect, preserve, retrieve: inquisitions depend on data storage, and data storage only improves. In 1987, Lawrence Weschler published an account of how the evidence of systematic torture in Brazil, conducted in the 1960s and 1970s by successive military governments, was finally brought to light. One of the investigators explained:

The Brazilian generals, you see, were technocrats. They were intent on doing things by the book, on following the forms, even if the results were often cruel and perverse. For example, they were obsessed with keeping complete records as they went along. They never expected anyone to delve into those records — certainly not in any systematic fashion. They never imagined they'd be held accountable to anyone. But the forms, the technicalities, required complete and well-ordered records, so they kept them. Now, in the early stages of an internee's *processo* — that's the Portuguese word for a military court proceeding — the authorities often had recourse to torture. This was partly because they were eager to extract as much information as quickly as possible so they would be able to make further arrests before the prisoner's friends and comrades could learn of his arrest and cover their tracks. But it was also an almost traditional reflex, going back to the days of slavery and the Inquisition.

An archive elicits conflicting thoughts and behaviors. The wish to preserve the past is a worthwhile instinct — but deciding what to preserve presents a challenge to basic honesty. Archives speak to a need for collective memory. They can inspire a certain humility. But they also reflect some measure of vanity — a high regard for the human enterprise. And then there's the matter of how archives are used. If open and accessible, they can foster transparency and understanding; if restricted or closed, they can become menacing, putting knowledge in the hands of some and not of others. Jacques Derrida's delirious and quirky *Archive Fever* exposes archives for what they are: dangerous, glorious, insidious, inebriating. They impose order on a reality that may in fact have none. By offering storage for memory, they make forgetting possible. But they can also be tools of control.

The very size of some archival repositories gives one pause. The Sumerian archives at Ebla survive in clay on 17,000 cuneiform fragments — and that's just the record of a single city, from 4,000 years ago. A medievalist friend once confessed his gratitude to the French Revolution, whose incendiary fervor caused the destruction of 90 percent of the archives of Carcassonne — he could never have completed his doctorate had they remained intact.

The National Archives of the United States has long since spread out from its central headquarters in Washington to some twenty satellite repositories throughout the country. The facility in College Park, Maryland, is the largest of them all. Gleaming white, with tinted glass, it could be the seat of a biotech company or an intelligence agency. Footpaths wind through an encircling forest of willowy trees — the kind of locale where Hollywood sets secret meetings, frosty exhalations curling above dark coats. Security is tight. ID badges are embedded with tiny transponders that tell your minders exactly where in the building you are. The penthouse floor is for classified material. From time to time you'll round a corner and be ambushed by a TV screen, which you are on.

The records on deposit here are not only American; archival administrators, especially imperial ones, are an acquisitive type. U.S. forces, occupying portions of Germany after World War II, took control over as much of the Third Reich's archives and other printed material as they could find. A portion of Adolf Hitler's personal library, retrieved from a salt mine near Berchtesgaden, is held at the Library of Congress. For decades, the archives of the Third Reich remained in American hands, though still on German soil, at a facility known as the Berlin Document Center. Eventually it was all microfilmed — a step up from cuneiform, but one that in a digital age seems nearly as antiquated.

The microfilms — 70,000 rolls — reside in the College Park facility, in Room 4050, which is the size of a small supermarket. Other materials from the BDC — original cards and files — sit in boxes on shelves in a different room, one the size of a football field. Some of them involve the lengthy process of "de-Nazification" — figuring out who had done what, and whether individuals should be allowed to return to their lives. On a recent visit, in the company of an archivist, I randomly picked out a file card from a box and found the notation "There are strong objections. Not recommended." Concentration camp records are here too. The shelving is automated, to save space. At the press of a button, it parts to let you in; people sometimes get trapped when the shelving closes. That is one instrument the Inquisition didn't think of. To give you some idea of the size of the College Park archive, each of its gigantic storage rooms is known as a stack; the facility contains forty-one of them. You can understand why the government wants to digitize its holdings, and also why the cost of doing so now approaches $1.4 billion, and will continue to rise.

Room 4050 has calm gray walls and floors, fluorescent lighting, and floor-to-ceiling rows of light-gray filing cabinets. If you know what you are looking for — say, the Nazi Party registration card for Herr Alfred Krautkammer — it is easy enough to locate: Look him up in the catalogue under NSDAP Collection, and you'll see that the relevant microfilm is in the series A3340-MFOK. The microfilms are arranged alphabetically according to the first name on each roll, and each roll is given a number. Find the number, pull out the box, put the roll on a reader. The archivist helping me had a sense of humor. As she described the search process, she compared it to Ionesco's "How to Prepare a Hard-Boiled Egg." Before long, the card appeared on the screen. Krautkammer, Alfred. A butcher by profession. Lived in Wiesbaden. Joined the Nazi Party in 1941.

It's a little disconcerting to view such material under these conditions — clean, orderly, antiseptic. I spent some time with the archivist scrolling through spools of microfilm. The cards flew by, hundreds, thousands, like illustrated cels on the way to becoming animation. Occasionally, we would pause for a closer look. Zoom, zoom, stop. Here was the membership card, filled in by typewriter, of a woman who joined the Nazi Party in late 1944, the war already lost. The archivist couldn't help herself; she said, "That wasn't very smart." Zoom, zoom, stop. Here was the card, filled out by hand, of a man who joined the party very early, in 1925. The script was elegant, a reminder that Germany was a country with mass public education and enviable standards of refinement. Civilization itself seems to be peering back from the card, as it peers back from the Inquisition. In El Greco's famous portrait, Cardinal Niño de Guevara, an inquisitor general of Spain, wears heavy round eyeglasses to indicate that he is an intellectual and a man of advanced ideas. This same man is the subject of the 1935 novella *El Greco Paints the Grand Inquisitor*, by Stefan Paul Andres, a parable of Nazi Germany.

The working conditions in Berlin are similar to those in College Park, but the surroundings have a history. For many years, the bulk of the material in the Berlin Document Center was lodged in the cavernous basements of a complex of villas at Wasserkafersteig 1, in Zelendorf, on the edge of the Grunewald, where Hermann Göring maintained his surveillance headquarters. The complex makes a cameo in Len Deighton's novel *Funeral in Berlin*. In the 1990s, after the reunification of Germany, when the archives came back into the physical possession of the German government, the millions of files were consolidated in another suburban location, at Finkensteinallee No. 63.

It is a grim assemblage of brick buildings inside a large gated compound, and might easily be mistaken for a sanitarium. The facility is surrounded by a leafy neighborhood of stout, respectable residences that lived through the war. The compound began its existence in the nineteenth century, as the Royal Prussian Cadet Institute; the Kaiser himself looked on as the cornerstone was laid. In the 1930s, it became a military barracks. An old photograph shows Hitler reviewing troops in what is now the weedy parking lot where I left my car. New buildings were added in the Nazi era, and remain to this day. The entrance to one of them — an indoor swimming pool, among the largest in the world when it was built — is flanked by heroic concrete statues of "German Man" and "German Woman," Teutonic versions of the winged bulls that guarded Sargon's citadel.

This is the largest federal archive in Germany. File cabinets spill out into Gothic hallways and what once were tiled washrooms. The subject matter ranges from routine administration of the Nazi state to its darkest undertakings. One series holds the records of the People's Court — some 50,000 items — concerning trials and convictions for treason. Another holds the files of the Rasse und Siedlungshauptamt (Race and Settlement Main Office), with dossiers on the racial background of married members of the SS and their spouses. Each person's file includes the results of a physical examination. Many include genealogical histories. To make certain of racial purity, some family trees were traced back to the sixteenth century.

Repressive regimes are record-keeping regimes. Repression demands administration. Seventy-five years ago, when modern data processing began to emerge, IBM's German subsidiary, with the knowledge of executives in America, provided the Nazi government with punch-card and tabulating machines by the thousands, which the company serviced and kept supplied. The machines were used initially to store information about the German population — including its Jewish component — and later to help manage the operations of extermination and labor camps. "The physician examines the human body and determines whether all organs are working to the benefit of the entire organism," an executive of IBM's German subsidiary observed at the opening of a new facility in Berlin in 1934. "We are very much like the physician, in that we dissect, cell by cell, the German cultural body." He added, "I feel it almost a sacred action."

The original membership rolls of the Nazi Party are all here at Finkensteinallee No. 63 — they are recorded on 11 million index cards. Party correspondence fills 1.3 million files. The personal dossiers on SS members take up another 350,000. To all this material in the Bundesarchiv must be added the archives from the German Democratic Republic — the former East Germany — a hybrid regime that for half a century blended features of both Nazi Germany and the Soviet Union, its postwar overlord.

The East German secret police, the Stasi, occupied a headquarters complex of more than a million square feet, divided among more than twenty buildings, which sprawl across several city blocks in the Lichtenberg district of East Berlin. The complex is modern, shabby, and soul-deadening in that particular East German way; the local authorities are trying to figure out what to do with it. Some of the buildings still serve as storage for Stasi archives, including official reports of the surveillance routinely conducted on millions of East German citizens.

The movie *The Lives of Others,* released in 2006, captures the bureaucratization of surveillance in East Germany at its most ordinary. But only the abstraction of numbers can capture the scale. At its peak, just before the fall of the Berlin Wall, in 1989, the Stasi had some 90,000 official employees. Over time, they compiled an archive containing, by one estimate, a billion sheets of paper. Like many bureaucracies, the Stasi was on autopilot for years. As one historian writes, "The daily activities of the spy world — the running of agents, catching spies, tracking enemies of the state, and making spy gadgets, to name just a few — led to the emergence of an insular spy culture, more intent on securing its power than protecting national security." The intramural machinations of cardinal-inquisitors would have translated very easily to Lichtenberg.

At the death of the hated Pope Paul IV, in 1559, the people of Rome stormed the headquarters of the Inquisition, freeing prisoners and destroying records. After the Berlin Wall came down, the people of East Berlin surged around the Stasi complex and eventually broke their way in. In this instance, the crowd was more interested in preserving records than in destroying them. Stasi operatives had burned or shredded what they could as the end drew near, but they could not overcome their own prowess: the archives had grown too vast. Desperate Stasi officials probably wished they had devoted some effort to developing a working prototype of Orwell's memory holes. Orwell described them:

> In the walls of the cubicle there were three orifices. To the right of the speakwrite, a small pneumatic tube for written messages; to the left, a larger one for newspapers; and in the side wall, within easy reach of Winston's arm, a large oblong slit protected by a wire grating. This last was for the disposal of waste paper. Similar slits existed in thousands or tens of thousands throughout the building, not only in every room but at short intervals in every corridor. For some reason they were nicknamed memory holes. When one knew that any document was due for destruction, or even when one saw a scrap of waste paper lying about, it was an automatic action to lift the flap of the nearest memory hole and drop it in, whereupon it would be whirled away on a current of warm air to the enormous furnaces which were hidden somewhere in the recesses of the building.

In the end, the Stasi managed to destroy only about 5 percent of its holdings before the East German regime collapsed. Many of the shredded documents have since been reconstructed, with the help of software that can select thin strands of paper from among a tangle of millions, and match the strands to one another.

Software for restoring shredded documents is one of only a few things the East Germans didn't think to invent, judging from exhibits on display in the Stasi Museum, a forlorn domain that occupies a small building in the interior of the Stasi complex. It seems to exist in some strange middle state between tragedy and kitsch. The museum shop is threadbare. The café offers little, served by a sullen matron with the demeanor of Rosa Klebb. The museum is the creation of a group called Anti-Stalinist Action, and comes across as what it is: not the work of professional curators but something homemade, a bitter labor of love.

Certain artifacts stand out for their sheer banality — beer mugs and shot glasses with the Ministry of State Security's coat of arms and the slogan "25 years of reliable protection." They look like items you'd pick up in State College or Ann Arbor. One area of the museum is devoted to ways of concealing cameras: in ties and buttons, thermoses and trees, watering cans and trash cans. The padding of a bra is pulled away to reveal a lens. There is a machine for steaming open letters, at a rate of six hundred an hour. The Stasi was well aware of smugglers' tricks. One display depicts confiscated Bible tracts, which had been discovered rolled up inside the inner tubes of bicycle tires. Along a wall by a window sit a number of sealed clear bottles that hold specimens of cloth. Stasi technicians had invented a device called the "smell chair," whose cushion was fitted with an absorbent replaceable cover. During interviews, persons of interest would be seated in the chair; when they left, a sample of cloth would be kept in a bottle for some later use, usually involving dogs — for instance, determining if a suspect had been in a certain room, or hunting someone down. In a corner of the main exhibit space stands a Stasi guardhouse, defaced with graffiti from the heady days of 1989. Painted on the front are the words *Freiheit fur Meine Akte* — "Freedom for my file."

The files have their freedom now, in a sense. All told, the archives at the old cadet institute — Nazi and East German combined — occupy some sixty linear miles of shelf space. There is so much documentation at the Berlin Document Center that a new repository is being built, an annex to the building in the complex that was once the headquarters of the Leibstandarte SS Adolf Hitler, the Führer's personal guard. The Reich's eagle has long since been removed. A graphic display explaining the project, in a makeshift structure near the entrance, has been given a technically correct yet blandly unrevealing title: "The New Building of the Federal Archives in Berlin — Located Between Contradictory Contexts of German History."

The reading rooms at the BDC — one in a structure known as

Building 901, another in a converted chapel nearby — can handle 150 researchers at a time. The workstations are always busy. As at any archive, there are lockers for coats and bags — a security precaution. There are forms to fill out, identification cards to produce. Officious librarians retrieve specific files. Some researchers are students and historians. Many are ordinary citizens with personal agendas. What happened to certain relatives? Who took the family's property? Or, maybe, nothing more complicated than What was in my file?

The Tunnel of Truth

Francis Walsingham would scarcely recognize the Britain of today. It is a liberal, secular democracy of a model kind. The United Kingdom is the nation in whose judicial system Julian Assange, the beleaguered founder of WikiLeaks, decided to place his trust when he found himself in legal peril. The monarch remains the head of an established church, but there are now far more practicing Catholics in England than there are practicing Anglicans. And there are all those Muslims, a relatively new element, some of whom have resorted to violence for political ends, as some Irish did during the past generation.

The system will protect itself: here Walsingham would be back on comfortable ground. Faced first with an insurgency in Northern Ireland, beginning in the early 1970s, and then with threats of various kinds from radical Islam, the British government began to modernize its apparatus of surveillance and data collection. It is today a global leader. Britain maintains the largest DNA registry in the world. It is also covered by a system of some 4 million closed-circuit television cameras, the most comprehensive system anywhere. The effort has been promoted by the government with the slogan "If you've got nothing to hide, you've got nothing to fear." In the autumn, when plant life thins, you can see that cameras have been in the flower boxes of clubs and hotels all along. Cameras linked to computers cover roads and highways. After Islamist terrorists unleashed a wave of attacks in London in July of 2005, the police were able to create a nearly continuous video montage of the suicide bombers as they drove in their car from Leeds to a train station outside London:

4 A.M.–5 A.M.: Speed cameras track the car heading south through the city's leafy suburbs. . . . The bombers join the southbound M1 at junction 40 and their progress is tracked as they journey south along the spine of England.

6:30 A.M.: After 160 miles on the M1, the Nissan Micra turns off at junction 11, arriving at Luton train station car park at around 6:50 A.M.

7 A.M.: The four don their military-style rucksacks in the increasingly busy car park . . . CCTV cameras, designed to capture car thieves, film the four engaged in a final prayer.

7:40 A.M.: The four bombers catch a Thameslink train, which winds through the affluent commuter belt of Hertfordshire towards King's Cross.

8:26 A.M.: The quartet are captured walking across the concourse of London's busiest station. They are chatting; Hussain is laughing. Minutes later, they are huddled in a final, earnest conversation.

The surveillance system is a comfort to some, up to a point. It is also a source of unease. Databases of various kinds — commercial, public, private, medical, biological — are connected as never before. Legal procedures provide the authorities with wide latitude to hold suspects for significant periods, and to deport undesirables with a minimum of due process. A British national identity card was scheduled to be phased in, but the scheme was put on hold in early

2011 — the idea engendered too much public opposition. Few doubt that the era of the identity card will one day come, and not just in Britain. Under a law passed in 2000, some 474 local governments and 318 government agencies are permitted to "self-authorize" the surveillance of British citizens — that is, they may, without the approval of a magistrate, have people followed, monitor their phone calls and e-mail, and record their activities surreptitiously with cameras. A woman in Dorset who became a target of such surveillance in 2008 was suspected, wrongly, of nothing more than sending her children to a school outside her district.

In 2012, London is scheduled to host the summer Olympics. Biometric identification is required for workers at major Olympics construction sites — everyone must negotiate iris and palm scanners. Security plans call for Royal Air Force drones, equipped with optical and other sensing devices, to cruise above Olympic venues at all times. Bomb-sniffing robots may mingle with the crowds. One idea that has been mentioned is the creation of a "tunnel of truth" — a passageway that would scan people attending the games for radiation, explosives, and biohazards, and at the same time use facial-recognition software to identify those who may be on watch lists.

Henry Porter, a columnist for the *Guardian* and the *Observer,* is one of the most persistent critics of a regime he fears is settling into place, as much through bureaucratic inertia and technological advance as through outright advocacy. Privacy erodes by degrees, each step sometimes seen as a sensible response to the circumstances and sometimes not seen at all. Porter's dystopian thriller *The Bell Ringers* conjures a Britain in which the surveillance measures that already exist are pushed just a little further along, given just a little more interconnection. You buy some modernity, and you cede some privacy. A famous line in Tacitus notes how eagerly the people of ancient Britain took up Roman customs and devices, observing, "The unsuspecting Britons spoke of such novelties as civilization, when in fact they were only a feature of their enslavement."

It can be hard to separate the two. The process for obtaining a reader's card to use the manuscript room at the British Library is easy, efficient, and swift. Much of it can be done online. A brief visit to a well-run office produces an actual card. The reading room itself is the most comfortable place imaginable, staffed by the same pallid, helpful clerks you'd have found there in 1950 or 1870. The rules are on a human scale. Four manuscripts at a time, no more! Pencils only, please! But CCTV cameras are everywhere, behind tasteful orbs of tinted glass. And I realized, as I checked the "past history" window of my account, that the library had a copy of my passport and driver's license, had my e-mail address, had a record of every item I had looked up or requested, and probably saw that I had once taken out a pen to make a quick note when the point of my pencil broke. It's a trade-off, and billions of people are making trade-offs of this sort every day.

A few years ago, I spent an afternoon with Admiral John Poindexter, a national security advisor under Ronald Reagan. The small study in his home was filled with memorabilia — from Annapolis, the navy, the White House. His pipes stood in racks. Poindexter was called out of retirement in 2002 to head up the U.S. government's Total Information Awareness Office, a visionary program to compile a vast database of personal information, including biometric and surveillance data, which could be analyzed by automated computer tools for patterns of suspicious activity. It was launched without much thought to public relations: its official seal depicted light from a Masonic eye falling ominously on planet Earth, above the Latin motto *Scientia est Potentia* — "Knowledge is Power." The program was quickly defunded.

Poindexter was unapologetic. If America is going to combat asymmetric warfare waged by terrorists, he explained, it needs a lot more information. The world has changed since the bipolar days of the Cold War. Back then, we knew where the threat was coming from. We knew where the Soviets' missiles were. We understood their communications systems. "Fast forward," Poindexter said, "to a situation where the U.S. is the only superpower, and you have all of these non-state actors out there, and some rogue states. You have a much more difficult problem."

Poindexter has often been portrayed as a caricature. He is in fact a thoughtful man. He laid out his thinking methodically. He professed concern for privacy, and described a "privacy app" that Total Information Awareness would have deployed, intended to offer some measure of protection. That said, he believed deeply in the potential of the effort he had launched, and believed just as deeply that some sacrifice of privacy would be a small price to pay. If you've got nothing to hide, you've got nothing to fear. "Strong privacy advocates would not agree with this," he said, "but my view is that if privacy is invaded, it only really becomes a problem if there are actions taken against the person as a result of invading that privacy. That's not a commonly held view." His personal opinion, he went on, was that "in today's dangerous world," the insistence on a right to privacy is "a luxury we probably can't afford."

Camp Justice

The age of Total Information Awareness is not here yet, nor is the regime imagined in Philip K. Dick's 1956 short story "The Minority Report," in which the authorities have developed the capacity to predict crimes before they happen, and make preventive arrests accordingly. In our world, justice and punishment are still mainly post-crime — mainly, but not entirely. There are times when people can legally be restrained because of fears that they represent a danger to themselves or others. There are times when people can be targeted simply because they belong to a class of persons perceived as threatening. And there are times when people can be subjected to extreme forms of interrogation, including what amounts to torture, because, it is argued, some greater harm will be prevented.

There is ample precedent in American history for "preemption." Starting in 1919, amid a Red Scare precipitated by the Bolshevik Revolution in Russia and a spate of bombings in the United States, the Justice Department launched the so-called Palmer Raids, named for A. Mitchell Palmer, the attorney general at the time. In a letter to the U.S. Senate, Palmer indicated that he had drawn up a list of 60,000 presumed radicals. He requested new legislation to suppress radical publications. The raids, led by the young J. Edgar Hoover, rounded up targeted individuals by the thousands. They were held in detention centers and often deported. The efforts enjoyed broad public support. In the words of a *Washington Post* editorial, "There is no time to waste on hairsplitting over infringement of liberties."

Beginning in 1942, shortly after the attack on Pearl Harbor, as many as 110,000 Japanese Americans were sequestered in internment camps without due process, on the grounds that, as a group, they represented a potential threat to the United States. The general in charge of the internment put it bluntly: "In the war in which we are now engaged, racial affinities are not severed by migration. *The Japanese race is an enemy race.*" The italics are his. Among other things, the internment underscored the value of careful data collection. Although the fact was long denied, the Census Bureau, whose records are normally confidential, provided assistance in tracking down Japanese Americans. Years later, Presidents Kennedy, Johnson, and Nixon would leverage another cache of confidential data — the files of the Internal Revenue Service — for their own political purposes.

A second and more sustained Red Scare commenced with the onset of the Cold War. The official reaction to it, though often referred to loosely as McCarthyism — after Senator Joseph McCarthy, who leveled damaging accusations at hundreds of individuals whom he suspected of being communists or harboring communist sympathies — was in large part undertaken by the FBI, now led by Hoover. Governments at every level set up boards to look into the loyalty of their employees. So did private companies. One scholar in the mid-

1950s estimated that 20 percent of all workers in the country had, as a condition of employment, "taken a test oath, or completed a loyalty statement, or achieved official clearance, or survived some undefined private scrutiny" — a far deeper penetration than any inquisition by the Church could claim.

McCarthy's efforts lost steam, and he was discredited, but the FBI carried on under the aegis of its secret COINTELPRO operation, which was directed mostly at leftist groups, civil rights activists, and, later, antiwar protesters. A prominent book on the subject — *The Boss,* by Athan G. Theoharis and John Stuart Cox — is subtitled *J. Edgar Hoover and the Great American Inquisition.* COINTELPRO personnel, the authors write, "were authorized to use subterfuge, plant agents provocateurs, leak derogatory information to the press, and employ other disruptive tactics to destabilize the operations of targeted groups." Meanwhile, the Central Intelligence Agency, whose charter prohibits any domestic national-security role, pursued a covert mail-opening program directed at Americans, compiling a database of 1.5 million names. Another secret CIA program, known as CHAOS, infiltrated a broad range of domestic antiwar organizations.

Hoover's convictions were absolute, and he had a high pulpit. He warned about America's "dangerously indulgent attitude toward crime, filth, and corruption." He denounced those he saw as "mortal enemies of freedom and deniers of God Himself." COINTELPRO was shut down in 1971, soon after its existence had been exposed by activists. CHAOS was quietly terminated in 1973, not long before its activities became the subject of a *New York Times* investigation. That same year, Richard Nixon remarked to an aide that Hoover "had a file on everybody." This was not quite true: Hoover had files on only 25 million people — at the time, one out of eight Americans.

Legislative oversight, like that provided by the Church Committee in the 1970s, has brought some abuses to light. But the combination of moral panic and existential fear is a potent one. In the aftermath of the 9/11 attacks, Congress passed the USA Patriot Act, which allows the authorities to conduct "sneak and peek" searches without immediately notifying subjects, permits access to business records "in connection with" counterterrorism investigations, and expands to the point of vagueness the meaning of "material support" for terrorism. Most of its provisions have been reauthorized. In 2002, the National Security Agency was secretly given license to tap telephone conversations between people in the United States and people abroad without obtaining a warrant beforehand. Legislation eventually gave some legal cover to this practice, though it has run into trouble in the courts.

No actions connected with the post-9/11 period have received more attention than the use of torture to elicit information from prisoners captured in the war on terrorism. These methods have been referred to by the euphemism "enhanced interrogation." The term brings to mind the euphemism for torture that the Roman Inquisition employed — *rigoroso esamine,* or "rigorous examination." Torture has been employed on detainees in Bagram prison, in Afghanistan, and at numerous black sites in other countries. In the minds of much of the world, the American regime of torture is crystallized in the single word "Guantánamo."

The detention facilities at Guantánamo are collectively known as Camp Delta. They were built after the U.S. invasion of Afghanistan, which was launched in response to the 9/11 attacks. The Afghanistan war rapidly produced prisoners by the hundreds — suspected Al Qaeda or Taliban fighters, all of them Muslim, some of them certainly dangerous, some of them old men or young boys. Roughly 750 detainees have been held at Guantánamo altogether; about 175 were still there in 2011. Camp Delta replaced Camp X Ray, the original facility, built years ago to hold Haitian boat people. The famous photograph of the first detainees arriving at Guantánamo, shackled and blindfolded, kneeling in their orange jumpsuits in an open-air passage between chain-link fences, was taken at Camp X Ray. That spot is now overgrown with vegetation. The camp has been abandoned.

Flowering vines climb the fences and creep along the barbed wire. Wooden watchtowers creak as you ascend by ladder for the view. The grass comes up to your waist; you can hear the rustle of rodents and reptiles at your feet, but can see nothing. On the perimeter of Camp X Ray stand two long wooden buildings, each divided into several rooms that were used in the early days to conduct interrogations. Tables and benches are fixed solidly to the floor. Bits of duct tape lie among the droppings of banana rats.

Guantánamo has been a focus of intense international criticism ever since the first prisoners arrived, in January 2002. Many reports, later confirmed in detail, concerned the use of torture during the interrogation of detainees. The nature of the legal regime at Guantánamo also provoked condemnation. The Guantánamo Bay Naval Base is considered U.S. territory, and federal law governs there in ways that are apparent to any visitor. Iguanas, for instance, are everywhere — on lawns, in parking lots, inside the detention facilities. They are a protected species under federal law. Signs on the roadways warn of a $10,000 fine for even the inadvertent killing of an iguana. And yet as far as the detainees are concerned, Guantánamo was chosen because it represented a "legal black hole": it was not part of the constitutional homeland, the Bush administration argued, or subject to the same legal standards that might obtain within that homeland. Detainees could therefore be subjected to any legal regime the authorities decided to implement.

In effect, Guantánamo was chosen because it was a place where it was legal to have no legal regime at all. Habeas corpus did not apply — until, after years had elapsed, the Supreme Court ruled that it must. Detainees did not have to be told why they were being held. Their captors did not have to justify holding them. Nor did they need to divulge the names of the detainees. Where and how they should stand trial, if trial was warranted, remained a matter of contention. Among other things, the abuse of prisoners has tainted much of the evidence. An area of tents and makeshift buildings at Guantánamo is known as Camp Justice; it's the place set aside for the proceedings called military commissions. The Bush administration originally envisaged a $100 million facility for this purpose, and then scaled the plans back to a $12 million courtroom. Spectators sit behind soundproof glass; testimony is relayed by audio feed on a twenty-second delay, and can be cut off if classified information is divulged. By the summer of 2011, only five detainees had made their way through the process.

In 2010, the technicians at Google Labs introduced a feature called the Books Ngram Viewer, which allows users to discover the frequency with which particular words have been employed in published books going back hundreds of years. The pool is large: some 500 billion words in more than 5 million digitized books (and covering several languages). If you search for the word "Guantánamo," you'll see that it underwent a sharp uptick during the past decade. You'll see the same pattern if you search for the word "inquisition." The two words have become tightly linked, in the United States and around the world. "The Guantánamo Inquisition." "Guantánamo's Inquisitors." "Waterboarding: From the Inquisition to Guantánamo." You don't have to look very hard.

"All Means Necessary"

To reach the Guantánamo Bay Naval Base, you must travel four hours by airplane on one of two flights that operate daily out of Fort Lauderdale. The trip would be shorter if the aircraft did not have to avoid Cuban airspace, making a large loop around the island and approaching from the south. The planes are small, and until recently did not have restrooms. The passengers are mainly military personnel and defense contractors. The airport occupies the smaller of Guantánamo's two peninsulas, on the leeward side. A short ferry ride takes you to the larger peninsula, on the windward side.

Not far from the landing, at Fisherman's Point, stands a stone monument with a bronze plaque. It commemorates the arrival here of Christopher Columbus in 1494. He was on his second voyage, with a fleet of seventeen ships, and had brought with him 1,200 colonists. The fleet also carried five *religiosos,* whose job it would be to serve the colonists and also bring the indigenous people into the bosom of the Church. Columbus had been looking for gold but found only fish, which Indians were cooking on the shore. The Spaniards took note of the many iguanas, not yet endangered. In that same year, the pope would divide the Western Hemisphere between Spain and Portugal. The Inquisition was paying attention to the New World, including Cuba, within decades.

Cuba achieved independence from Spain in 1902, after the Spanish-American War, and the United States, wanting a naval base, took a perpetual lease on about forty-five square miles of territory on the two peninsulas enclosing Guantánamo Bay. Under the terms of the lease, the U.S. government pays Cuba $4,085 a year. Fidel Castro, protesting the U.S. presence, has for fifty years refused to cash the checks, reportedly keeping them in a drawer. The naval base is cut off from the rest of Cuba by hills. At night a sine curve of floodlit fencing marks the ridgeline. The hills also cut off the area from rain, making conditions at Guantánamo dry and hot. Military vehicles carry coolers filled with bottled water. So do civilians in their own cars, which are referred to as POVs, for "personally owned vehicles." The Indians left behind massive shell heaps known as middens. If American forces leave middens, they will consist of Dasani bottles.

The U.S. government does not issue detailed maps of the detention facilities at Guantánamo, and any aerial pictures of the base taken by passengers on incoming aircraft are deleted by security personnel. Pictures taken by departing passengers are fine. A Renaissance censor must be making the rules. In 2010, a Stanford University archaeologist named Adrian Myers used Google Earth images from 2003 and 2008 to map in detail the rapid growth of Camp Delta, from the makeshift facilities that existed on 9/11 to the permanent structures built since then. The newest buildings are modeled directly on "supermax" prisons in the United States. Camp 5, one of the maximum-security facilities, is a replica of a prison in Terre Haute, Indiana. Camp 6, another maximum-security facility, replicates a prison in Lenawee, Michigan. Khalid Sheikh Mohammed and other high-value prisoners are held in Camp 7, which is off by itself. Camp 4 is the most relaxed of the facilities. In the detainee library, I noticed several complete sets of Harry Potter and also a copy of Friedrich Nietzsche's *Will to Power,* and wondered if hard-line members of Congress knew about either of these selections.

Imperial spores carry the imprint of the homeland. The Indies, declared Columbus, were to be governed "according to the custom and practice of Castile." Guantánamo in this sense is no different from any other American outpost. It has strip malls, fast-food restaurants, and residential communities that look like any suburb. Ramps on the buildings and cuts in the sidewalks indicate that the Americans With Disabilities Act is very much in force. Signs caution against sexual harassment. Psychological counseling is a phone call away. There are Protestant and Catholic churches, but you can also find a rabbi or an imam if you need one.

You can't escape the religious overtones at Guantánamo. A single kitchen the size of a warehouse, presided over by a no-nonsense Filipina (a "third-country national," or TCN, as such workers are called), prepares meals for troops and detainees alike. Pasta is boiled in industrial pots that tip mechanically, as if at a steel mill. Half the operation is *halal,* to ensure the delivery of "culturally appropriate" meals to Muslim prisoners. Military personnel uniformly refer to their task as "the mission." In the camps, the *adhan,* the call to prayer, is broadcast five times a day. I watched from a guard tower one morning before daybreak as a group of twenty detainees assembled quietly and knelt toward *qibla,* the direction of Mecca. Their rhythmic chant was still in my ears when I entered the military mess hall at Camp America a few minutes later. A flat-screen TV dominated the wall at each end. One screen showed CNN. The other showed an evangelical preacher delivering a homily. Soldiers listened as they ate. When I sat down for breakfast with the guards who had been with me in the tower, they bowed their heads in silent prayer before cutting into their pancakes. They, like their captives, have God on their minds, if not on their side. These two religions of the book seem to have arrived at something of an impasse.

It was not always clear why many of the detainees were there — a fact underscored by an assortment of classified documents pertaining to Guantánamo that were made public in 2011. Some detainees had been picked up on the battlefield in Afghanistan, and a significant number were certainly combatants or terrorists. Many others were the victims of denunciation by third parties whose motives remain opaque, or were simply caught up in sweeps and slapped with a label by soldiers who understood neither their language nor their culture. A few were apprehended on tips, at remote locations around the world. Some took a circuitous route, having been rendered to obliging countries for torture and interrogation before being flown to Cuba. To an extent, Guantánamo became a self-fulfilling prophecy: men who were not radical when captured became radicalized by captivity. One of Francis Walsingham's spies, Maliverny Catlyn, observed a similar phenomenon in English prisons in the 1580s, where Catholics were detained in large groups: "If you mean to stop the stream, choke the spring. Believe me, the prisons of England are very nourishers of papists."

Very early on — within months of 9/11, Guantánamo was the site where issues of torture and criminal justice converged, seizing the full attention of officials at the highest levels of the White House and the Pentagon. The British lawyer Philippe Sands has laid out an indisputable time line. First the administration decided, in February of 2002, to abrogate the Geneva Conventions regarding

detainees. Then it created a legal justification for torture by defining the term in such a way—it must produce pain "equivalent in
intensity to the pain accompanying serious physical injury, such as
organ failure, impairment of bodily function, or even death"—that
most acts of torture fell outside it. This standard was embodied in
the so-called torture memos drafted in 2002 by the Justice Department lawyers John Yoo and Jay Bybee; those documents did for
the twenty-first century what the papal bull *Ad extirpanda* did for
the thirteenth. With that threshold in place, the Bush administration drew up a list of techniques—including isolation, twenty-hour
interrogations, nudity, hooding, standing for long periods of time,
deprivation of light and sound, the use of dogs—and conveyed the
list to interrogators on the scene. This list was given sanction in the
famous memo on which Donald Rumsfeld, the secretary of defense,
scrawled, "I stand for 8–10 hours a day. Why is standing limited to 4
hours?"

In late 2002 and early 2003, the techniques were employed over a
period of seven weeks on a detainee who went by the number 063,
and is now known to be Mohammed al-Qahtani. Transcripts of the
interrogations were eventually leaked to the press. The transcriber
had taken note of al-Qahtani's reactions at various points in the interrogation process, and Sands strung them together for emphasis:

Detainee began to cry. Visibly shaken. Very emotional. Detainee
cried. Disturbed. Detainee began to cry. Detainee bit the IV tube
completely in two. Started moaning. Uncomfortable. Moaning.
Began crying hard spontaneously. Crying and praying. Very agitated. Yelled. Agitated and violent. Detainee spat. Detainee proclaimed his innocence. Whining. Dizzy. Forgetting things. Angry.
Upset. Yelled for Allah. Urinated on himself. Began to cry. Asked
God for forgiveness. Cried. Cried. Became violent. Began to cry.
Broke down and cried. Began to pray and openly cried. Cried out
to Allah several times. Trembled uncontrollably.

The resemblance to Inquisition transcripts — "Oh, dear God!" — is hard to miss. In another parallel with Church practice, medical personnel were always present; they witnessed the questioning firsthand. The administration would attempt to blame brutal interrogations on "rogue elements" or, in the case of Guantánamo, on "an aggressive major general." It is true that, for a time, the interrogators at Guantánamo, operating without guidance, often amateurs, and under extreme pressure to show results, improvised as best they could. They gleaned ideas from the Fox drama 24. The Jesuits should be grateful that Richard Topcliffe did not have television. But the explicit sanction of torture, and the demand that it be used, came from above.

The administration never voiced second thoughts. In its resolution approving military action after 9/11, Congress had authorized the use of "all means necessary" — a deliberately open-ended phrase that would be interpreted to include domestic surveillance and other efforts. "All" meant "all." When it came to interrogation, the permissible techniques would be extended, in some cases, to include waterboarding, physical abuse, and threats of death. The interrogation techniques, it was said, had "worked." The information gathered had "saved innocent lives." That assessment has never been documented. In 2008, the director of the FBI, Robert Mueller, was asked whether extreme forms of interrogation had produced intelligence that disrupted any attacks on America. He replied, "I don't believe that has been the case." Efficacy aside, the only demonstrated concern has been for semantics and legality, narrowly understood, not the justice and legitimacy of the enterprise itself. Michael V. Hayden, President Bush's outgoing director of the CIA, told Leon Panetta, the incoming director, "I've read some of your writings while you've been out of government. Don't ever use the words CIA and torture in the same paragraph again. Torture is a felony, Leon. Say you don't like it. Say it offends you. I don't care. But just don't say it's torture. It's a felony."

Razor v. Music

Clive Stafford Smith, a human rights lawyer, was speaking with a young intern, a high school student named Will, when I caught up with him at his home in Symondsbury, Dorset. Stafford Smith had given Will the job of listing all the forms of abuse employed at Guantánamo and then finding the Spanish terms for the same techniques from the Inquisition, assuming he could find a match. He had found a corresponding term for just about everything, he said, but had stalled on "extraordinary rendition." I suggested *relajado al brazo secular* — relaxing penitents to the secular arm for punishment. It wasn't perfect, but it captured the idea of getting someone else to do your dirty work for you. Will said he would look into it.

Stafford Smith, lanky and voluble, is the British-born but American-trained director of Reprieve, an organization he founded to oppose the death penalty and defend prisoners on death row. After 9/11, as Guantánamo began to fill, Reprieve offered assistance to the families of some of the detainees. It also joined efforts in the United States to mount legal challenges to the detention system, challenges that eventually met with success in a series of Supreme Court rulings. One of Stafford Smith's clients is Binyam Mohammed, a onetime Guantánamo detainee from Ethiopia, whose civil suit wrested an admission from the British government that it had colluded with the United States in the application of torture.

The village of Symondsbury nestles in a quiet vale. From high ground it has a view of the sea. The church, on a slope, goes back to the fourteenth century. Wildflowers grow among the tombstones. The village is about as far from Guantánamo, psychologically, as it is possible to get. This was the setting in which Stafford Smith recalled a conversation with Binyam Mohammed.

"The whole argument over the definition of torture," he said, "is another one of these semantic debates that allowed the Bush administration to do horrible things. When you take some of the things like sleep deprivation or like loud music that Rumsfeld would disparage — I had no idea how pernicious that stuff was, really. If you keep someone awake for ten or eleven days, they just die.

"And the music! Binyam Mohammed enlightened me on that one. If you ask someone if they'd rather have a razor blade taken to their penis or have loud music played at them, everyone goes for the music. Binyam had the razor blade in Morocco and the loud music in Kabul. He said he would rather go with the razor blade because physical pain has a beginning and end; mental pain, you start losing your mind. The way he put it was, Would you rather lose your power of sight, as in be blinded, or lose your mind, as in go insane? When you reframe the question that way, suddenly the whole thing turns right around in your head."

All told, Stafford Smith has by now spent perhaps nine months living in Guantánamo, interviewing detainees and preparing cases. When he is not out of the country, he commutes once a week from Symondsbury to Reprieve's offices in London, in the legal warren among the Inns of Court. It is a cluttered place, ranging over several floors, and has become a gathering spot for many of the former detainees now living in England.

In 2010, the British government agreed to an out-of-court settlement with fifteen former detainees and one man still being held at Guantánamo. All of them are British citizens or legal British residents who have alleged complicity by MI5 and MI6 in their mistreatment. The amount of the settlement, though not known, runs into the millions of dollars.

7

WITH GOD ON OUR SIDE

The Inquisition and the Modern World

The Church has no fear of historical truth.

— POPE JOHN PAUL II, 1998

We know you're wishing that we'd go away,
But the Inquisition's here and it's here to stay.

— MEL BROOKS, *HISTORY OF THE WORLD: PART I*, 1981

Making Martyrs

ABOUT A YEAR AGO, I returned to Rome to spend some time with Msgr. Alejandro Cifres, who after more than a decade is still in charge of the Inquisition archives at the Vatican. Some things had not changed. The shop Euroclero still stood across the street, beyond the gates, selling chalices and cassocks and resplendent liturgical garments for clerics of every rank. It has been Josef Ratzinger's tailor for many years. The windows of the Palazzo del Sant'Uffizio still bore their heavy bars. The studded wooden doors at the entrance were as welcoming as ever. But there seemed to be more cars and fewer Vespas parked outside. And there had been other changes. For one thing, the monsignor's boss, Cardinal Ratzinger, had taken a new job, and had moved from his office upstairs to quarters on the top floor of the Apostolic Palace, above the northern arm of Bernini's colonnade. The papal apartments, a ten-room suite that had long been in a state of disrepair, received a thorough renovation. Shelving was installed for the pope's personal library of 20,000 books. Water pipes, encrusted with lime, were replaced. A German company was brought in to remodel the kitchen. Some of the papal rooms had been using 125-volt outlets. Everything is 220 volts now, the Italian standard.

The rooms housing the Inquisition archives have been remodeled too; Msgr. Cifres had been a busy man, and had become a building contractor as well as an archivist. The Vatican city-state is confined within tight boundaries. It will not soon be rolling back the Risorgimento in a war of expansion. The only place it can grow is down. Of course, another city exists there already, an ancient Roman one. Below the Holy Office lies a cemetery and whatever is left of an amphitheater, the Circus of Nero, where many Christians went to their deaths. This little plot of ground has been making martyrs of Christians ever since. Nero's mother, Agrippina, lived in the neighborhood; the frescoed walls of what may have been her villa were discovered in 1999, when the Vatican built an underground parking garage to handle crowds for the upcoming Jubilee. When the archive decided, in 2003, that it must have more space, it added two new levels underneath the palazzo. The excavations went down twenty feet below the existing basement, and produced as much marble as dirt. ("And some bones," Cifres notes matter-of-factly.) Fragments of columns and cornices and pediments and tombstones now line the hallways. They had to go somewhere.

The new underground space is modern—the walls clinically white, the atmosphere regulated by science. Instruments in the corners keep track of temperature and humidity. There is room to grow. The documents are stored on automated metallic bookshelves twelve feet high, like the ones at the U.S. National Archives. Cifres showed me how they work, but did not make a joke about torture. The facility could be the Social Security Administration or MI6, except that the floors are marble, the files are labeled in a fine Renaissance hand, and crucifixes grace the walls. One section holds official maps of the old Jewish ghettos in Italian cities. In another are architectural plans for Inquisition offices that would one day be built throughout the Papal States. Elsewhere are shelves of Hebraic material, confiscated over the years, and an early printed copy of Nicholas Eymerich's manual for inquisitors.

Certain items in the Archivio reappeared, like old friends. I was glad to see the two mahogany card catalogues on their wooden stand — the Index of Forbidden Books. I opened up the box labeled "A–K" and touched the soft, worn edges of the cards. It is hard to believe that any volume in these two catalogues would make anyone's jaw drop today. Carlo Botta's *Storia d'Italia dal 1719 al 1814*? Jacobus Ode's *Comentarius de angelis*?

Upstairs, the old archive space has been turned into conference rooms and reading rooms. There is actually a reception area now, with an alcove for the mandatory lockers where researchers must lodge their belongings. The condemnation of Descartes won't be disappearing in a tote bag. By Vatican standards, the Archivio is a busy place. Well over a hundred researchers applied to work here last year. I opened a door and came in upon half a dozen scholars in front of laptops, each with a bundle of documents unwrapped on a desk. They turned as one to look when the door creaked open, and then returned as one to their labors.

"What are they working on?" I asked Msgr. Cifres later. "Censorship, mostly," he said. And the trial of Galileo. And, from a later period, the Modernist controversy. Also, he went on, now that the Holy Office archives are accessible up through 1939, anything having to do with fascist Italy and Nazi Germany is getting more and more attention. He paused, thinking about what he might have missed. "And of course apparitions," he said. Apparitions are reported more frequently than you might imagine, and bishops typically consult the

CDF on how to proceed. In December 2010, just before Christmas, a bishop in Wisconsin affirmed that the Virgin Mary had most likely appeared to a Belgian immigrant woman near Green Bay in 1859. (A vision of the Virgin in Akita, Japan, was affirmed by Ratzinger himself in 1988.) The scholars at the CDF, from universities around the world, focus mainly on sterner stuff. The biggest project under way is the publication of all Inquisition documents relating to science and natural philosophy. The first four volumes, under the series title The Catholic Church and Modern Science, were published in 2010 and cover the years from the start of the Inquisition to the execution of Giordano Bruno. The editors find it "inconceivable" that the Church's policies of "preventive control" could have failed to dampen intellectual life. Galileo is up next.

In the monsignor's office, above his desk, hangs an oil painting of Robert Bellarmine. Below it is a signed photograph of Pope Benedict XVI. On a library table lie several books on the Arts and Crafts movement and the work of William Morris, which is Cifres's other passion. At his small apartment in the Vatican, the décor is all Arts and Crafts — the furniture, the wallpaper, the drapes. Morris died in 1896, the same year in which Pope Leo XIII issued his bull *Apostolicae Curae*, which declared ordinations by the Anglican Church "absolutely null and utterly void." The condemnation of Anglican Orders, as this action is known, is the subject of the monsignor's doctoral thesis, which he hopes to complete soon. So Cifres spends a lot of time, intellectually, in the 1890s, when he is not in the 1590s.

But he is also solidly in the twenty-first century. There is a computer in his office, and he is eager to show off the database and retrieval system he has created. The organizational tree of the Inquisition archives now exists online in skeletal form — you can start with a given year, narrow it down to a particular department, then to a specific case, and then to the files of a certain cardinal-inquisitor on that case. Bit by bit, the content of the individual documents is being stirred in. Eventually, you will be able to search documents by word as easily at the Holy Office as in any other database. I asked Cifres if other parts of the Vatican were similarly advanced. He was happy to report that some congregations had adopted this very system. The Vatican Library was also digitizing its collection. And the Archivio Segreto? He offered a resigned smile, which I took to be the equivalent, in curial terms, of falling off his chair. Apparently it was still in the . . . well, pick your century. Cifres had developed his database with the help of a collaborator, Marco Pizzo, at Rome's Museo del Risorgimento, and some software consultants. The system is called SHADES (the awkward acronym is derived from "software for historical archives description"). One wishes that he'd found a way to call it HADES. Universities around the world can apply for access. Bernard Gui would have been impressed, and perhaps a little envious.

"Not Our Favorite Subject"

When Pope John Paul II agreed to open most of the Inquisition archives to scholars, in 1998, he referred to the Inquisition as "a tormented phase in the history of the Church," and he maintained on more than one occasion that "the Church has no fear of historical truth." His successor, Pope Benedict XVI, has said much the same thing. Both popes, whatever their merits and deficiencies, made good on promises to give historians far greater access to the documents in the Vatican's possession. To be sure, they closed the door at the papacy of Eugenio Pacelli — Pius XII — whose silence during World War II, as evidence mounted of German genocide, has drawn both abiding scorn and uneasy apologetics. Those archives, and everything since, remain sealed. But that is the big exception. When David Kertzer wished to examine the materials in the Edgardo Mortara case, the Vatican's initial reaction was, as he recalls, "That's not our favorite subject." But the staff proved helpful to him nonetheless. Those four volumes in the series The Catholic Church and Modern Science are first-class works of scholarship. Oddly, the four-volume set comes with a refrigerator magnet depicting Pope Benedict XVI — an attempt at branding, maybe, or perhaps official acknowledgment of the reality of magnetism. One can see this change in outlook regarding the archives as a belated recognition of the value of transparency and free inquiry — never the Holy See's strong point — or as a defensive move in the ongoing war over the ownership of history. No doubt it has elements of both.

To the extent that it was a defensive move, it was probably a smart one. The credibility of the Church on the Inquisition is meager, and partisans who jump to the Church's defense tend to come across as blinkered and naive. The "pleasant surprises" that Cardinal Silvestrini was hoping for have not materialized. But independent scholars have added texture and nuance to the seven-hundred-year story of the Inquisition. They have put it into a social context. They have documented its unhappy consequences but also shown its limitations — the wide gap between plans and performance, ambitions and competence. The Inquisition emerges in a somewhat fuller light. It seems to have executed a smaller percentage of defendants than most secular courts did. It attempted to codify its practices and place restrictions on its behavior. In other ways, the Inquisition emerges as more disturbing than ever — because it could persist for so long in such a mindless way, sustained and perpetuated by larger forces that no one could quite perceive, let alone understand, much less control. At the same time, it comes across as a bureaucracy like any other, subject to the same myopic imperatives, the same petty ambitions and animosities, that one finds in *Dilbert* or *The Office*.

That scholarship would have taken this turn — cutting the Inquisition somewhat down to size — should not be surprising. That is what frequently happens when hard facts collide with a mythic reputation. To cite a different example: with the opening of official archives in Moscow, after the collapse of communism, historians have ventured a view of the inner workings of the Soviet state as in some respects more "normal" than one might have thought — still a fearsome construct, but one in which factors we would recognize as interest groups, politics, and even public opinion had to be taken into account. Modern scholars of the Inquisition disagreed with one another on many points before the archives were opened, and they continue to have their battles. How effective was censorship? Did the Inquisition hold Spain back? But the availability of new raw material has allowed them to play out their arguments on firmer terrain.

The Inquisition may not have been "the eye that never slumbered," as Prescott put it, but it did leave wounds that never heal. When the archives were at last opened, a looming question was whether the pope would at some point formally apologize for the Inquisition, perhaps in the course of the Jubilee Year, 2000. At a conclave of historians and theologians that marked the occasion, Carlo Ginzburg rose to comment. All eyes turned to him. Ginzburg is the sort of man who attracts attention — those eyebrows! — and the opening of the archives was an event he had played a role in.

Eamon Duffy remembers the moment clearly: "Ginzburg said, 'This is all very well.' He said, 'What I didn't hear the pope say today, and what I haven't heard anybody in this discussion say, is that the Catholic Church is *ashamed* of what it did. Not *sorry.* Sorry is easy. I want to hear the Catholic Church — I want to hear the pope — say he is *ashamed.*' There was a tremendous round of applause from the historians. Not from the theologians."

"Sorry" was in fact not so easy. A priest in Indiana recently collaborated with a software company to create an iPhone app that can help people examine their consciences and make a confession. You can type in certain generic biographical descriptors (for instance, "priest," "age seventy-five"), and it will run through the Ten Commandments with your category in mind, asking questions it deems relevant to your situation ("Have I been lazy, halfhearted, or cynical in my ministry?" "Do I hold any resentments against God?" "Have I engaged in sexual fantasies?"). But there isn't a prompt along the lines of "Did I help, abet, or otherwise enable, a centuries-long worldwide inquisition?" The papal apology, when it did come, had been maneuvered into place slowly, over a period of years, and with careful rhetorical adjustments along the way. The process began with a pastoral letter titled "As the Third Millennium Draws Near," released in 1994, when the pope acknowledged the actions of "children" of the Church who had "departed from the spirit of Christ and His Gospel." It continued in 1998 with the document "We Remember: A Reflection on the Shoah," in which the pope offered repentance on behalf of the "sons and daughters" of the Church who had stood by as the Holocaust unfolded. At last, in a penitential service at St. Peter's in the Jubilee year itself, the pope asked forgiveness for all transgressions committed by the "children of the Church" during the past 2,000 years. The references to "children" and "sons and daughters" seemed to leave the Church's leadership out of the picture. The formulaic parsing was widely noticed. At least there was no reference to "rogue elements" or "an aggressive major general."

The wounds never heal: Every year in Rome's Campo dei Fiori, where a grim, hooded statue of Giordano Bruno rises above the market stalls, secularists and freethinkers gather on February 17, the day of Bruno's execution, to mark his legacy and attack the Church. The statue was controversial when erected, in 1889 — a deliberate thumb in the eye of the papacy by a newly reunited Italy. Anticlerical activists shouting "Death to the butchers of the Inquisition!" had taken to the streets to press for a monument; most of Italy's civil government attended the unveiling. Today, roses are frequently left at the statue's base. In 2000, on the 400th anniversary of Bruno's death, demonstrators in the square mounted a raucous reenactment of the execution. Men in black hoods were on hand to serve as *confortatores* to the condemned man — playing the role of the clerics who accompanied heretics to the stake, hoping to win a last-minute reconciliation (which did not, however, include a stay of execution).

More open wounds: In 1992, on the 500th anniversary of the expulsion of the Jews from Spain, King Juan Carlos joined Israel's president, Chaim Herzog, in prayer at Beth Yaakov, the Madrid synagogue. The synagogue could not open its doors until 1968, after Spain lifted restrictions on non-Catholic places of worship. Spain, as it happens, was also the last nation in the European Union to recognize Israel. The king acknowledged that his country had known periods of "intolerance and persecution," but stopped short of an outright apology. His gesture of reconciliation was not enough for some. That same year, the Spanish parliament approved legislation giving Judaism, Islam, and the various Protestant denominations the same status in law that Roman Catholicism had long enjoyed.

For their part, Muslims — who are far more numerous than Jews in Spain, and whose presence is today far more politically charged — have sought an apology for the expulsion order of 1609, though as yet to no avail. Former prime minister José María Aznar, a conservative, has opposed any apology. He said at a conference in Washington, "I support Ferdinand and Isabella." So there is still plenty of fuel for the pyre, and no shortage of people willing to apply the flame.

The Inquisitorial Impulse

Meanwhile, there is the phenomenon itself to consider — not the recurring debate over the historical Inquisition but the recurring behavior that brings inquisitions into existence. Call it the inquisitorial impulse. It springs from certainty — from unswerving confidence in the rightness of one's cause. But conviction alone is never enough. What separates an inquisition from other forms of intolerance is its staying power. It receives institutional support — creating its own or relying on what exists. It goes on and on. Today, the basic elements that can sustain an inquisition — bureaucracy, communications, the tools of surveillance and censorship — are more prevalent and entrenched, by many orders of magnitude, than they were in the days of Gregory IX or Tomás de Torquemada. None of them will be reduced in significance in the years ahead. They will only become more powerful.

THE BUREAUCRATIC MACHINE

Bureaucracy is a human artifact, and for all its negative reputation, it provides the management and inertia that keep modern societies operating. Armies and airports, highways and schools, all run on bureaucracy. Every payment by any government is the product of a bureaucracy. Spain's vast colonial empire was relatively weak because its bureaucratic structures were modest; the strong bureaucratic traditions of China, in contrast, go back 5,000 years.

One rule of thumb about bureaucracies, however, is that they tend to expand: their mission becomes broader, their personnel become more numerous, and their reason for existence becomes the fact that they already exist. Over time, bureaucratic procedures affect more and more areas of life, from the conduct of a classroom to the boarding of an airplane to the final moments in intensive care. And over time, more and more people find themselves invested in particular bureaucracies, because their livelihoods depend on them. The growth has been especially pronounced in the area of domestic and national security. A 2010 *Washington Post* report found that in the United States, some 1,271 government organizations and 1,931 private companies now exist to deal with national-security concerns — amounting to an "alternative geography" of America that is "hidden from public view and lacking in thorough oversight." Bureaucracies become closed systems. They tend to restrict access to the information they control to those with official clearance. They are intent on autonomy.

Security experts have long criticized the methods used by the Transportation Security Administration — the government agency that oversees screening at airports — as inefficient and largely pointless, even as the methods have become more invasive, mindless, and routine. An individual's name can be added to the official U.S. terrorism watch list as the result of a single tip that is "deemed credible." That list, which holds some 440,000 names, is secret, and people cannot discover if their names are on it. The TSA continues to add layers of scrutiny. Recounting his experience with the new "back-scatter" x-ray body-scan machines, the columnist Dave Barry described in a radio interview how he had been subjected to a physical examination after being informed that the machine had detected a condition the security guards referred to as a "blurred groin." In April 2011, a six-year-old girl was made to undergo an "enhanced pat down" at an airport in New Orleans, an episode that caused controversy when video of the search was posted on YouTube. The TSA responded that "the security officer in the video followed current standard operating procedures," which is undoubtedly true, and the point.

In primitive states, procedures rarely have much longevity. In more advanced states, the organs of government grind on, often impervious to attempts at control. That characteristic marks even well-intended measures. Some years ago, in an issue of *The American Prospect* on the subject of "The Inquisitorial State," the columnist Anthony Lewis described how the appointment of special prosecutors and independent counsels with open-ended mandates and deep pockets had led to a culture of obsessive investigation. The rationalists of the Enlightenment conceived of government as a machine, something that had "levers" and "wheels" and "springs" and that, if properly built, could run with minimal intervention. The problem, it turns out, is making it stop.

In the end, bureaucracies take on lives of their own. That is why, for a century, the Inquisition censors on the wharves of that harbor in Portugal dutifully checked every incoming ship for contraband books, and wrote up the prescribed reports, even though their searches turned up nothing. Observing the gradual transformation of "government into administration, of republics into bureaucracies," Hannah Arendt commented, "Bureaucracy is the form of government in which everybody is deprived of political freedom, of the power to act; for the rule by Nobody is not no-rule, and where all are equally powerless we have a tyranny without a tyrant."

UNDER OBSERVATION

In the late 1990s, the Federal Bureau of Investigation implemented a program that employed "packet sniffing" software to monitor certain e-mail and other communications. The effort was probably doomed the moment it became widely known that the software's code name was Carnivore. The National Security Agency, the U.S. intelligence arm chiefly responsible for tracking messages and data transmitted through the Internet, the telephone, and other electronic means, runs a similar program, commonly known as Echelon. Various lists circulating on the Internet purport to identify some of the thousands of keywords that trigger the NSA's attention. They include some words you'd expect, such as "assassinate," "cybercash," and "small-pox," and some you might not, such as "unclassified," "nowhere," and "Trump."

In the aftermath of 9/11, efforts like Carnivore and Echelon were joined by Total Information Awareness. That program was formally dismantled, but similar initiatives survive under different names. So do other kinds of monitoring. In 2007, Deputy Attorney General James B. Comey, testifying before the Senate Judiciary Committee, recounted an episode that had occurred three years earlier, when the White House sought to get authorization for a domestic surveillance program by the NSA that the Justice Department believed was illegal. The attorney general, John Ashcroft, was in intensive care after surgery, but the White House counsel and the White House chief of staff arrived unexpectedly at his bedside to obtain his signature. Comey had gotten there first, and Ashcroft refused to sign. But surveillance of this sort continues. The potential for "deep packet" inspection — drilling far down into electronic communications for sought-after information — is embedded in various kinds of computer software. The U.S. government insisted on having a point of access in case of need. Washington is not alone in this capability. Systems can be bought off the shelf, and companies will provide bespoke systems to seemingly any customer. The government of Iran has been eager to investigate the activities of political dissidents. In 2008, Iran set up a sophisticated inspection system with the help of Siemens and Nokia.

Advances in surveillance are rarely walked back. They become institutionalized, and then normalized, creating a new status quo and a platform for whatever the next steps might be. Jack Balkin, of Yale University Law School, has pointed out that powers granted by acts of Congress in the period after 9/11 — the Authorization of the Use of Military Force of 2001, the Patriot Act of 2001, the Military Commissions Act of 2006, the Protect America Act of 2007, the 2008 amendments to the Foreign Intelligence Surveillance Act — have, taken together, "created a basic framework for the National Surveillance State," which in turn could lead to "emergency government as a normal condition of politics." National-security cases aside, the number of state and federal requests for wiretap authorization keeps growing; it reached a record high of 3,194 in 2010, up by a third over the previous year. Of that number, a single request for authorization was denied by a judge.

Monitoring is not merely an act of policy. It is abetted by everyone, because it is built into the way we run our lives. A member of Germany's Green Party recently made public a graphic display of his personal movements over a six-month period. It was based on longitude and latitude data that had been automatically tracked by his cell phone on 35,000 distinct occasions. On the basis of the proximity of a user's cell phone to the cell phones of other people, together with the user's location and the duration of his conversations, and without listening in, service providers can analyze patterns of personal interaction — identifying your circle of friends, discerning when conversations touch on political topics, even predicting if you're about to jump to a different phone company. "Computer vision" systems are now employed in prisons, at shopping malls, in intensive care units; they can recognize faces, monitor expressions, assess behavior. They are used by Hollywood to test audience reactions. They are used by hospitals to remind employees to wash their hands. They can distinguish among emotions. A new Google app called Goggles allows users to photograph an object or scene and then search the Internet for matches. Google drew the line, for now, at facial recognition, but the capability exists.

ACCESS DENIED

Censorship today occurs in many new ways, but the old ways are still very much alive. The expurgation of a work of history by Philipp Camerarius in the sixteenth century has an analogue in the revision of school textbooks by the Texas State Board of Education in the twenty-first. Under the new Texas guidelines, approved in 2010, textbooks must emphasize that the Founding Fathers were people of religious faith; must deemphasize the doctrine of separation of church and state; must assert that the Civil War was fought mainly over states' rights, not slavery; must give ample consideration to the views of Confederate President Jefferson Davis; must downplay criticism of Senator Joseph McCarthy; and must include positive references to the Moral Majority, the Heritage Foundation, and the National Rifle Association. A proposal to rename the slave trade "the Atlantic triangular trade" did not pass, nor did a proposal that textbooks must use Barack Obama's middle name, Hussein.

In the short term, do changes like these threaten the freedom of any university historian in Cambridge or Berkeley (or Austin)? Of course not. In our lifetime, no scholar will feel constrained to alter so much as a comma. No professor will be purged. But in the long term? The changes in Texas affect 5 million students a year in the state's grammar schools and high schools. Additional changes will be implemented every decade, when the textbooks come up for review. Meanwhile, the Texas requirements will ripple outward: the Texas market is so large that publishers often turn local demands into national standards. Fifty years will pass, a century. The intellectual elite may remain free to say what it wishes. But what will have happened to popular opinion in the meantime? And what will that future elite have grown up knowing?

Examples of censorship like those above — campaigns against this book or that; campaigns to include one set of ideas and exclude another — are by now almost antiquated. They are sideshows. Corporations and the government may soon have the capacity to achieve similar ends in a more systematic way. In 2010, the investment-banking firm Goldman Sachs decreed that profanity was no longer to be used in e-mails sent by its employees, and backed up its policy by installing software to detect any breaches. In 2009, Amazon discovered that it did not have the rights to editions of Orwell's *1984* and *Animal Farm* that readers had downloaded onto their Kindles. With the push of a button, Amazon was able to delete those books remotely from all Kindles worldwide. No one questioned that Amazon needed to act — it was in breach of copyright. But many were surprised that it could make books simply disappear from people's hands. The fact that the episode involved these particular novels was an irony lost on no one.

Much has been made of the role of Twitter, Facebook, and other social media in fostering democratic upheavals in Iran, Egypt, Tunisia, and elsewhere — as if the last barriers to the free flow of communication and information are inevitably destined to disappear. Cyber analysts are not so sure. Yes, it's usually possible to get around so-called first-generation filtering — whereby governments attempt to erect firewalls at key Internet choke points in order to screen out whatever they deem undesirable. But "second-generation filtering" — whereby governments (or other entities) themselves attack sources of information in various ways — is another story. A popular revolution overthrew the government of Hosni Mubarak, in Egypt, but the most important lesson from the episode may be that before it did so, the Egyptian authorities managed to shut down the entire Internet in the country with relative ease. In Iran, whose Islamic government has also been a target of protests fueled by online social networks, the authorities used access to Twitter and Facebook to collect names and trace relationships.

The Internet has long had its utopian theorists. Its dystopian pessimists deserve attention. In his book *The Net Delusion*, Evgeny Morozov asks, "What if the liberating potential of the Internet also contains seeds of depoliticization and thus dedemocratization?" Elsewhere he writes, "A Twitter revolution is only possible in a regime where the state apparatus is completely ignorant of the Internet and has no virtual presence of its own. However, most authoritarian states are now moving in the opposite direction, eagerly exploiting cyberspace for their own strategic purposes." In China, the government "harmonizes" Web sites that traffic in content it considers inappropriate — that is, it shuts them down. In the United States, well-meaning measures to ensure the transparency of government operations have been bent to a different use. When a University of Wisconsin historian began commenting in a blog on statewide political matters, his opponents cited his status as a state employee and demanded, under the state's open-records law, that he release all the private e-mails he had ever written from his university e-mail account containing words such as "Republican," "union," "collective bargaining," "recall," and "rally." Leverage can be exercised in other ways. Opinion varies widely on the merits of WikiLeaks, which in 2010 made public hundreds of thousands of classified U.S. government documents. The organization has not been charged with any crime, but soon after the first disclosures, and at the urging of a powerful senator, Amazon dropped WikiLeaks material from its servers. Separately, several major financial companies, including Visa, MasterCard, and PayPal, announced that they would no longer process contributions to WikiLeaks. The flow of information — and money — is subject to choke points, and it's not always clear who controls the valves.

The organization Freedom House publishes an annual survey of freedom of expression worldwide. According to its 2010 survey, the world has seen eight consecutive years of setbacks. Severe controls of some sort on the press and on the Internet are more the rule than the exception; only one person in six lives in a country without them. As a study published in the independent British publication *Index on Censorship* recently pointed out, "No longer is it easy to hide from slow-moving and inept bureaucracies in the vast pools of information flows." Wealthy Catholic families in Reformation England once kept "priest holes" in their manor houses to hide itinerant Jesuits. Priest holes on the Internet are not very secure.

Us Against Them

Americans pride themselves on being a nation with no established religion, where the state does not interfere in religious activities. And yet the level of hostility toward "the other" — or, in milder form, the level of nervousness and suspicion — is on the rise. It is not just a matter of religion, of course. Bill Bishop, in his book *The Big Sort,* describes how more and more Americans are choosing to live, work, and play almost exclusively with people "like themselves." This is a natural tendency, but it diminishes exposure to any contrary outlook while elevating the primacy of one's own. The Internet makes the pursuit of this sort of epistemic closure increasingly easy. Users of a search engine called SeekFind will be directed only to sites consistent with evangelical Christianity. Users of a site called I'mHalal will be directed only to sites consistent with Islam.

Religion remains a central front. In Texas in 2004, a plank in the Republican Party platform made an explicit reference to "the myth of the separation of church and state" and declared that "the United States of America is a Christian nation." An evangelical tone suffuses the modern American military, particularly the Army officer corps. In public life, the "Christian nation" theme is hard to miss. When President Obama made a state visit to Turkey in 2009, he told his audiences there: "We do not consider ourselves a Christian nation or a Jewish nation or a Muslim nation; we consider ourselves a nation of citizens who are bound by ideals and a set of values." Angry rejoinders were instantaneous. Newt Gingrich, the former speaker of the House, called the president's remarks "fundamentally misleading about the nature of America." Fox News host Sean Hannity described the comments as "a disgrace." A year later, Sarah Palin professed bewilderment at "hearing any leader declare that America isn't a Christian nation." At rallies, Palin calls on an army of "prayer warriors" to smite her foes, and she encourages the identification of herself with the biblical figure Esther. In 2011, the governor-elect of Alabama, Robert Bentley, stated that he considered himself a "brother" to others only if "you're a Christian, and if you're saved, and if the Holy Spirit lives within you." Prominent ministers have laid the blame for 9/11 and Hurricane Katrina on homosexuality and secularism, and identified the cause of the 2010 earthquake in Haiti as a long-ago "pact with the devil."

The proposed building of an Islamic cultural center in lower Manhattan, within several blocks of Ground Zero — the site of the World Trade Center, destroyed by Islamist terrorists — brought out similar feelings. The cultural center, which was to include a mosque, had been advanced by a moderate imam named Feisal Abdul Rauf, who embraces a vision of an Islam that lives peacefully within the American tradition. Rauf had been sent on overseas missions by the Bush administration to explain American ideas of religious pluralism. The cultural center was to be named Cordoba House, the reference being to Córdoba in Spain, the symbolic embodiment of *convivencia*. The facility conformed to local ordinances and had received a unanimous green light from New York City's Landmarks Preservation Commission.

Though concentrated in a handful of communities nationwide, Muslims make up less than 1 percent of the U.S. population. But the idea of an Islamic facility near "hallowed ground" inflamed passions. Political leaders and other prominent figures raised their voices against it. So did the venerable Anti-Defamation League. The ADL's historical mission is to "put an end forever to unjust and unfair discrimination against, and ridicule of, any sect or body of citizens" — but in this instance, the organization explained, the anguish of the grieving families "entitles them to positions that others would categorize as irrational or bigoted." Bryan Fischer, an official with the American Family Association, went further, arguing that there should be "no more mosques, period" in the United States, because "each Islamic mosque is dedicated to the overthrow of the American government."

Opposition to Islamic facilities broke out in California, Tennessee, Wisconsin, and elsewhere. A church in Gainesville, Florida — the Dove World Outreach Center — announced plans to gather copies of the Koran and hold a public bonfire. The church's pastor said it was his intention to "send a message to Islam and the pushers of sharia law: that is not what we want." He burned a Koran and sent his message; riots in Afghanistan, which broke out in response, left ten people dead and eighty-three wounded.

President Barack Obama and New York Mayor Michael Bloomberg, among others, spoke out forcefully in support of First Amendment rights. They noted that many of the earliest European settlers had been motivated by a quest for the religious freedom they could not find at home. Part of the very genius of the American idea was that removing religion from the constitutional structure allowed religious beliefs of all kinds to flourish without provoking endless violence. Such voices did not seem to be getting the best of the argument. Obama himself was painted as, in effect, a *converso*, and possibly a backsliding one at that. The evangelist Franklin Graham remarked that Obama had been born from "the seed of Islam." In late summer of 2010, a CNN/Opinion Research Center poll found that 70 percent of Americans were opposed to the Cordoba House project.

The matter did not stop with Cordoba House. In November 2010, in Oklahoma, an amendment to the state constitution that would ban any consideration of sharia law in rulings by state-court judges won approval from 70 percent of all voters. The ballot initiative was quickly struck down by a federal judge, but legislators in a number of other states, including Arizona, Florida, South Carolina, and Utah, introduced bills to similarly restrict any use of sharia law. Frank Gaffney, the president of the Center for Security Policy and a supporter of such legislation, said, "I think you're seeing people coalesce around legislation of the kind that was passed in Oklahoma."

THE ONE TRUE PATH

Finally, there is the matter of moral certainty—the indispensable ingredient. Moral certainty ignites every inquisition and then feeds it with oxygen. One might argue that there's less moral certainty in the world today than there was fifty (or five hundred) years ago. The power of the Church is vastly diminished. The power of the great secular "isms"—communism, fascism—has dissipated. Moral certainty lacks the institutional base it once had. But as a personal matter—as what individuals actually believe—it is as pervasive as ever, even if certainties are in collision. Moral certainty underlies the idea of a "clash of civilizations" between Islam and the West. Surveys consistently find that a large proportion of Americans—about a third—believe the Bible to be unerringly true in all particulars—the "actual word of God" and something to be "taken literally." After authorizing the invasion of Iraq, President George W. Bush was asked if he had consulted his father, a former president, for advice as he weighed his decision. Bush answered that he had not—but that he had consulted "a higher power." For some, the higher power is not God per se but the forces of history, or democracy, or reason, or technology, or science, or a subset of science such as evolutionary psychology or genetics—and these people are no less certain in their convictions. Sometimes it's even hard to tell the various parties apart: one mutates into another in surprising ways. How different are the certainties of the ancients from those of the moderns? Writing in *The New Yorker* some years ago, Louis Menand posited the breakdown of traditional monotheism into "genetic polytheism," in which personal behavior is attributable to an individualized genetic pantheon. Where once there was a god of anger, now there is a gene of aggression. Where once there was a god of wine, now there is a gene of alcoholism. In ancient Greece, Phobos was the god of fear. Today he is gene SLC6A4, whose specific Olympian dwelling place is chromosome 17q12.

There's another way of looking at the certainty issue — by flipping it on its head. The presumption is now widespread, though rarely articulated in these terms, that a lack of certainty is unacceptable. It is the presumption that if we only knew enough, and paid enough attention, and applied sufficient resources, then ills of all kinds would disappear. Anti-terrorism measures are built on this assumption, and so new forms of search and surveillance are added continually to older ones. U.S. foreign policy has long been premised on the assumption that a threat to America anywhere is a threat to us everywhere. Though its proponents failed to consider that taking action entails as much uncertainty as taking no action, the policy of pre-emption, articulated by the Bush administration, was built on the proposition that uncertainty cannot be countenanced. The catalyzing moment was caught by the writer Ron Suskind, reporting on Vice President Dick Cheney:

Cheney listened intently, hard-eyed, clamped down tight. When the briefing finished, he said nothing for a moment. And then he was ready with his "different way."

"If there's a one percent chance that Pakistani scientists are helping al Qaeda build or develop a nuclear weapon, we have to treat it as a certainty in terms of our response," Cheney said. He paused to assess his declaration. "It's not about our analysis, or finding a preponderance of evidence," he added. "It's about our response."

So, now, spoken, it stood: a standard of action that would frame events and responses for years to come. The Cheney Doctrine. Even if there's just a one percent chance of the unimaginable coming due, act as if it is a certainty.

The Seventh Virtue

As I left the Inquisition archives on my last visit, Msgr. Cifres walked with me out the door and into the courtyard. We stood for a few moments near the fountain at its center. This is not one of Rome's exuberant, splashing fountains; it's subdued, perhaps slightly abashed. I looked around the courtyard to get my bearings. "Where was Giordano Bruno held?" I asked Cifres. He gestured with a wave of his arm to the eastern side of the palazzo. "All the prison cells were over there," he said, "but during the renovations in the 1920s, that wing was demolished and then rebuilt." The dungeons, it was felt, could be dispensed with. It is just a bureaucracy now. I asked Cifres about the Friends of the Inquisition Archives initiative — had that program gotten anywhere? No, he said, for some reason it had never found much traction. What can you do?

In the waning years of the Roman Empire, a lawyer-turned-littérateur named Aurelius Clemens Prudentius composed the epic poem *Psychomachia,* about a contest between good and evil. It eventually became popular, and in the Middle Ages influenced a number of better-known works, such as the morality play *Everyman* and the allegorical poem *Piers Ploughman.* It was Prudentius who developed the list of the "seven heavenly virtues" — which did battle in his epic with the "seven deadly vices." The first six of the heavenly virtues are charity, temperance, chastity, diligence, patience, and kindness. At the bottom of the list, appropriately enough, is humility. The "greatest of these," Paul observed of the core Christian virtues, is charity.

That is the standard view of all Christian denominations. It is a constant refrain of the Gospels and a central message of most religions. Stripped of divine sanction, it is a cherished secular value.

But if the first virtue, charity, summons us to our better natures, it is the seventh virtue, humility, that protects us from our baser ones. A few years ago, the political philosopher Michael Sandel published a small book called *The Case for Imperfection*. Its ostensible focus is on genetic engineering and other scientific methods for ensuring that the human beings who walk the planet are as good as they can be—as close to perfect as we can make them. But the larger purpose is to raise a question: Is perfection even desirable? Yes, of course, it is a worthy goal to diminish disease, incapacity, and other afflictions. But the quest for perfection goes well beyond such efforts, even as we disagree on what "perfection" actually means.

More to the point, Sandel asks, shouldn't we pause to consider the contribution that imperfection makes to the betterment of the human condition? Our individual qualities and flaws are distributed unevenly. For now, they are also distributed randomly. We deserve neither full credit for what is good about ourselves nor full blame for what is bad. No one does. This aleatory quality—each of us in some sense represents a throw of nature's dice—has important consequences. Rightly understood, it puts a premium on what we do have in common: to begin with, our moral equality as beings, regardless of specific attributes. Because all of us come up short in some dimension, it conduces to tolerance. "One of the blessings of seeing ourselves as creatures of nature, God, or fortune is that we are not wholly responsible for the way we are," Sandel writes. "The more alive we are to the chanced nature of our lot, the more reason we have to share our fate with others."

The Inquisition—any inquisition—is the product of a contrary way of seeing things. It takes root and thrives when moral inequality is perceived between one party and everyone else. Inquisitions invite members of one group—national, religious, corporate, political—to sit in judgment on members of another: to think of themselves, in a sense, as God's jury. Fundamentally, the inquisitorial impulse arises from some vision of the ultimate good, some conviction about ultimate truth, some confidence in the quest for perfectibility, and some certainty about the path to the desired place — and about whom to blame for obstacles in the way.

These are powerful inducements. Isaiah Berlin warned against them:

> To make mankind just and happy and creative and harmonious forever — what could be too high a price to pay for that? To make such an omelette, there is surely no limit to the number of eggs that should be broken — that was the faith of Lenin, of Trotsky, of Mao, for all I know, of Pol Pot. Since I know the only true path to the ultimate solution of the problems of society, I know which way to drive the human caravan; and since you are ignorant of what I know, you cannot be allowed to have liberty of choice even within the narrowest limits, if the goal is to be reached. You declare that a given policy will make you happier, or freer, or give you room to breathe; but I know that you are mistaken, I know what you need, what all men need; and if there is resistance based on ignorance or malevolence, then it must be broken and hundreds of thousands may have to perish to make millions happy for all time. What choice have we, who have the knowledge, but to be willing to sacrifice them all?

This way of thinking is not new. We would have encountered one version of it during the Medieval Inquisition, another during the French Revolution. Modernity itself is not the culprit, but it is an accomplice. It transforms an impulse into a process.

Some ills have cures of a conventional kind. We can change a law, tweak a regulation, implement a program. The inquisitorial impulse is impervious to such interventions. Legal restrictions can always be finessed (and the Inquisition itself, in any case, was always "legal"). The capacities of surveillance are heading in one direction only, regardless of what any law might say. No matter what happens to the nation-state, bureaucracies are permanent and ever more pervasive. They operate with more autonomy every day.

I think often of that conversation with Francisco Bethencourt, when he explained that what ultimately sent the Inquisition into decline (we were talking specifically about the Spanish and Roman Inquisitions) was something that had no physical existence at all: the slow advance of Enlightenment notions of tolerance, freedom of conscience, and freedom of expression. Enlightenment and Inquisition have faced off against each other in countless ways over centuries, but I came across a small, symbolic example one afternoon at the British Library. I had gone there to look at Bernard Gui's *Liber Sententiarum* — his *Book of Sentences* — but affixed to the front of the manuscript was a sheaf of eighteenth-century correspondence bearing on how the manuscript had come into the library's hands. The philosopher John Locke had played a central role; he came across the manuscript in the south of France, alerted the historian Philipp van Limborch to its existence, and eventually managed to find a buyer for it. "When you see what it contains," Locke wrote to Limborch, "I think you will agree with us that it ought to see the light. For it contains authentic records of things done in that rude age which have either been forgotten or purposefully misrepresented." Locke's ideas about religious toleration turned on the very idea of uncertainty: human beings can't know for sure which truths are "true," and in any case, attempting to compel belief only leads to trouble.

Tolerance and free expression did not spread everywhere, or at the same pace anywhere. Locke's contemporary, Jonathan Swift, published much of his most acerbic writing anonymously, fully aware of the potential consequences if his authorship became known. (Even so, he was denied ecclesiastical preferment in England, and shunted off to a sinecure in Dublin.) But the gradually accruing power of an idea that takes hold can have all the force of physical reality.

The philosopher John Searle has written about this in several of his books — he calls the process "the construction of social reality." It's easy enough to see how aspects of the physical world come to be accepted as givens: rock is hard; water flows downhill; death comes to us all. It is less easy to understand how social conventions — for instance, that the slips of paper known as money possess value — come to enjoy the same universal acceptance. But they do. Some of them are more durable than the tangible world itself. Societies change from one political form into another; civilizations crumble into dust; new technologies transform ordinary life from one generation to the next — but certain agreed-upon ways of thinking live on. The notion that one can own pieces of the physical world — private property — has sunk in deeply. So has the very idea of "rights."

Inquisitions have a tangible component and a notional component. On the one hand, there are the laws, the bureaucracies, the surveillance, the data-gathering, the ways of meting out punishment and applying force. One can imagine "reforms," "restrictions," "guidelines," and "safeguards" in all these areas, to keep abuses in check. Some already exist, to limited effect. Individuals and organizations all around the world are engaged in efforts to enact legal curbs of one kind or another. I wish them well.

On the other hand, there is the idea that some single course is right, that we can ascertain what it is, and that we should take all necessary measures to compel everyone in that direction. Samuel Johnson once remarked of someone he knew that the man "seems to me to possess but one idea, and that is a wrong one." The drafters of the U.S. Constitution — fearful of rule by one opinion, whether the tyrant's or the mob's — created a governmental structure premised on the idea that human beings are fallible, fickle, and unreliable, and sometimes to be feared. Triumphalist rhetoric about the Constitution ignores the skeptical view of human nature that underlies it. The Church itself, in its more sober teachings on certitude and doubt, has always raised a red flag: Human beings are fallen creatures. Certitude can be a snare. Doubt can be a helping hand. Consider a list of theologians who have found themselves targets of the Holy Office — Teilhard de Chardin, John Courtney Murray, Yves Congar — only to be "surrounded with a bright halo of enthusiasm" at some later point, as Cardinal Avery Dulles once put it. When the Church says it has "no fear of historical truth," the point it should be trying to convey is this: it has no fear because if historical truth demonstrates anything, it is that we will keep taking the wrong path — and to acknowledge that fact keeps us on the right one. Humility is the Counter-Inquisition's most effective ally. It can't be legislated, but it can come to be embraced.

Passing from the courtyard of the Holy Office and back through the heavy studded doors, I turned around for a look at the façade. Pope Pius V, who built the palazzo, had put a bold inscription there — in effect, the Inquisition's mission statement. Translated from the Latin, the inscription declared: "Pius V Pontifex Maximus constructed this home for the Holy Inquisition in 1569 as a bulwark of the Catholic faith, in order that adherents of heretical depravity might be utterly restrained."

I noticed for the first time that the inscription is in fact no longer there. The marble scroll on which it was placed has been scraped and polished, shorn of any words at all. French troops, I later learned, had removed the inscription during Napoleon's occupation. The marble today looks shiny but unnatural, like skin that has burned and then healed. Some things can be erased. Some things cannot be. And some things shouldn't be. In this instance, I was grateful for the attempt, and grateful for the scar.

ACKNOWLEDGMENTS

God's Jury has evolved and matured during the course of more than a decade, and owes a debt to many people. Chief among them are the historians who gave generously of their time and their guidance. They include Francisco Bethencourt, Eamon Duffy, Carlo Ginzburg, Peter Godman, Henry Kamen, David Kertzer, Emmanuel Le Roy Ladurie, William Monter, Edward Peters, and John Tedeschi. Msgr. Alejandro Cifres, who oversees the Inquisition archives at the Vatican, was unfailingly helpful. I am also grateful to many Jesuit friends and Catholic theologians who offered assistance and perspective along the way, and in certain cases provided insights drawn from personal experience of unhappy interactions with the authorities in Rome.

Over the years I have discussed aspects of this book, sometimes sharing drafts of work in progress, with a wide circle of people who have particular knowledge or particular judgment: Karen Barkey, Mark Bowden, Fredric Cheyette, Lawrence Douglas, Paul Elie, James Fallows, David Friend, Robert D. Kaplan, Corby Kummer, Toby Lester, Gail Kern Paster, Tom Ricks, Philippe Sands, Eric Schlosser, Benjamin Schwarz, Clive Stafford Smith, Scott Stossel, Doug Stumpf, Charles Trueheart, Alan Wolfe, and Robert Wright. In a category by themselves are the three editors I've had the privilege of working for as *God's Jury* took shape: William Whitworth and the late Michael Kelly at *The Atlantic Monthly*, and Graydon Carter at *Vanity Fair*.

Finally, I would like to thank those involved in making the book itself: Andrea Schulz, my editor at Houghton Mifflin Harcourt; the late Peter Davison, who encouraged the idea for this book to begin with; Anton Mueller, who got the idea off the ground; Martha Spaulding, a longtime friend and colleague, who has copyedited virtually every word I've written for more than thirty years; Raphael Sagalyn, my friend and agent over that same period of time; the illustrator Edward Sorel, another friend and frequent collaborator; and Cullen Nutt, who has served ably in the role of both researcher and sounding board. Special thanks are due to my assistant, Keenan Mayo, and to the staff of the Boston Athenaeum, where significant portions of this book took form.

My wife, Anna Marie, always the first and best reader, has subjected *God's Jury* to her typical "*rigoroso esamine,*" and it is to her that the book is dedicated.

NOTES

1. Standard Operating Procedure

page

1   *"No one goes in"*: Chadwick, *Catholicism and History*, p. 89. The archivist was Msgr. Francesco Rosi-Bernardini.

    "Theology, sir": Miller, *The Crucible*, p. 67.

2   *in the words of the Apostolic Constitution*: Apostolic Constitution (*Pastor bonus*), translated by Francis C. C. Felly, James H. Provost, and Michel Thériault. Canadian Conference of Catholic Bishops, 1998.

    plenty of rulings of its own: Congregation for the Doctrine of the Faith, "Instruction *Dignitas Personae* on Certain Bioethical Questions," September 8, 2008; Congregation for the Doctrine of the Faith, "Considerations Regarding Proposals to Give Legal Recognition to Unions Between Homosexual Persons," June 3, 2003; "Vatican Tells Parishes Not to Open Archives to LDS Church," *Catholic News Agency*, May 7, 2008; Congregation for the Doctrine of the Faith, "Declaration on the Unicity and Salvific Universality of Jesus Christ and the Church—*Dominus Jesus*," August 6, 2000.

3   *Holocaust-denying bishop*: Peter Walker, "Profile: Richard Williamson," *Guardian*, February 25, 2009.

    use of condoms: Richard Owen, "Pope Says Condoms Are Not the Solution to AIDS—They Make It Worse," *The Times* (London), March 17, 2009.

    indigenous peoples: Gina Doggett, "Pope Once Again in Damage Control Mode," Agence France Presse, May 23, 2007.

    once introduced the visiting Ratzinger: Peter Steinfels, "Cardinal Is Seen as Kind, if Firm, Monitor of Faith," *New York Times*, February 1, 1988.

    a Ratzinger fan site: http://www.popebenedictxvifanclub.com/faq.html.

4   *so that work could be completed*: Pastor, *History of the Popes*, vol. 17, p. 289.

    When I first set foot: My first visit to the Archivio della Congregazione per la Dottrina della Fede took place in 2000. It was followed by visits in 2001, 2004, and 2010. The account here and elsewhere in this book is based on all four visits and on conversations on each occasion with Msgr. Alejandro Cifres Giménez, the director of the archives.

    vast underground bunker: Richard Owen, "The Vatican Offers a Glimpse of Its Most Secret Archives," *The Times* (London), January 8, 2010.

5 *the convenience of modern historians:* Chadwick, *Catholicism and History*, p. 9.

6 *"some pleasant surprises":* Bruce Johnston, "Vatican to Open Up Inquisition Archives," *Daily Telegraph*, January 12, 1998.

7 *"No one expects":* "The Spanish Inquisition," *Monty Python's Flying Circus*, series 2, episode 15.

Mel Brooks dance number: History of the World: Part 1 (1981), produced, written, and directed by Mel Brooks.

"comedy is tragedy plus time": Crimes and Misdemeanors (1989), written and directed by Woody Allen.

Cokie Roberts was asked: Good Morning America, December 3, 1998.

media scrutiny of Sarah Palin's record: "Fox Special Report with Brit Hume," September 2, 2008.

captains of finance who were summoned to testify: Stanley Bing, "The Inquisition Convenes in Washington," Fortune.com., January 12, 2010.

8 *"I had to learn who Torquemada was":* 20/20, ABC News, November 25, 1998.

singling out Bobby: "The Visible Vidal," *Gay and Lesbian Review Worldwide*, vol. 17, no. 2, March 2010.

criticizing the tactics: Taki, "Rats and Heroes," *The Spectator*, 15/22 December, 2001.

writing about the sex-abuse scandal: Maureen Dowd, "Should There Be an Inquisition for the Pope?," *New York Times*, March 31, 2010.

continued . . . for seven hundred years: The brief summary that follows of three main phases of the Inquisition is based on a variety of sources, including Lea, *A History of the Inquisition of the Middle Ages*; Kamen, *The Spanish Inquisition*; Lea, *A History of the Inquisition of Spain*; Bethencourt, *The Inquisition*; Black, *The Italian Inquisition*; and Peters, *Inquisition*.

9 *the only Belgian song ever to hit No. 1:* Rachel Helyer Donaldson, "New Film Tells Tragic Story of the Singing Nun," *The First Post*, April 29, 2009.

shortage of combustible material: Kamen, *The Spanish Inquisition*, p. 213.

10 *the victim was a Spanish schoolmaster:* Lea, *A History of the Inquisition of Spain*, vol. 4, p. 461.

11 *pressing to have Queen Isabella declared a saint:* Isambard Wilkinson, "Spain Seeks Sainthood for Isabella," *Daily Telegraph*, April 23, 2003.

a fertile recruiting ground for bishops and cardinals: Bethencourt, *The Inquisition*, p. 136.

12 *"No death certificate has ever been issued":* William Monter, "The Inquisition," in Hsia, ed., *Companion to the Reformation World*.

the rise of a metaphorical Inquisition: Peters, *Inquisition*. The subject occupies much of the book, but see in particular pp. 189–262, 296–315.

13 *cited the Inquisition in his summation:* Robert H. Jackson, "Summation for the Prosecution," International Military Tribunal, July 26, 1946.

the Grand Inquisitor delivers a scathing indictment: Dostoyevsky, *The Brothers Karamazov*, pp. 248–262.

14 *He heard nothing for nearly twenty years:* The details of this episode are recounted in a letter to the author from Carlo Ginzburg, February 25, 2001.

15 *"Naturally," said a Vatican official:* Anne Jacobson Schutte, "Palazzo del Sant'Uffizio: The Opening of the Roman Inquisition's Central Archive," *Perspectives*, American Historical Association, May 1999.

"We know all the sins of the Church": Alessandra Stanley, "Vatican Is Investigating the Inquisition, in Secret," *New York Times*, October 31, 1998.

by two conclaves of Inquisition scholars: The account, here and elsewhere, of the conferences that marked the opening of the archives is based on conversations with people who attended, among them John Tedeschi, Eamon Duffy, and William Monter.

John Paul asked the historians: "Vatican Prepares Apology for Inquisition," Agence France Presse, November 1, 1998.

deeds done by the followers of the Church: Francis A. Sullivan, "The Papal Apology," *America*, April 8, 2000.

17 *Doubt occupies an oddly exalted status:* J. B. Nugent, "Doubt," *New Catholic Encyclopedia*, pp. 883–884.

a placard over the doorway: Chadwick, *Catholicism and History*, p. 135.

18 *Greene's work came under intense Vatican scrutiny:* Peter Godman, "Graham Greene's Vatican Dossier," *Atlantic Monthly*, July/August 2001.

I came across two polished wooden boxes: Images of the card catalogues are presented in Cifres and Pizzo, *Rari e Preziosi*, pp. 142–145.

the very document that abolished the Index: "Abolizione dell'Indice dei libri prohibiti," *L'Osservatore Romano*, June 15, 1966.

Cardinal Ratzinger . . . raised an eyebrow: Elisabeth Rosenthal, "Don't Count Pope Among Harry Potter Fans," *New York Times*, July 16, 2003.

19 *"Very well, Potter":* Rowling, *Harry Potter and the Order of the Phoenix*, p. 631.

"an eye that never slumbered": Prescott, *History of the Reign of Philip II*, p. 362.

20 *"the real scandal isn't what's illegal . . .":* Edwin Diamond, "The Kinsley Report," *New York Magazine*, August 4, 1986.

presented with a copy of his confession: Harry Fiss, "The Interpreter," *New York Times Magazine*, May 2, 1999.

22 *adopted as his motto:* "Religion: The Cardinal's Setback," *Time*, November 23, 1962.

an influential study: Moore, *Formation of a Persecuting Society*. Moore argues that the persecution of a variety of groups in medieval Europe reflected a systemic social outlook.

23 *"the very fabric of reality":* Given, *Inquisition and Medieval Society*, p. 214.

a Franciscan inquisitor once confided: James B. Given, "The Inquisitors of Languedoc and the Medieval Technology of Power," *American Historical Review*, vol. 24, no. 2 (April 1989), pp. 336–359.

"We persecuted the seeds of evil": Dietrich von Niem, *On Schism*, quoted in Peters, *Inquisition*, p. 303.

2. A Stake in the Ground

25 *"scuttling about in hiding like crabs":* Pope Gregory IX, from the decretal *Ille humani generis*, in Peters, *Heresy and Authority in Medieval Europe*, pp. 196–198.

"You, so and so": Gui, *The Inquisitor's Guide*, p. 176.

26 *like other dualists, the Cathars believed:* The general account here of Cathar beliefs and the Albigensian Crusade is drawn from a number of sources, notably Le Roy Ladurie, *Montaillou*, pp. viii–xi; Lea, *A History of the Inquisition of the Middle Ages*, vol. 1, pp. 89–208; Peters, *Heresy and Authority in Medieval Europe*, pp. 103–107. Full-length recent accounts of the crusade include Weiss, *The Yellow Cross*, and O'Shea, *The Perfect Heresy*. Specific references are cited accordingly.

27 *Their name may come from the Greek:* O'Shea, *The Perfect Heresy*, p. 270. The derivation of the name remains a matter of some debate.

The most zealous adherents . . . Ordinary Cathars: Le Roy Ladurie, *Montaillou*, pp. viii–xi; Costen, *The Cathars and the Albigensian Crusade*, p. 76.

28 *the romantic quest continues to animate:* See, for instance, *The Treasure of Montségur*, by Sophy Burnham (HarperCollins, 2002), and *The Judas Apocalypse*, by Dan McNeil (Publish Press, 2008).

29 *Specific moments, recorded by the inquisitors:* Oldenbourg, *Massacre at Montségur*, pp. 356–364.

"crushed the head of the dragon": Lea, *A History of the Inquisition of the Middle Ages*, vol. 2, p. 43.

30 *"lower than God but higher than man":* Tierney, *The Crisis of Church and State, 1050–1300*, p. 128.

31 *"They gave the finger":* Gui, *The Inquisitor's Guide*, p. 9.

Several years later, Pope Lucius III: Peters, *Inquisition*, p. 47.

"Forward, then, most valiant soldiers of Christ!": Lea, *A History of the Inquisition of the Middle Ages*, vol. 1, p. 152.

as the geographer David Harvey once noted: The point is made in Harvey, *The Condition of Postmodernity*. Quoted in Cullen Murphy, "Feudal Gestures," *Atlantic Monthly*, October 2003.

pronounced an anathema against his enemies: "Dr. Ayman al-Zawahiri: The Path of Doom," Arabic-language video released on August 27, 2009. Transcript available at www.nefafoundation.org.

32 *in a public statement soon after the 9/11 attacks:* Manuel Perez-Rivas, "Bush Vows to Rid World of 'Evil-doers,'" CNN.com, September 16, 2001.

painted the words: Jeff Sharlet, "Jesus Killed Mohammed," *Harper's*, May 2009.

recounted a prayer session: Robert D. Kaplan, "Five Days in Fallujah," *Atlantic Monthly*, July/August 2004.

made reference to a Muslim warlord: "U.S. Is 'Battling Satan,' Says General," BBC News, October 17, 2003; William M. Arkin, "The Pentagon Unleashes a Holy Warrior," *Los Angeles Times*, October 16, 2003.

ended a speech . . . with these words: Ricardo Sanchez, "Military Reporters and Editors Luncheon Address," Washington, D.C., October 12, 2007.

33 *you'll frequently come across this injunction:* The T-shirts are available online from many retailers, including the California-based company Special Forces Gear (http://www.specialforces.com/store/customer/home.php).

first attributed to a papal legate: Sumption, *The Albigensian Crusade*, p. 93; O'Shea, *The Perfect Heresy*, p. 85.

a hundred men from the nearby town of Bram: O'Shea, *The Perfect Heresy*, p. 106; Pegg, *A Most Holy War*, pp. 100, 109; Sumption, *The Albigensian Crusade*, pp. 111, 128–129.

34 *The inquisitorial process had a long history:* The general account here of the origins and conduct of the *inquisitio* is drawn from a number of sources, including Lea, *A History of the Inquisition of the Middle Ages*, vol. 1, pp. 399–429; Given, *Inquisition and Medieval Society*, pp. 5–22; Peters, *Heresy and Authority in Medieval Europe*, pp. 189–215; Peters, *Inquisition*, pp. 12–67; and Baldini and Spruitt, *Catholic Church and Modern Science*, pp. 34–38. Other specific references are cited accordingly.

did not need to wait for someone to file a complaint: Given, *Inquisition and Medieval Society*, p. 22.

35 *Traveling light . . . set about conducting trials:* Peters, *Inquisition*, pp. 58–59.
    inquisitors in the Lauragais region: Pegg, *The Corruption of Angels*, p. 3.

36 *a man named Arnaud Sicre:* Le Roy Ladurie, *Montaillou*, p. 286.
    medieval words for some distances: Hackett, *World Eras*, vol. 4, *Medieval Europe*, pp. 126–128.
    Politically the continent was fractured: Given, *Inquisition and Medieval Society*, p. 16–17.

37 *local folkways of yesteryear were very much alive:* See, for instance, Thomas, *Religion and the Decline of Magic*. Also Jacques Le Goff, "Culture clericale et traditions folkloriques dans la civilization merovingienne," *Annales* 22 (1967), pp. 780–791.
    his beliefs regarding the dead: Le Roy Ladurie, *Montaillou*, p. 348.
    "feelings of alienation" and "expanded curiosity": Edward Peters, "Notes Toward an Archeology of Boredom," *Social Research* vol. 42, no. 3 (1975), pp. 493–511.

38 *The papal chanceries become busier and busier:* Blouin, ed., *Vatican Archives*, p. xviii.
    a trial in Venice, held at the Basilica of San Marco: John T. Noonan, "Gratian Slept Here: The Changing Identity of the Father of the Systematic Study of Canon Law," *Traditio* 35 (1979): 145–172.

39 *the parable of the wedding banquet:* Gospel According to Luke, 14:23.
    an injunction to deal with heresy by brute force: Garry Wills, "Augustine's Hippo: Power Relations (410–417), *Arion*, vol. 7, no. 1 (Spring–Summer 1999), pp. 98–119.
    At the Council of Tarragona: John H. Arnold, "Lollard Trials and Inquisitorial Discourse," in Given-Wilson, ed., *Fourteenth Century England II*, p. 83.
    standards of what is acceptable are gradually eroded: Daniel Patrick Moynihan, "Defining Deviancy Down," *American Spectator*, vol. 62, no. 1 (Winter 1993), pp. 17–30.

40 *pamphlet prepared by the U.S. Army:* "How to Spot a Communist," U.S. First Army, 1955. (http://www.niu.edu/~rfeurer/labor/How%20to%20Spot%20a%20Communist.pdf.) The Pentagon withdrew the pamphlet after the American Civil Liberties Union objected to its content.
    interrogated at Philadelphia International Airport: "Lawsuit Claims Pomona College Student Was Detained by TSA over Arabic Flashcards," *Los Angeles Times*, February 10, 2010.

41 *some 75 million pages of records:* Mary Williams Walsh, "Who Owns the Nazi Paper Trail?" *Los Angeles Times*, June 30, 1994.
    the first generation of IBM punch-card systems: The story is told at length in Black, *IBM and the Holocaust*.
    To give some idea of the scale: Given, *Inquisition and Medieval Society*, p. 25.
    consider a household item . . . the desk dictionary: Paul Luna, "Not Just Another Pretty Face: The Contribution of Typography to Lexicography," *Dictionary Design*, February 18, 2009.

42 *to prove his claim to the overlordship of Scotland:* Given, *Inquisition and Medieval Society*, p. 34.
    inquisitors were more practical and inventive . . . easy cross-referencing: The revolution in the technology of documentation is considered at length in Given, *Inquisition and Medieval Society*, pp. 25–51.

43 *Bonet was caught in a lie. . . . "tedious frequency":* Given, *Inquisition and Medieval Society*, p. 39.
    instruction manuals . . . conduct interrogations: Given, *Inquisition and Medieval Society*, p. 46.

44 *Eco continues, describing the inquisitor's bearing:* Eco, *The Name of the Rose*, pp. 369–370.

rose rapidly . . . burned in public: Gui, *The Inquisitor's Guide*, p. 8.

45 *Over a period of fifteen years:* James Given, "A Medieval Inquisitor at Work," in Cohn and Epstein, eds., *Portraits of Medieval and Renaissance Living*, pp. 207–232.

which now resides in the British Library: M.A.E. Nickson, "Locke and the Inquisition of Toulouse," *British Museum Quarterly*, vol. 36, no. 3/4 (Autumn 1972), pp. 83–92.

It begins with a list . . . Then come the details: British Library, Add. MS. 4697.

Some of the accused . . . more than forty of the living: Given, *Inquisition and Medieval Society*, p. 69.

An itemized accounting of expenses: Lea, *A History of the Inquisition of the Middle Ages*, vol. 1, p. 553.

46 *This sort of moral delicacy . . . During the past decade:* "Fact Sheet: Extraordinary Rendition," American Civil Liberties Union, December 6, 2005.

a Canadian citizen, Maher Arar: Jane Mayer, "Outsourcing Torture," *The New Yorker*, February 14, 2005. See also Stephen Grey, "The Agonizing Truth About CIA Renditions," *Salon*, November 5, 2007.

A throng would gather: Lea, *A History of the Inquisition of the Middle Ages*, vol. 1, pp. 391–393.

47 *Gui's most productive day:* Given, *Inquisition and Medieval Society*, p. 75.

Gui was a prodigious writer: Gui, *The Inquisitor's Guide*, p. 14.

Out of this decree grew a modest confession industry: Given, *Inquisition and Medieval Society*, p. 45.

The notion of a "slippery slope": Mario Rizzo and Glen Whitman, "The Camel's Nose Is in the Tent: Rules, Theories and Slippery Slopes," *UCLA Law Review* vol. 51, no. 2 (2003), pp. 539–592. See also Eugene Volokh and David Newman, "In Defense of the Slippery Slope," *Legal Affairs*, March–April 2003.

48 *One English essayist recalls:* Charles Moore, "The Spectator's Notes," *Spectator*, February 19, 2011.

The Dominicans preached everywhere . . . As one historian concludes: M. Michele Mulcahey, "*Summae Inquisitorum* and the Art of Disputation: How the Early Dominican Order Trained Its Inquisitors," in *Praedicatores, Inquisitores*, Acts of the 1st International Seminar on the Dominicans and the Inquisition, 2002, pp. 145–156.

49 *its members came to be known:* Edward Peters, "Quoniam abundavit iniquitas: Dominicans as Inquisitors, Inquisitors as Dominicans," *Catholic Historical Review*, vol. 91, no. 1 (2005), pp. 105–121.

"just as all diseases": Gui, *The Inquisitor's Guide*, p. 31.

"It must be noted": Gui, *The Inquisitor's Guide*, p. 71.

50 *granted wide latitude to inquisitors:* Lea, *A History of the Inquisition of the Middle Ages*, vol. 1, pp. 424–429.

Half a millennium later: Joseph Abrams, "Despite Reports, Khalid Sheikh Mohammed Was Not Waterboarded 183 Times," Fox News, April 28, 2009.

current and historical interrogation practices: Educing Information, Intelligence Science Board, National Defense Intelligence College, Washington, D.C., 2006.

51 *It warns interrogators:* FM 2-22.3. *Human Intelligence Collector Operations*, Department of the Army, 2006, section 9-6.

he might sit with a large stack of documents: Morellet, *Abrege du Manuel des Inquisiteurs*, pp. 100–101.

"file and dossier approach": FM 2-22.3, section 8–15.

Another technique suggested by Eymerich: Morellet, *Manuel des Inquisiteurs*, p. 99.

52 *when the interrogator senses the source is vulnerable*: FM 2-22.3 section 8-17.

Another way to break the impasse: Morellet, *Manuel des Inquisiteurs*, p. 102.

"rapid-fire interrogation": FM 2-22.3, section 8-16.

Eymerich writes a script: Morellet, *Manuel des Inquisiteurs*, p. 101.

53 *the "emotional-futility" approach*: FM 2-22.3, section 8-13, 8-14.

torture techniques developed very early: Guilaine and Zammit, *The Origins of War*, pp. 56–60.

"Torture him, how?": Aristophanes, *The Frogs*, lines 624–628.

Mexican drug cartel: Anderson Cooper 360 Degrees, CNN, March 26, 2009.

54 *Torture had been used . . . clear and definitive end point*: Peters, *Torture*, pp. 40–46.

56 *laid down more rules than civil magistrates did*: This was true for the Medieval, Spanish, and Roman Inquisitions. See, for instance, Peters, *Inquisition*, p. 92; Kamen, *The Spanish Inquisition*, p. 172; and Pérez, *The Spanish Inquisition*, pp. 146–147.

if inquisitors absolved one another: Peters, *Torture*, p. 236.

"mature and careful deliberation": Lea, *History of the Inquisition of the Middle Ages*, vol. 1, p. 424.

"intensely moral places": Michael Ignatieff, "The Truth About Torture," *New Republic*, December 9, 1985.

57 *"I'd cut down every law"*: Bolt, A Man For All Seasons, p. 66.

The landscape of Montaillou: Weiss, *The Yellow Cross*, pp. 21–23.

58 *The inquisitor was Jacques Fournier*: The particulars of the investigation and the history of Fournier's Register are concisely laid out in Le Roy Ladurie, *Montaillou*, pp. vii–xvii.

Bernard Gui showed up to watch: Le Roy Ladurie, *Montaillou*, p. xiii.

59 *"rock star" . . . compared his youthful looks*: Cantor, *Inventing the Middle Ages*, p. 165.

60 *the fingernails of the dead*: Le Roy Ladurie, Montaillou, p. 31.

a night of passion: Le Roy Ladurie, *Montaillou*, p. 159.

a pithily nihilistic philosopher: Le Roy Ladurie, *Montaillou*, p. 171.

61 *In Lent, toward vespers*: Le Roy Ladurie, *Montaillou*, pp. 8–9.

Ms. Lewinsky called Ms. Currie: Starr, *The Starr Report*, p. 126.

62 *Straight away I made love*: Le Roy Ladurie, *Montaillou*, p. 167.

At the White House: Starr, *The Starr Report*, pp. 66–68.

When Pierre Clergue: Le Roy Ladurie, *Montaillou*, p. 173.

She also showed him an email: Starr, *The Starr Report*, p. 108.

64 *Papal inquisitors were involved*: Read, *The Templars*, pp. 265–266.

"according to ecclesiastical constitutions": Read, *The Templars*, p. 290; Barber, *The Trial of the Templars*, p. 198.

3. Queen of Torments

65 *The most ardent defenders of justice*: Kamen, *The Spanish Inquisition*, p. 163.

"I wish to interrogate him!": Rowling, *Harry Potter and the Order of the Phoenix*, p. 745.

In Leonard Bernstein's version: Candide (1956), lyrics by Richard Wilbur and John Latouche.

66 *the final justice of God:* Maureen Flynn, "Mimesis of the Last Judgment: The Spanish Auto de Fe," *Sixteenth Century Journal,* vol. 22, no. 2 (1991), pp. 281–297.

The living prisoners wore: Anderson, *Daily Life During the Spanish Inquisition,* pp. 73–74.

the scene in Seville . . . carried off by plague: The events surrounding the first auto-da-fé of the Spanish Inquisition are described in a number of sources, including Roth, *The Spanish Inquisition,* pp. 41–46; Lea, *A History of the Inquisition of Spain,* vol. 1, pp. 163–164; Kamen, *The Spanish Inquisition,* p. 47.

Hojeda produced a report: Pérez, *The Spanish Inquisition,* p. 19.

67 *an American tourist named Aaron Stigman:* Henry Roth, "The Surveyor," *The New Yorker,* August 6, 1966.

"They'd have me burned at the stake": Coulter, *Godless: The Church of Liberalism,* p. 184.

it enjoyed the positive reinforcement: Lea, *A History of the Inquisition of the Middle Ages,* vol. 1, p. 223.

brought on by heat stroke: http://www.stjoancenter.com/topics/Death_by_Heat_Stroke.html

68 *might die from smoke inhalation:* Merritt M. Birky and Frederic B. Clarke, "Inhalation of Toxic Products From Fires," *Bulletin of the New York Academy of Medicine,* vol. 57, no. 10 (December 1981), 997–1013.

the simple act of breathing: Bruce M. Achauer, M.D., et al., "Pulmonary Complications of Burns," *Annals of Surgery,* vol. 177, no. 3 (March 1973), pp. 311–319.

exhausted the available oxygen: James B. Terrill, et al., "Toxic Gases From Fires," *Science,* vol. 200, no. 23 (June 1978), pp. 1343–1347.

catastrophic damage to nerves and tissue: Prahlow, *Forensic Pathology,* pp. 488, 496; Robert R. Frantz, "Firestorms and Wildfires," in Hogan and Burstein, eds., *Disaster Medicine,* p. 230.

Michael Servetus . . . endured a lingering death: Lawrence and Nancy Goldstone, *Out of the Flames,* pp. 3–4.

a bag of gunpowder: John Tedeschi, "A New Perspective on the Roman Inquisition," in Bujanda, *Le Controle des Idées à la Renaissance,* pp. 25–26.

solicitation of sex by clergy: A detailed recent study of the subject, based on the records of more than 200 cases heard by tribunals of the Spanish Inquisition, is Stephen Haliczer's *Sexuality in the Confessional.*

69 *constituting perhaps 2 percent of the population:* Population figures as a whole for this period are inexact, and establishing the size of subpopulations is problematic. Estimates of the Jewish population as a percentage of the Spanish population tend to vary between 1 and 3 percent. See Gitlitz, *Secrecy and Deceit,* pp. 73–74; Kamen, *The Spanish Inquisition,* p. 8.

the etymology is not certain: Netanyahu, *The Marranos of Spain,* p. 59 (fn 153).

a vast computerized database: The scholars who have compiled the database are Gustav Henningsen, Jaime Contreras, and Jean-Pierre Dedieu. See William Monter, "The Inquisition," in Hsia, ed., *A Companion to the Reformation World,* pp. 255–271.

systematic about censorship: Peters, *Inquisition,* pp. 95–96.

70 *a Spanish censor at work:* "A Censored Second Folio," *Folger,* Spring 2011; Sidney Lee, "Shakespeare and the Inquisition," in Boas, ed., *Elizabethan and Other Essays,* pp. 184–195.

under the monarchy's control: Peters, *Inquisition*, p. 97.

71 *a new Grand Mosque of Granada:* Charles M. Sennott, "Seeking Madrid motives in a cradle of Muslim glory," *Boston Globe,* March 28, 2004.

more than 600 mosques . . . Iberia as a whole: Anthony Celso, "The Tragedy of Al-Andalus: The Madrid Terror Attacks and the Islamicization of Spanish Politics," *Mediterranean Quarterly,* vol. 16, no. 3, pp. 86–101. See also Victoria Burnett, "Spain's Many Muslims Face Dearth of Mosques," *New York Times,* March 16, 2008.

the 2004 Madrid train bombings: "The 3/11 Madrid Bombings: An Assessment After 5 Years," International Security Studies Program, Woodrow Wilson International Center for Scholars, April 10, 2009.

"They have a grander vision": Charles M. Sennott, "Seeking Madrid motives in a cradle of Muslim glory," *Boston Globe,* March 28, 2004.

Spanish bishops turned down a request: Elizabeth Nash, "Spanish bishops fear rebirth of Islamic kingdom," *The Independent,* January 5, 2007.

a campaign to remove the word "mosque": Rachel Donadio, "Debate Over a Monument's Name Echoes a Historic Clash of Faiths," *New York Times,* November 4, 2010.

Had this battle gone differently: Gibbon is quoted in Menocal, *The Ornament of the World,* pp. 55–56.

72 *an itinerant cobbler from Montaillou:* Le Roy Ladurie, *Montaillou,* p. 296; Weiss, *The Yellow Cross,* p. 290.

disagree on just how cordial: For a recent account see Menocal, *The Ornament of the World.*

"a relationship between unequals": Kamen, *The Spanish Inquisition,* p. 4.

you'll hear the claim made: Alan S. Kaye, "Two Alleged Arabic Etymologies," *Journal of Near Eastern Studies,* vol. 64, no. 2 (2005), pp. 109–111.

Josef Ratzinger on the cover of the magazine: Peter Seewald, "Dios tiene un agudo sentido del humor," *El Semanal,* February 18, 2001.

73 *at a meeting in the Alhambra:* Kamen, *The Spanish Inquisition,* p. 31.

"In our land": Sachar, *Farewell España,* p. 70.

In England, Jews were considered royal property: Mundill, *The King's Jews,* pp. xi, 12, 72–74, 146.

74 *in 1609 . . . shunned as "Christians":* Pérez, *The Spanish Inquisition,* pp. 47–50; Anderson, *Daily Life During the Spanish Inquisition,* p. 116.

Expulsion . . . has never gone out of use: An overview of the subject can be found in Benjamin Schwarz, "The Diversity Myth," *Atlantic Monthly,* May 1995.

"Please, O King, what is it that you want from your subjects?": Rubin, *Isabella of Castile,* p. 299; Netanyahu, *Don Isaac Abravanel,* pp. 55–56.

Abravanel offered the king: Rubin, *Isabella of Castile,* p. 299.

74 *managed to wring a single concession:* Menocal, *Ornament of the World,* pp. 248–249.

impossible to get an accurate fix: A lower figure is given by Kamen, *The Spanish Inquisition,* pp. 23–24; a higher figure is given by Sachar, *Farewell España,* pp. 71–72; a middle range is offered by Pérez, *The Spanish Inquisition,* pp. 35–36.

"Do not grieve over your departure": Kamen, *The Spanish Inquisition,* p. 8.

77 *birthright citizenship was a new target:* Julia Preston, "Citizenship as Birthright Is Challenged on the Right," *New York Times,* August 7, 2010.

"If a Catholic mom were to give birth": Media Matters Institute, "Keith Larson on 14th Amendment . . . ," August 8, 2010.

77 *highlighted the national-security angle:* Walid Zafar, "Rep. Gohmert Warns of Baby Terrorists," *Political Correction,* June 25, 2010.

according to opinion polls: "Public Evenly Split on Changing 14th Amendment?" *Washington Post,* August 11, 2010.

state legislators unveiled a proposal: Rachel Slajda, "Birthright Citizenship Foes Want Two-Tiered Birth Certificates," *TPM Muckraker,* January 7, 2011.

that would deny birthright citizenship outright: Eric Kleefeld, "Vitter, Rand, Propose Amendment to Pare Back Birthright Citizenship," *Talking Points Memo,* January 27, 2011.

78 *the Black Death was good for one thing:* Gottfried, *The Black Death,* p. 94.

distilled in the person of Ferrand Martínez: Gitlitz, *Secrecy and Deceit,* pp. 6–7; Lea, *A History of the Inquisition of Spain,* vol. 1, pp. 103–111.

a phenomenon they call "epistemic closure": The term comes from philosophy and has been used in a political sense by Julian Sanchez of the Cato Institute, among others. Patricia Cohen, "No Closure in the 'Epistemic Closure' Debate," *New York Times,* April 26, 2010.

79 *anti-Jewish riots . . . a choice:* Gitlitz, *Secrecy and Deceit,* pp. 7–8.

A significant proportion: Again, getting a fix on the numbers is difficult and controversial. See Gitlitz, *Secrecy and Deceit,* pp. 7–8, 28, 74; Peters, *Inquisition,* p. 82; Netanyahu, *The Origins of the Inquisition in Fifteenth-Century Spain,* pp. 1097–1098.

Sixtus . . . had other distractions: Duffy, *Saints and Sinners,* pp. 185–186; Lea, *A History of the Inquisition of Spain,* pp. 157–160.

80 *laid down strict guidelines . . . "the most extraordinary bull":* Kamen, *The Spanish Inquisition,* p. 49; Lea, *A History of the Inquisition of Spain,* vol. 1, pp. 233–234.

whose prerogatives pushed royal power: Kamen, *The Spanish Inquisition,* p. 50.

One historian notes that: Quoted in Mark Thurner, "Modern Inquisitions: Peru and the Colonial Origins of the Civilized World (review)," *Journal of Colonialism and Colonial History* 7, no. 1 (2006), pp. 107–110.

Like state bureaucracies everywhere: Irene Silverblatt, "Colonial Conspiracies," *Ethnohistory,* vol. 53, no. 2 (April 2006), pp. 259–280.

81 *Torquemada has achieved a form of meta-existence:* Torquemada appears in Longfellow's poem "The Theologian's Tale; Torquemada" (1863) and in Hugo's play *Torquemada* (1882). Electric Wizard's song "Torquemada 71" can be found on the band's 2008 album *Witchcult Today.* Marlon Brando played Torquemada in the 1992 movie *Christopher Columbus: The Discovery.* The webcomic *Pibgorn* is available at http://www.gocomics.com/pibgorn.

Torquemada was born: For details of the inquisitor general's life, see Lea, *A History of the Inquisition in Spain,* vol. 1, pp. 173–179; Kamen, *The Spanish Inquisition,* pp. 47–53, 137–139; Pérez, *The Spanish Inquisition,* pp. 28–30.

Whether he himself had Jewish ancestry: Netanyahu, *The Origins of the Inquisition in Fifteenth Century Spain,* pp. 431–434, 1249–1250 (fn 60).

82 *"Full of pitiless zeal":* Lea, *A History of the Inquisition of Spain,* vol. 1, p. 174.

Inquisitors would come to a town . . . in Toledo alone: Kamen, *The Spanish Inquisition,* p. 57.

83 *"The edicts of grace":* Kamen, *The Spanish Inquisition,* p. 57.

And the deck was stacked: Details of the tribunal process in Spain are described in Kamen, *The Spanish Inquisition,* pp. 166–172, 177–178, 184–185; Llorente, *A Critical History of the Inquisition,* pp. 62–70; Pérez, *The Spanish Inquisition,* pp. 135–136.

Conviction rates: Pérez, *The Spanish Inquisition*, p. 149.

84 *penalties varied . . . the most feared penalty*: Kamen, *The Spanish Inquisition*, pp. 193–213.

Disease could decimate a fleet: Crowley, *Empires of the Sea*, pp. 77–78.

contrived to define horse-smuggling as a "crime of faith": Monter, *Frontiers of Faith*, pp. 86–89.

85 *They were thick upon the ground*: Bethencourt, *The Inquisition*, p. 75.

five stages of dying: Kübler-Ross, *On Death and Dying*, pp. 34, 44, 72, 75, 99.

86 *The names the instruments have been given*: A brief survey of the available tools is provided by Kerrigan, *The Instruments of Torture*.

87 *In the so-called Bybee memo*: The Bush administration's various memos relating to torture can be found at http://www.propublica.org/special/missing-memos.

Following Aquinas, the inquisitors: Sullivan, *The Inner Lives of Medieval Inquisitors*, pp. 184–189.

"The major downside": Alan M. Dershowitz, "The Torture Warrant: A Response to Professor Strauss," *New York Law School Law Review*, vol. 48, no. 1–2 (2004), pp. 275–294.

Torture might once have been limited: Peters, *Torture*, pp. 63–64.

88 *illustrates a moral slide . . . intelligence of a lesser kind*: Andrew Sullivan, "Torture Creep," *The Dish*, May 5, 2011.

the Greater and Lesser Stress Traditions: Rejali, *Torture and Democracy*, pp. 295–296.

"interrogators get sneaky": Rejali, *Torture and Democracy*, p. 9.

Before a session began . . . minutely detailed account: Peters, *Torture*, p. 57.

89 *Lea reproduces one such account*: Lea, *A History of the Inquisition of Spain*, vol. 3, pp. 24–25.

the recognition, well understood by modern interrogators: Mark Bowden, "The Dark Art of Interrogation," *Atlantic Monthly*, October 2003.

90 *Under duress, eight of the ten defendants*: Gisli Gudjonsson, "Confession," *New Scientist*, November 20, 2004.

confessed to crimes they had not committed: John Schwartz, "Confessing to Crime, but Innocent," *New York Times*, September 13, 2010; Brandon L. Garrett, "Getting It Wrong: Convicting the Innocent," *Slate*, April 13, 2011.

Three main forms of torture were employed: For a fuller overview of the basic techniques, see Pérez, *The Spanish Inquisition*, pp. 146–148; Lea, *A History of the Inquisition of Spain*, vol. 3, pp. 16–22; Kamen, *The Spanish Inquisition*, 187–191.

The first technique . . . the Queen of Torments: Peters, *Torture*, p. 68.

allowed to drop with a jerk: Kamen, *The Spanish Inquisition*, p. 190; Rejali, *Torture and Democracy*, p. 296.

91 *John McCain was subjected to a version of it*: "The Candidates: John McCain," MSNBC, February 27, 2008.

One prominent case is that of Manadel al-Jamadi: Jane Mayer, "A Deadly Interrogation," *The New Yorker*, November 14, 2005.

92 *The recording secretary preserved the moment*: Kamen, *The Spanish Inquisition*, p. 191.

"Even a small amount of water in the glottis": Rejali, *Torture and Democracy*, p. 279.

"A review of contemporary cases": Ole Vedel Rasmussen, "Medical Aspects of Torture," *Danish Medical Bulletin*, vol. 37, supplement no. 1 (January 1990), pp. 1–88.

The CIA has acknowledged . . . no more than five "sessions": Joseph Abrams, "Despite Reports, Khalid Sheikh Mohammed Was Not Waterboarded 183 Times," Fox News, April 28, 2009.

93 *simply a "continuance"*: Lea, *A History of the Inquisition of the Middle Ages*, vol. 1, p. 427.

   in order to experience the reality of waterboarding: Christopher Hitchens, "Believe Me, It's Torture," *Vanity Fair*, August 2008.

   U.S. forces used various forms of water torture: Rejali, *Torture and Democracy*, p. 280.

94 *a vivid account*: Alleg, *The Question*, pp. 46–50.

   "a dunk in the water": "Bush Enters Cheney Torture Row," BBC News, October 28, 2006.

   That wasn't always so . . . Eventually, the work of prominent historians: See, for instance, Baer, *History of the Jews in Christian Spain*; Roth, *History of the Marranos*; and Beinart, *Conversos on Trial* and *The Expulsion of the Jews from Spain*. The larger point about the historiography of the Inquisition is made by Kamen, *The Spanish Inquisition*, pp. 309–312, and Peters, *Inquisition*, p. 324.

95 *"Benzion looms above his son"*: David Remnick, "The Outsider," *The New Yorker*, May 25, 1998.

   His father . . . Jabotinsky wing of the movement: Caspit and Kfir, *Netanyahu: The Road to Power*, p. 14.

   Netanyahu came to Palestine . . . professor at Cornell: Caspit and Kfir, *Netanyahu: The Road to Power*, pp. 13–39.

96 *in withering terms*: Netanyahu, *The Origins of the Inquisition*, p. 930.

   "I knew where the quemadero was": Henry Roth, "The Surveyor," *The New Yorker*, August 6, 1966.

   "incredible romance": Roth, *A History of the Marranos*, p. xxiii.

   He speaks in precise paragraphs: Conversation with Benzion Netanyahu, June 2000.

97 *upon meeting him face-to-face*: The interview with Henry Kamen recounted in this chapter took place in Barcelona in September of 2000. The arc of the argument presented here is based on that conversation, on his book *The Spanish Inquisition*, and on follow-up correspondence.

98 *Kamen agrees . . . and they by him*: Henry Kamen, "The Secret of the Inquisition," *New York Review of Books*, February 1, 1996.

99 *"green purgatory of rural society"*: Le Roy Ladurie, *The Mind and Method of the Historian*, p. 215.

101 *What turns a society . . . from one thing into another?*: Kamen, *The Spanish Inquisition*, p. 320.

102 *"fleet of misery and woe"*: Sachar, *Farewell España*, p. 73.

   trying to get a handle on the number: Bethencourt, *The Inquisition*, p. 444.

4. That Satanic Device

103 *"in the mood to give it a good censoring"*: Godman, *The Saint as Censor*, p. 3.

104 *in a second-floor room*: Blackwell, *Galileo, Bellarmine, and the Bible*, p. 1; Shea and Artigas, *Galileo in Rome*, pp. 193–195.

105 *"under an almost unbearable strain"*: Tedeschi, *The Prosecution of Heresy*, pp. 10–11.

   "characters like that of Paul re-appear": Ranke, *The Ecclesiastical and Political History of the Popes of Rome*, vol. 1, p. 287.

106 *"He favoured above all other institutions"*: Ranke, *The Ecclesiastical and Political History of the Popes of Rome*, vol. 1, pp. 313–314.

   a Roman mob sacked the original headquarters: Setton, *The Papacy and the Levant*, vol. 4, pp. 718–720.

eleven ancient aqueducts: Aicher, *Guide to the Aqueducts of Ancient Rome*, p. 29.

pulled away the stonecutters and masons: Pastor, *History of the Popes*, vol. 17, pp. 288–289.

a vast, fortresslike structure: Coffin, *Pirro Ligorio*, pp. 77–78.

107 *"is a lofty hall with gloomy frescoes"*: Hare, *Walks in Rome*, vol. 2, p. 276.

"gloomy and forbidding pile of massive masonry": Nevin, *Vignettes of Travel*, pp. 362–366.

something of a historical accident: The vicissitudes of the Vatican archives in the early nineteenth century are described in Chadwick, *Catholicism and History*, pp. 14–30. See also John Tedeschi, "A 'Queer Story': The Case of the Inquisitorial Manuscripts," *Proceedings of the Royal Irish Academy* (1986), pp. 67–74, and H. R. Trevor-Roper, "The Papal Papers," *New York Review of Books*, May 31, 1979. For an overview of Vatican records more generally, see Blouin, ed., *Vatican Archives: An Inventory and Guide to Historical Documents of the Holy See*, pp. xv–xxxiv.

The documents that tell the story: An overview of the sources and their locations can be found in John Tedeschi, "The Organization and Procedures of the Roman Inquisition," in Tedeschi, *The Prosecution of Heresy*, pp. 127–157; and John Tedeschi, "The Status of the Defendant before the Roman Inquisition," in Guggisberg, Moeller, and Menchi, eds., *Kertzerverfolgung im 16. und frühen 17. Jahrhundert*, pp. 125–146.

108 *Gone were the days when a Renaissance pontiff*: Duffy, *Saints and Sinners*, p. 185.

To reduce the cost of transportation: Blouin, *Vatican Archives*, p. xxi.

109 *the designer sunglasses, the red Prada shoes*: Colm Tóibín, "Among the Flutterers," *London Review of Books*, vol. 32, no. 16 (August 2010).

he is indeed an intellectual: The point is made forcefully in Allen, *Cardinal Ratzinger*. See also Garry Wills, "A Tale of Two Cardinals," *New York Review of Books*, April 26, 2001.

110 *he led the way up the spiral staircase*: The account here reflects conversations with Peter Godman at the Archivio, before the premises were refurbished, in 2000 and 2001; other quotations from Godman, unless specified, are from these or later conversations in 2004 and 2010, and e-mail correspondence.

112 *"we labor in equivocation"*: Godman, *The Saint as Censor*, p. 24.

113 *Petrarch . . . one of the great book collectors*: Elton, *The Great Book-Collectors*, pp. 41–53; Robinson, *Petrarch*, p. 26.

began distributing his library: Elton, *The Great Book-Collectors*, p. 57; Saygin, *Humphrey, Duke of Gloucester*, p. 83.

"the Ripoli Press charged three florins": Quoted in Eisenstein, *The Printing Revolution in Early Modern Europe*, pp. 15–16.

It is estimated that scribes copied out: Eltjo Buringh and Jan Luiten Van Zanden, "Charting the 'Rise of the West': Manuscripts and Printed Books in Europe, A Long-Term Perspective From the Sixth Through Eighteenth Centuries," *The Journal of Economic History*, vol. 69, no. 2 (2009), pp. 409–445.

Thanks to the revolution in typography: Goldstone, *Out of the Flames*, pp. 22–29.

114 *central to civic space*: Eisenstein, *The Printing Revolution*, p. 14.

"a scholar, deep in meditation in his study": Yates, *The Art of Memory*, p. 131.

"It is a mystery to me": Quoted in Eisenstein, *The Printing Revolution*, p. 168.

"competing for space": Eisenstein, *The Printing Revolution*, pp. 168–171.

115 *"able to send their messages from beyond the grave"*: Eisenstein, *The Printing Revolution*, pp. 174–175.

as a young seminarian in the 1960s: Carroll, *Constantine's Sword*, p. 319.

the experience of China: James Fallows, "'The Connection Has Been Reset,'" *Atlantic Monthly*, March 2008.

115 *An uneasy compromise was eventually reached:* David Barboza and Miguel Helft, "A Compromise Allows Both China and Google to Claim a Victory," *New York Times*, July 10, 2010.

116 *activists seek to remove books they deem offensive:* Office of Intellectual Freedom, American Library Association.

A school board on Long Island: Jennifer Barrios, "Board Bans 2 Books from Reading List," *Newsday*, December 5, 2007.

A school in Alabama: "Profanity, Sex Trigger Book-banning Efforts," *Birmingham News*, September 29, 2008.

two male penguins who adopt an egg: "Schools Chief Bans Book on Penguins," *Boston Globe*, December 20, 2006.

A Kentucky statute still in force: Frank E. Lockwood, "'Infidel' Texts Banned in Schools; Educators Say They Follow State Law," *Lexington Herald-Leader*, August 5, 2006.

Fahrenheit 451 has been challenged: Kristin Tillotson, "If You Read, the Terrorists Will Win," *Minneapolis Star-Tribune*, December 2, 2005; "Ray Bradbury's *Fahrenheit 451* Banned," *New Internationalist*, December 1, 2006.

"The lust to suppress": Hentoff, *Free Speech For Me — But Not For Thee*, p. 1.

117 *"brought their books together and began burning them":* Acts of the Apostles, 19:19–20.

the philosopher Peter Abelard: Abelard, *Historia Calamitatum*, p. 44.

In his several Bonfires of the Vanities: Duffy, *Saints and Sinners*, p. 197; Pastor, *History of the Popes*, vol. 5, pp. 205–207.

by a determined cardinal: Black, *The Italian Inquisition*, p. 169.

what was believed to be the last existing copy: Goldstone, *Out of the Flames*, pp. 3–4.

fell to the Master of the Sacred Palace: Godman, *The Saint as Censor*, pp. 8–9.

118 *he examined all books before publication:* Black, *The Italian Inquisition*, p. 159.

potential incursion of censorship on the Internet: John Walker, "The Digital Imprimatur," *Knowledge, Technology, and Policy*, vol. 16, no. 3 (Fall 2003), pp. 24–77.

"not in full conformity with the Catholic faith": "Vatican Orders Bishop to Remove Imprimatur," *National Catholic Reporter*, February 27, 1998.

Johnson had not sought an imprimatur: John L. Allen, Jr., "U.S. Bishops Blast Book by Feminist Theologian," *National Catholic Reporter*, March 30, 2011; "Johnson: Bishops' Condemnation Came Without Discussion," *National Catholic Reporter*, March 31, 2011.

In 1542, with the formal establishment . . . both congregations: Black, *The Italian Inquisition*, pp. 160–161, 179.

119 *"As soon as there were books or writing of any kind":* Catholic Encyclopedia. http://www.newadvent.org/cathen/03519d.htm.

"tempting cups of poison": John Thavis, "Index of Forbidden Books: A Tome Gathering Dust for 25 Years," Catholic News Service, June 14, 1991.

the Catholic Daughters of America: Hamburger, *Separation of Church and State*, p. 412.

summarizing and cataloguing the contents: Thomas Henegan, "Secrets Behind the Forbidden Books," *America*, February 7, 2005. See also http://www.buchzensur.de, the Web site of Hubert Wolf's project on the Roman Inquisition and the Congregation of the Index in the Modern Age.

120 *The Inquisition's response took many forms:* Useful overviews of the Church's regime of censorship can be found in Baldini and Spruitt, *Catholic Church and Modern Science*, vol. 1, pp. 103–128; Bethencourt, *The Inquisition*, pp. 221–236; Godman, *The Saint as Censor*, pp. 3–48; Black, *The Italian Inquisition*, pp. 158–207.

symptomatic of Church attitudes: Tedeschi, *The Prosecution of Heresy*, p. 276.

one sixteenth-century censor wrote privately: Peter Godman, "Inside the Archives of the Inquisition," *Times Literary Supplement*, January 16, 1998.

what George Orwell . . . would call "memory holes": Orwell, *1984*, p. 38.

121 *a typewritten memo from the British embassy:* Timothy Garton Ash, "Orwell's List," *New York Review of Books*, September 25, 2003.

in Milwaukee, the local bishop: "Roman Catholics: End of the Imprimatur," *Time*, December 29, 1967.

"The maintenance of a structure": Bethencourt, *The Inquisition*, p. 230.

122 *A marginal notation in his hand:* Godman, *The Saint as Censor*, p. 208.

If a book was on the list: Tedeschi, *The Prosecution of Heresy*, p. 275.

every reference to coitus: Black, *The Italian Inquisition*, p. 170.

Over the years, they would proscribe: Thomas Henegen, "Secrets Behind the Forbidden Books," *America*, February 7, 2005.

clumsily blotted out: some examples are reproduced in Bethencourt, *The Inquisition*, pp. 224–225.

An inquisitor in Padua: Black, *The Italian Inquisition*, p. 169.

books published in German or English: Godman, *The Saint as Censor*, p. 47.

Uncle Tom's Cabin *came under scrutiny:* Thomas Henegen, "Secrets Behind the Forbidden Books," *America*, February 7, 2005.

the works of Hegel and Kant: Peter Godman, "Inside the Archives of the Inquisition," *Times Literary Supplement*, January 16, 1998.

escaped completely: Thomas Henegen, "Secrets Behind the Forbidden Books," *America*, February 7, 2005.

123 *Bellarmine came close to having one of his own works . . . condemned:* Godman, *The Saint as Censor*, p. 227.

But, Tedeschi writes, there was more: Tedeschi, *The Prosecution of Heresy*, pp. 273–319.

124 *would seek the services of a friendly bishop:* "Roman Catholics: End of the Imprimatur," *Time*, December 29, 1967.

no new editions of his work were published there: Bethencourt, *The Inquisition*, p. 236.

In Spain, whose Inquisition mounted its own censorship effort: Bethencourt, *The Inquisition*, p. 233.

125 *the Inquisition's eventual campaign against the vernacular:* Black, *The Italian Inquisition*, pp. 175–177.

interviewed during the filming of his 1966 epic: Lillian Ross, "The Bible in Dinocitta," *The New Yorker*, September 25, 1965.

were virtually annihilated: Fenlon, *Heresy and Obedience in Tridentine Italy*, pp. 74–75.

Inventories of books confiscated in Spain: Bethencourt, *The Inquisition*, p. 233.

"major imponderables": Black, *The Italian Inquisition*, p. 207.

126 *Writing about the limits on intellectual freedom in China:* James Fallows, "'The Connection Has Been Reset,'" *Atlantic Monthly*, March 2008.

127 *"that most terrible, because most insidious, of ghosts":* Godman, *The Saint as Censor*, p. 230.

The remains of Galileo Galilei: Rachel Donadio, "A Museum Display of Galileo, the Heretic, Has a Saintly Feel," *New York Times*, July 23, 2010.

An analysis of Galileo's tooth: "How We Found the Lost Relics of Galileo," Museo Galileo, June 8, 2010.

128 *"sad misunderstanding"*: John Thavis, "Pope Says Church Erred in Condemning Galileo," Catholic News Service, November 2, 1992.

against the backdrop of what had happened to Giordano Bruno: The particulars of the Bruno case are discussed concisely in Black, *The Italian Inquisition*, pp. 182–186, and Blackwell, *Galileo, Bellarmine, and the Bible*, pp. 45–48, and at greater length in Rowland, *Giordano Bruno*, pp. 244–277.

renowned . . . for his capacious recall: Rowland, *Giordano Bruno*, pp. 62–63.

a book by Erasmus hidden in a privy: Rowland, *Giordano Bruno*, p. 75.

an infinity of stars and planets: Rowland, *Giordano Bruno*, pp. 109–112, 215–221.

129 *"constellation of the ignorant"*: Pastor, *History of the Popes*, vol. 24, p. 206.

but summaries survive: Rowland, *Giordano Bruno*, p. 248.

His interactions with the formidable Robert Bellarmine: Godman, *The Saint as Censor*, pp. 176–178.

was haunted ever afterward: Rowland, *Giordano Bruno*, pp. 12–13; Blackwell, *Galileo, Bellarmine, and the Bible*, p. 48; Black, *The Italian Inquisition*, p. 185.

"with great caution": Blackwell, *Galileo, Bellarmine, and the Bible*, p. 266.

agreed on one thing . . . on good terms with popes: Blackwell, *Galileo, Bellarmine, and the Bible*, pp. 166–170.

130 *It was a pragmatic accommodation*: Godman, *Saint as Censor*, pp. 214–220.

"Concern for truth had evolved": Blackwell, *Galileo, Bellarmine, and the Bible*, p. 177.

131 *There was a charitable organization in Rome*: John Tedeschi, "A New Perspective on the Roman Inquisition," in Bujanda, *Le Controle des Idées à la Renaissance*, pp. 26–27.

Throughout the peninsula, the total number executed: Bethencourt, *The Inquisition*, p. 444.

Trials . . . followed the usual pattern in certain ways: John Tedeschi, "The Status of the Defendant before the Roman Inquisition," in Guggisberg, Moeller, and Menchi, eds., *Kertzerverfolgung im 16. und frühen 17. Jahrhundert*, pp. 125–146.

132 *he would most likely be taken aback*: John Tedeschi, "Carlo Ginzburg e le fonti," a paper delivered on the twenty-fifth anniversary of the publication of The Cheese and the Worms, in Colonnello and Del Col, *Uno Storico, un Mugnaio, un Libro*, pp. 23–28.

at the beginning of his academic career: Many of the personal details in this account were provided by Ginzburg in correspondence with the author, February 2001.

133 *"How could I have let such an obvious fact escape me?"*: Carlo Ginzburg, "Witches and Shamans," *New Left Review*, July/August 1993, p. 79.

"the persecuted, not the persecutors": Quoted in Tony Molho, "Carlo Ginzburg: Reflections on the Intellectual Cosmos of a 20th-century Historian," *History of European Ideas*, vol. 30, no. 1 (2004), pp. 121–148.

He was so excited by the discovery: Carlo Ginzburg, "Witches and Shamans," *New Left Review*, July/August 1993, pp. 80–81.

He was granted access, grudgingly: Personal communication with Carlo Ginzburg. See also Carlo Ginzburg, "Witches and Shamans," *New Left Review*, July/August 1993, pp. 75–85.

134 *"The benandanti spoke, often without being urged to"*: Ginzburg, Carlo, "Witches and Shamans," *New Left Review*, July/August 1993, p. 82.

"mental rubbish of peasant credulity": Trevor-Roper, *The European Witch-Craze*, p. 116.

135 *published throughout Europe*: Russell, *Witchcraft in the Middle Ages*, p. 79.

typical chapter heading: Kors and Peters, *Witchcraft in Europe*, pp. 198–199.

Much of this advice: Mackay, *The Hammer of Witches*, p. 11.

"strange amalgam": Anthony Grafton, "Say Anything," *The New Republic*, November 5, 2007.

the book's taxonomy of beliefs and practices: A concise overview of the *Malleus* and its impact can be found in Mackay, *The Hammer of Witches*, pp. 1–39.

would eventually cross the ocean: Demos, *The Enemy Within*, p. 69.

136 *"The study of actual interrogations":* Mackay, *The Hammer of Witches*, p. 31.

the genre known as microhistory: See Carlo Ginzburg, "Microhistory: Two or Three Things That I Know About It," *Critical Inquiry*, vol. 20, no. 1 (August 1993), pp. 10–35.

supported a vast book-making industry: Grendler, *The Roman Inquisition and the Venetian Press*, p. 12.

137 *"artful mind," "these were the angels":* Ginzburg, *The Cheese and the Worms*, pp. 12, 5–6.

"remnants of the thinking of others": Ginzburg, *The Cheese and the Worms*, p. 61.

"There was once a great lord": Ginzburg, *The Cheese and the Worms*, p. 49.

138 *Although he was condemned to prison:* Ginzburg, *The Cheese and the Worms*, pp. 93–95.

or even architectural: Bethencourt, *The Inquisition*, p. 443.

returned to Montereale and resumed his work: Ginzburg, *The Cheese and the Worms*, p. 93.

"losing many earnings": Del Col, *Domenico Scandella*, p. 129.

"Can't you understand": Ginzburg, *The Cheese and the Worms*, p. 103.

"He will argue with anyone": Ginzburg, *The Cheese and the Worms*, p. 2.

"things that would astonish": Del Col, *Domenico Scandella*, p. 20.

139 *"Your reverence must not fail to proceed":* Ginzburg, *The Cheese and the Worms*, p. 128.

and pronounced it acceptable: Weinberg and Bealer, *The World of Caffeine*, p. 40.

In Montereale today . . . fountain outside: John Tedeschi, "Carlo Ginzburg e le fonti," in Colonnello and Del Col, *Uno Storico, un Mugnaio, un Libro*, pp. 23–28.

140 *"provided the prime example":* Bethencourt, *The Inquisition*, p. 448.

John Locke put it like this: Locke, *A Letter Concerning Toleration*, pp. 33, 53.

"The Inquisition was extinguished": Conversation with Francisco Bethencourt, June 2010.

141 *abolished during the Napoleonic Era . . . to those few acres:* Peters, *Inquisition*, pp. 119–120; Kertzer, *The Kidnapping of Edgardo Mortara*, pp. 261–262.

the home of a Jewish couple . . . to baptize him: Kertzer, *The Kidnapping of Edgardo Mortara*, pp. 37, 40–41.

142 *"There must be some mistake":* Kertzer, *The Kidnapping of Edgardo Mortara*, p. 5.

The boy was taken to Rome . . . conducted the first Sabbath service: Kertzer, *The Kidnapping of Edgardo Mortara*, pp. 86–87, 89–90, 124, 295, 298.

"sat outside the Chief Rabbi's office": Kertzer, *The Kidnapping of Edgardo Mortara*, p. 304.

5. The Ends of the Earth

143 *"Where is the stairway to heaven?":* Richard E. Greenleaf, "The Inquisition in Eighteenth-Century New Mexico," *New Mexico Historical Review*, vol. 60, no. 1 (1985), pp. 29–60.

"This is the man who would like to see me": Aczel, *The Jesuit and the Skull*, p. 211.

144 *The things below . . . have not disappeared:* Tobias and Woodhouse, *Santa Fe: A Modern History*, pp. 231–235; La Farge, *Turn Left at the Sleeping Dog*, pp. 377–380; Lovato, *Sante*

Fe Hispanic Culture, pp. 4, 23–29, 98–119; "City Changes, Family Remains," *Santa Fe New Mexican*, December 5, 2010.

mass grave for Indians: Santo Invisibles, "Santa Feans Call for Truth in Public Celebration of Religious Conquest," Arizona Indymedia, September 5, 2010.

145 *ordering the execution:* Kessell, Hendricks, and Dodge, eds., *To the Royal Crown Restored*, pp. 532–533.

After a brief investigation, archaeologists determined: Tom Sharpe, "Talks With Tribes Delay Civic Center," *Santa Fe New Mexican*, September 25, 2005; Laura Banish, "Committee Will Reconsider Burial Permit," *Albuquerque Journal*, October 11, 2005; Associated Press, "Sweeney Center Dig Experts: Remains May Not Be Tesuque's," October 21, 2005; Laura Banish, "Caught Off Guard," *Albuquerque Journal*, November 6, 2005; Tom Sharpe, "City, Tribe, Reach Deal on Civic Center," *Santa Fe New Mexican*, December 16, 2005; David Alire Garcia, "Digging in the Dirt," *Santa Fe Reporter*, May 16, 2007.

begun painting it red: Geoff Grammer, "Cross of the Martyrs: Third Year for Vandals' Message in Red," *Santa Fe New Mexican*, August 24, 2010.

an inscription on an obelisk: Santo Invisibles, "Santa Feans Call for Truth in Public Celebration of Religious Conquest," Arizona Indymedia, September 5, 2010.

147 *highlights, marginal notations, and underlinings:* Lester, *The Fourth Part of the World*, p. 251.

deeply religious, even obsessively so: Details of the spiritual life of Christopher Columbus and other information about his outlook and ambitions are drawn from Lester, *The Fourth Part of the World*, pp. 295–296; Pauline Moffitt Watts, "Prophecy and Discovery: On the Spiritual Origins of Christopher Columbus's 'Enterprise of the Indies,'" *American Historical Review*, vol. 90, no. 1 (1985), pp. 73–102; Delno West, "Christopher Columbus and His Enterprise to the Indies: Scholarship of the Last Quarter Century," *William and Mary Quarterly*, vol. 49, no. 2 (1992).

"parish priests or friars": "Columbus's Letter to the King and Queen of Spain, 1494," Medieval Sourcebook, http://www.fordham.edu/halsall/source/columbus2.html.

popularized by a Harvard Business School professor: The professor was Theodore Levitt; the article that gave the term new currency was "Globalization of Markets," *Harvard Business Review*, May–June 1983.

148 *the trip from Rome to Alexandria and back:* Fergus Millar, "Emperors, Frontiers, and Foreign Relations, 31 B.C. to A.D. 378," *Britannia* 13 (1982), pp. 1–23.

"messengers of the lord": Dutton, *Carolingian Civilization*, pp. 65–66.

transport by sea could occur over longer distances: Parry, *The Discovery of the Sea*, pp. 20–47, 165–171; Lester, *The Fourth Part of the World*, pp. 218–249.

149 *as Edward Gibbon wrote:* Gibbon, *The Decline and Fall of the Roman Empire*, vol. 1, p. 50. *The Spanish Empire was no different . . . institutions of crown and church:* J. H. Plumb's introduction to Parry, *The Spanish Seaborne Empire*, pp. 21–22; Parry, *The Age of Reconnaissance*, p. 239.

150 *many* conversos *in the New World . . . Columbus numbered:* Gitlitz, *Secrecy and Deceit*, p. 54; Meyer Kayserling, "America, the Discovery of," JewishEncyclopedia.com.

sometimes encouraged . . . made the prohibition largely a dead letter: Gitlitz, *Secrecy and Deceit*, pp. 55, 60.

151 *in cities around the world:* Charles H. Cunningham, "The Ecclesiastical Influence in the Philippines (1565–1850)," *American Journal of Theology*, vol. 22, no. 2 (April 1918), pp. 161–186; Scholes, *Church and State in New Mexico*, p. 9.

"the most important ecclesiastical court in the New World": Scholes, *Church and State in New Mexico*, pp. 9–10.

Some years ago, the Bancroft Library: Gillian C. Boal, foreword to Faulhaber and Vincent, *Exploring the Bancroft Library*, p. 57.

152 *a vivid sense of the range of transgressions*: "Survey of Mexican Inquisition Documents," Bancroft Library, University of California, Berkeley; http://bancroft.berkeley.edu/collections/latinamericana/inquisitionsurvey.html.

some two hundred people were investigated: Stanley Hordes, "The Inquisition and the Crypto-Jewish Community in Colonial New Spain and New Mexico," in Perry and Cruz, eds., *Cultural Encounters*, p. 208.

left behind a deeply personal and affecting memoir: Liebman, *The Enlightened*, pp. 23–33, 49–50, 133.

153 *A* converso *community was by then a palpable reality*: Stanley M. Hordes, "The Crypto-Jewish Community of New Spain, 1620–1649: A Collective Biography," doctoral dissertation, Tulane University, 1980; Stanley M. Hordes, "The Inquisition and the Crypto-Jewish Community in Colonial New Spain and New Mexico," in Perry and Cruz, eds., *Cultural Encounters*, pp. 210–211.

The Inquisition stepped in: the statistics here and the general unfolding of events are drawn from Stanley M. Hordes, "The Crypto-Jewish Community of New Spain, 1620–1649: A Collective Biography," doctoral dissertation, Tulane University, 1980; Stanley M. Hordes, "The Inquisition and the Crypto-Jewish Community in Colonial New Spain and New Mexico," in Perry and Cruz, eds., *Cultural Encounters*, pp. 207–217.

154 *the oldest European road in America*: Moorhead, *New Mexico's Royal Road*, pp. 8–27.

New Mexico's only significant connection: Preston and Esquibel, *The Royal Road*, pp. 3–34; Moorhead, *New Mexico's Royal Road*, p. 55.

155 *A great convoy*: Moorhead, *New Mexico's Royal Road*, pp. 32–33.

hundreds of people . . . documents of government: Simmons, *Spanish Pathways*, pp. 16–18.

records are held at the Archivo General: Kate Doyle, "'Forgetting Is Not Justice': Mexico Bares Its Secret Past," *World Policy Journal*, Summer 2003, pp. 61–72.

one of the first things interrogators did: Stanley M. Hordes, "The Crypto-Jewish Community of New Spain: 1620–1649: A Collective Biography," doctoral dissertation, Tulane University, 1980.

the first American historian to become intimately familiar: Richard E. Greenleaf, "France Vinton Scholes (1897–1979): A Personal Memoir," *Hispanic American Historical Review*, vol. 60, no. 1 (1980), pp. 90–94.

after background checks to confirm their doctrinal fealty: France V. Scholes, "The First Decade of the Inquisition in New Mexico," *New Mexico Historical Review*, vol. 10, no. 3 (1935), p. 200.

156 *took evidence in cases of every kind*: The incidents recounted here are cited in France V. Scholes, "The First Decade of the Inquisition in New Mexico," *New Mexico Historical Review*, vol. 10, no. 3 (1935), pp. 195–241.

wash her private parts with water: Richard E. Greenleaf, "The Inquisition in Eighteenth Century New Mexico," *New Mexico Historical Review*, vol. 60, no. 1 (1985), pp. 29–60.

157 *"The very simplicity of political, social, and economic conditions"*: Scholes, *Church and State in New Mexico*, p. 193.

sometimes employed special messengers: Scholes, *Church and State in New Mexico*, pp. 32, 38, 110, 124.

158 *his murder was an affront to civil authority*: Scholes, *Church and State in New Mexico*, pp. 115–191.

"the largest mass beheading": Pacheco, *Ghosts, Murder, Mayhem*, p. 75.

In the 1660s, the tribunal brought formal charges: Kessell, *Kiva, Cross, and Crown*, pp. 171–207.

159 *they rose up in a coordinated attack*: For a concise description of the Pueblo Revolt, see Knaut, *The Pueblo Revolt of 1680*, pp. 3–15.

"having expressed views on religion": Quoted in James, *In and Out of the Old Missions of California*, p. 52.

confiscated four copies of a game: Chapman, *A History of California*, p. 373.

the "mad poet" of New Mexico: Richard E. Greenleaf, "The Inquisition in Eighteenth Century New Mexico," *New Mexico Historical Review*, vol. 60, no. 1 (1985), pp. 38–39.

harassed but not killed: Richard E. Greenleaf, "The Inquisition in Eighteenth Century New Mexico," *New Mexico Historical Review*, vol 60, no. 1 (1985), pp. 29–60.

160 *suspected of owning a book by Voltaire*: Bancroft, *A History of California*, vol. 19, pp. 659–660.

weren't known for reading books: Bancroft, *A History of California*, vol. 19, pp. 659–660.

a man was denounced — by his mother: J. R. Spell, "Rousseau in Spanish America," *Hispanic American Historical Review*, vol. 15, no. 2 (1935), pp. 260–267.

"ferret out French and English catechisms": Richard E. Greenleaf, "North American Protestants and the Mexican Inquisition, 1765–1820," *Journal of Church and State*, vol. 8, no. 2 (1966), pp. 186–199.

Inquisition in New Mexico appointed a censor: Richard E. Greenleaf, "The Inquisition in Eighteenth Century New Mexico," *New Mexico Historical Review*, vol. 60, no. 1 (1985), pp. 29–60.

A decree arrived in California: Bancroft, *A History of California*, vol. 19, pp. 659–660.

161 *in an isolated region of Portugal*: Gitlitz, *Secrecy and Deceit*, p. 53.

immigrants from the Azores: Gitlitz, *Secrecy and Deceit*, p. 47.

the so-called Jewish Indians of Venta Prieta: Raphael Patai, "The Jewish Indians of Mexico," *Jewish Folklore and Ethnology Review*, vol. 18, no. 1–2, pp. 2–12; Raphael Patai, "Venta Prieta Revisited (1965)," *Jewish Folklore and Ethnology Review*, vol. 18, no. 1–2, pp. 13–18.

got to their desired destination: Ross, *Acts of Faith*, pp. 1–25; Joel Millman, "Texas Rabbi Claims Mexico Is Playing Host to a Lost Tribe," *Wall Street Journal*, June 15, 2000.

162 *certain practices among small groups of Hispanics*: Hordes, *To the Ends of the Earth*, pp. 244–245; Schulamith C. Halevy, "Manifestations of Crypto-Judaism in the American Southwest," *Jewish Folklore and Ethnology Review*, vol. 18, no. 1–2, pp. 68–76.

"cross-cultural commonplace": Judith S. Neulander, "The New Mexico Crypto-Jewish Canon: Choosing to Be 'Chosen' in Millennial Tradition," *Jewish Folklore and Ethnology Review*, vol. 18, no. 1–2 (1996), pp. 19–58.

Her conclusion parallels Patai's: Judith S. Neulander, "The New Mexico Crypto-Jewish Canon: Choosing to Be 'Chosen' in Millennial Tradition," *Jewish Folklore and Ethnology Review*, vol. 18, no. 1–2 (1996), pp. 19–58; Judith S. Neulander, "Crypto-Jews of the Southwest: An Imagined Community," *Jewish Folklore and Ethnology Review*, vol. 16, no. 1 (1994), pp. 64–68; Debbie Nathan and Barbara Ferry, "Mistaken Identity? The Case of New Mexico's 'Hidden Jews,'" *Atlantic Monthly*, December 2000.

163 *They are also able to show*: Kunin, *Juggling Identities*, p. 107.

Genealogical research by Hordes: Hordes, *To the Ends of the Earth,* pp. 273–279; Kunin, *Juggling Identities,* p. 105.

left Spain and Portugal by the thousands: Gitlitz, *Secrecy and Deceit,* p. 54.

genetic evidence as well: Simon Romero, "Hispanics Uncovering Roots as Inquisition's 'Hidden Jews,'" *New York Times,* October 29, 2005; Hordes, *To the Ends of the Earth,* pp. 271–273.

an unusually high incidence . . . disproportionately susceptible: Jeff Wheelwright, "The 'Secret Jews' of San Luis Valley," *Smithsonian,* October 2008.

held on to elements of their faith: Gitlitz, *Secrecy and Deceit,* pp. 35–64.

164 *showed themselves to be shrewd observers and advisors:* Joseph S. Sebes, S.J., "China's Jesuit Century," *Wilson Quarterly,* Winter 1978, pp. 170–183.

what today would be called comparative religion: See Hunt, Jacob, and Mijnhardt, *The Book That Changed Europe.*

"I seek Christians and spices": Duffy, *Portuguese Africa,* p. 104.

165 *To this day, it enjoys:* "Goa's Per Capita Highest, Bihar's Lowest in FY '10," *The Hindu,* March 9, 2011.

forcing him to find other quarters: Saraiva, *The Marrano Factory,* pp. 350–351.

the faithful managed to save their idols: Paul Axelrod and Michelle A. Fuerch, "Flight of the Deities: Hindu Resistance in Portuguese Goa," *Modern Asian Studies,* vol. 30, no. 2 (1996), pp. 387–421.

sent a substantial payment to Pope Paul IV: Saraiva, *The Marrano Factory,* pp. 342–352.

166 *the Inquisition held twenty-seven autos-da-fé in Goa:* Saraiva, *The Marrano Factory,* pp. 342–352.

printing presses were kept out of Brazil: James E. Wadsworth, "In the Name of the Inquisition: The Portuguese Inquisition and Delegated Authority in Colonial Pernambuco, Brazil," *The Americas,* vol. 61, no. 1 (2004).

One petty dispute in Angola: Birmingham, *Portugal and Africa,* pp. 63–81.

two hundred years after their executions: Ioan Grillo, "Mexican Church to Review Cases of Excommunicated Independence Heroes," Catholic News Service, October 16, 2007; "Better Late Than Never," *The Mex Files,* September 1, 2009; "Church: Independence Heroes Died As Catholics," McClatchey–Tribune Regional News, August 31, 2009.

167 *refused to recognize . . . and withdrew:* Kertzer, *Prisoner of the Vatican,* p. 3.

who opened up . . . who re-established: Duffy, *Saints and Sinners,* p. 313; "Vatican Observatory," Vatican City State, http://www.vaticanstate.va/EN/Other_Institutions/The_Vatican_Observatory.htm.

preserved in a motion picture . . . first pope whose voice survives in a recording: "Recording of Pope Leo XIII, 1903," How to Be a Retronaut, April 3, 2010. http://www.howtobearetronaut.com/2010/04/recording-of-pope-leo-xiii-1903.

169 *followed the progress of its drafting and editing:* "Democracy and the Labour Problem," *North-Eastern Daily Gazette,* April 30, 1891.

"The Standard's Rome correspondent": "The Pope's Encyclical," *Yorkshire Herald,* May 16, 1891.

"the expression of his century": "Pope Leo's Anniversary," *New York Times,* March 3, 1895.

the perfect Latin edition of the works of Thomas Aquinas: Cullen Murphy, "All the Pope's Men," *Harper's,* June 1979.

170 *eighty beliefs that Catholics must condemn:* Duffy, *Saints and Sinners,* p. 295.

These included the belief: http://www.papalencyclicals.net/Pius09/p9syll.htm.

that provoked Lord Acton's famous remark: Dalberg-Acton, *Essays on Freedom and Power*, p. 364.

"towards power and against freedom": Owen Chadwick, "Lord Acton at the First Vatican Council," *Journal of Theological Studies*, vol. 27, no. 2 (1977).

that is to say, its name was retired: Peters, *Inquisition*, p. 120.

"The interests of the Inquisition were increasingly focused outward": Collins, *From Inquisition to Freedom*, p.14.

conservative and controlling mind-set of this period: "Censorship of Books": http://www .newadvent.org/cathen/03519d.htm; "inquisition": http://www.newadvent.org/cathen/ 08026a.htm.

171 *what would come to be called Modernism:* A useful introduction to the controversy and some of its participants can be found in Ratté, *Three Modernists.*

made the sign of the cross over his grave: Kerr, *Twentieth-Century Catholic Theologians,* pp. 2–5.

hurled the word "anathema": Pius X, "*Pascendi Dominici Gregis*: On the Doctrine of the Modernists," September 8, 1907. http://www.papalencyclicals.net/Pius10/p10pasce.htm.

"lengthy and ferocious": Duffy, *Saints and Sinners*, pp. 328–329.

172 *"There is a twofold and serious difficulty":* King, *Spirit of Fire*, p. 106.

173 *"never say or write anything against":* King, *Spirit of Fire*, p. 107.

"I weighed up the enormous scandal": King, *Spirit of Fire*, p. 108.

"in order to be free of it": Robert Nugent, "From Silence to Vindication: Teilhard de Chardin and the Holy Office," *Commonweal*, October 25, 2002.

"burned at the stake": Aczel, *The Jesuit and the Skull*, p. 211.

"you may count on me": Aczel, *The Jesuit and the Skull*, p. 205.

174 *a stern and public condemnation:* "Monitum," *L'Osservatore Romano*, July 1, 1962, translation provided by the conservative Catholic organization Tradition in Action. http:// www.traditioninaction.org/ProgressivistDoc/A_121_teilhardCondemned.html.

Pope Benedict made a positive reference: John L. Allen, Jr., "An Evolutionary Leap for Teilhard?" *National Catholic Reporter*, August 7, 2009.

in order to escape a libel action: Andrew Johnson, "Shirley Temple Scandal Was Real Reason Greene Fled to Mexico," *The Independent*, November 18, 2007.

The documents in the case: The details of the case of Graham Greene and the quotations from documents in the archives are drawn from Peter Godman, "Graham Greene's Vatican Dossier," *Atlantic Monthly*, July/August 2001.

175 *personal collection of more than 120,000 volumes:* "The De Luca Collection," Vatican Library, March 17, 2009.

177 *still kept books on the Index in a locked cage:* Pascal de Caprariis, "The Cage" (letter to the editor), *Boston College Magazine*, Winter 2011.

177 *by the pseudonymous Xavier Rynne:* Rynne's reporting was eventually collected and published in the single volume *Vatican Council II.*

178 *"No one should be judged and condemned":* Allen, *Cardinal Ratzinger*, pp. 64–65.

"prejudged every question" . . . signed his name: Gibson, *The Rule of Benedict*, pp. 184–185.

"soon had the effect on Ratzinger": Garry Wills, "A Tale of Two Cardinals," *New York Review of Books*, April 26, 2001.

179 *his right to teach as a Catholic theologian:* Victor L. Simpson, "Theologian Stripped of Teaching Post," Associated Press, December 18, 1979.

neither "suitable nor eligible": Merrill McLoughlin, "The Pope Gets Tough," *U.S. News &*

World Report, November 17, 1986; "Catholic U. Is Upheld in Firing Priest," Associated Press, March 1, 1989.

179 *"in disagreement with the teaching of the Church":* Gibson, *The Rule of Benedict,* p. 197.

Dominican priest . . . was silenced for a year: "Rebel Priest Sentenced to Year of Silence," *Los Angeles Times,* October 19, 1988; "Vatican Expels Factious Priest From Dominicans," *Los Angeles Times,* March 6, 1993.

took the extreme step of excommunicating a Sri Lankan priest: Celestine Bohlen, "Excommunicated Priest Is Reunited with Vatican," *New York Times,* March 5, 1998.

the litany of names goes on: Many of the cases from the 1980s and 1990s are discussed in Collins, *From Inquisition to Freedom,* and Reese, *Inside the Vatican;* some of them, and others as late as 2005, are taken up in Gibson, *The Rule of Benedict.*

putting Catholic universities on a tighter leash: Reese, *Inside the Vatican,* pp. 258–259.

180 *compared it to what he had endured at the hands of the Nazis:* Quoted in Cahalan, *Formed in the Image of Christ,* p. 10.

offers this vignette from another case: Gibson, *The Rule of Benedict,* p. 200.

181 *after years of confrontation:* Laurie Goodstein, "Vatican Is Said to Force Jesuit off Magazine," *New York Times,* May 7, 2005.

referred to the procedures of the Congregation: "Due Process in the Church," *America,* April 9, 2001.

182 *Reese consulted with Cardinal Avery Dulles:* Apart from various printed sources, the account of the events surrounding the firing of Thomas Reese is drawn from an interview with Reese in February 2011, and subsequent communications.

talking with Hans King: Cullen Murphy, "Who Do Men Say That I Am?" *Atlantic Monthly,* December 1986.

They met at Castel Gondolfo: Gibson, *The Rule of Benedict,* p. 186.

6. War on Error

184 *"Without torture I know we shall not prevail":* Hutchinson, *Elizabeth's Spymaster,* p. 72.

"Politics is not religion": Camus, *The Rebel,* p. 302.

185 *an exasperated president of Brown University had noted:* Biographical details about Lea and the history of the Lea Library are drawn from Edward Peters, "Henry Charles Lea and the Libraries Within a Library." http://www.library.upenn.edu/exhibits/rbm/at250/history/ep.pdf. See also Edward Peters, "Henry Charles Lea (1825–1909)," in Helen Damico and Joseph Zavadil, eds., *Medieval Scholarship: Bibliographic Studies on the Formation of a Discipline,* vol. 1, History, pp. 89–100.

186 *he was by any standard a professional:* Bethencourt, *The Inquisition,* pp. 13–15.

place the study of the Inquisition on a sound historical footing: For a concise introduction to the work of Sarpi, Limborch, and Llorente, see Bethencourt, *The Inquisition,* pp. 3–12; and Peters, *Inquisition,* pp. 269–272, 275–287.

which encompassed all the inquisitions: Peters, *Inquisition,* pp. 275–276.

187 *John Calvin's Genevan Consistory:* The records of the Consistory are the focus of an ambitious and ongoing scholarly publishing project. See Kingdon, ed., *Registers of the Consistory of Geneva in the Time of Calvin.*

188 *harbored the suspicions of his class and time toward Roman Catholicism:* Edward Peters, "Henry Charles Lea: Jurisprudence and Civilization," Digital Proceedings of the Law-

rence J. Schoenberg Symposium on Manuscript Studies in the Digital Age (2010). http://
repository.upenn.edu/cgi/viewcontent.cgi?article=1024&context=ljsproceedings.

"have not paused to moralize": Edward Peters, "Henry Charles Lea: The Historian as Re-
former," *American Quarterly*, vol. 19, no. 1 (1967), pp. 104–113.

"inherited a fully fledged apparatus of persecution": Vincent P. Carey, "Voices for Tolerance in the War on Error," in Carey, ed., *Voices for Tolerance in an Age of Persecution*, pp.
17–29.

189   *begins the book by calmly remarking an irony*: Timerman, *Prisoner Without a Name, Cell
Without a Number*, pp. vii–viii.

"fish food . . . intensive therapy": Feitlowitz, *A Lexicon of Terror*, pp. 55, 59.

"appeared to consist of professional bureaucrats": Marchak, *God's Assassins*, p. 148.

the immense governmental effort involved: Marchak, *God's Assassins*, p. 9.

190   *The comment came from Eamon Duffy*: Quotations from Eamon Duffy, unless otherwise
specified, are from a conversation with the author, February 2010.

192   *The house owned by Sir Francis Walsingham*: Hutchinson, *Elizabeth's Spymaster*, pp. 97–
98.

193   *attempts to depose her*: Hutchinson, *Elizabeth's Spymaster*, p. 23.

194   *To meet the threat. . . . "It was now treason"*: Williams, *The Later Tudors*, pp. 289–291,
411–413, 467–471.

an unwise pamphleteer will lose his right hand . . . deposition scene: Williams, *The Later
Tudors*, pp. 411–412.

some 130 Catholic priests: Williams, *The Later Tudors*, p. 475.

"To the English": Peters, *Inquisition*, pp. 140–141.

195   *"use not so many questions"*: Lord Burghley's letter to Archbishop Whitgift, 1584, in Tanner, *Tudor Constitutional Documents*, p. 373.

Nor did his jailers employ just the rack: Hutchinson, *Elizabeth's Spymaster*, pp. 72–73.

captured vividly in the documents: See, for instance, Landsdowne MS 97, Item 10; Har-
leian MS 360, fol. 65; Add. MS 48,023 fols. 110–111; Add. MS 48,029, fols. 121–141.

196   *Looking in a bound volume for something else*: The volume is Add. MS 63,742.

a brutal interrogator: Hutchinson, *Elizabeth's Spymaster*, p. 75.

left the country . . . and was ordained: Law and Bagshaw, *A historical sketch*, p. 20 (fn 2);
Purdie, *The Life of Blessed John Southworth*, p. 3.

197   *"Xpofer Southworth sonne to Sr John Southworth"*: Law and Bagshaw, *A historical sketch*,
p. 136.

3,000 paid informers in Paris alone: Cyrille Fijnaut and Gary T. Marx, "The Normaliza-
tion of Undercover Policing in the West," in Fijnaut and Marx, eds., *Undercover*, pp.
1–28.

"When three people are chatting in the street": Stead, *The Police of Paris*, p. 49.

police controlled the organs of censorship: Stead, *The Police of France*, pp. 30–31.

198   *France in the 1790s . . . "a revolting Inquisition"*: Stead, *The Police of France*, pp. 46–50.

The czars . . . Prussia created: Reith, *The Blind Eye of History*, pp. 238–249; Clive Emsley,
"Control and Legitimacy: The Police in Comparative Perspective Since circa 1800," in
Emsley, Johnson, and Spierenburg, eds., *Social Control in Europe*.

Putin, the security operations were rebuilt . . . "We are in power now": Soldatov and Borogan, *The New Nobility*, pp. 23–35, 63–73; Amy Knight, "The Concealed Battle to Run
Russia," *New York Review of Books*, January 13, 2011.

199   *"The chief principle of a well-regulated police state"*: Groebner, *Who Are You?*, pp. 228–
229.

"Note-taking and record-keeping were prescribed": Richard E. Greenleaf, "North American Protestants and the Mexican Inquisition, 1765–1820," *Journal of Church and State*, vol. 2, no. 2 (1966), pp. 186–199.

200   *"The Brazilian generals, you see, were technocrats"*: Lawrence Weschler, "A Miracle, a Universe," *The New Yorker*, May 25 and June 1, 1987.

survive . . . on 17,000 cuneiform fragments: "Ebla: The State Archives," Italian Archaeological Mission in Syria. http://www.ebla.it/escavi_gli_archivi_di_stato.html.

201   *A portion of Adolf Hitler's personal library*: Timothy W. Ryback, "Hitler's Forgotten Library," *Atlantic Monthly*, May 2003.

202   *why the government wants to digitize its holdings*: Lisa Rein, "Cost to Build Digital Archive of US Records Could Hit $1.4b," *Washington Post*, February 4, 2011.

203   *an intellectual and a man of advanced ideas*: Scholz-Hänsel, *El Greco*, pp. 46–48.

lodged in the cavernous basements of a complex of villas: Some early history of the Berlin Document Center, and an account of the debate over the transfer of control of the archives to German hands, is provided by Gerald Posner, "Secrets of the Files," *The New Yorker*, March 14, 1994.

a grim assemblage of brick buildings: An overview of the history of the complex, from which some details here are drawn, is available at http://www.bundesarchiv.de/bundesarchiv/dienstorte/berlin_lichterfelde/index.html.en.

204   *The subject matter ranges from routine administration*: James S. Beddie, "The Berlin Document Center," in Wolfe, ed., *Captured German and Related Records*, pp. 131–142.

IBM's German subsidiary . . . provided the Nazi government: Black, *IBM and the Holocaust*, pp. 7–16.

"The physician examines the human body": Black, *IBM and the Holocaust*, p. 50.

205   *authorities are trying to figure out*: Wiebke Hollersen, "Former Stasi Headquarters Provide Headache for Berlin," *Spiegel Online*, June 3, 2010.

At its peak, . . . the Stasi: Andrew Curry, "Piecing Together the Dark Legacy of East Germany's Secret Police," *Wired*, January 2008.

"The daily activities of the spy world": Macrakis, *Seduced by Secrets*, p. 3.

206   *"In the walls of the cubicle there were three orifices"*: Orwell, *1984*, pp. 38–39.

Many of the shredded documents have since been reconstructed: Douglas Heingartner, "Back Together Again," *New York Times*, July 17, 2003; "Software to Reveal Stasi Secrets," *BBC News*, May 10, 2007; Andrew Curry, "Piecing Together the Dark Legacy of East Germany's Secret Police," *Wired*, January 2008.

207   *a device called the "smell chair"*: Elizabeth Gudrais, "The Seductions of Snooping," *Harvard Magazine*, July–August 2008.

208   *began to modernize its apparatus of surveillance*: "Lords: Rise of CCTV Is a Threat to Freedom," *The Guardian*, February 6, 2009.

"you've got nothing to fear": Daniel J. Solove, "Why Privacy Matters Even If 'You've Got Nothing to Hide,'" *The Chronicle of Higher Education*, May 15, 2011.

209   *a nearly continuous video montage*: Mark Townsend, "The Real Story of 7/7," *The Guardian*, May 7, 2006.

wide latitude to hold suspects for significant periods: William Langewiesche, "A Face in the Crowd," *Vanity Fair*, February 2008.

210   *too much public opposition*: S. A. Mathieson, "Minister Destroys National Identity Register," *The Guardian*, February 10, 2011.

permitted to "self-authorize" the surveillance of British citizens: Sarah Lyall, "Britons Weary of Surveillance in Minor Cases," *New York Times*, October 25, 2009.

negotiate iris and palm scanners: "Biometrics Screening for Olympics Workers," *The Times* (London), March 5, 2008.

to cruise above Olympic venues: "RAF Drones to Be Used for 2012 Olympics Security," *Herald* (Scotland), January 9, 2008; "Expect the Drones to Swarm on Britain in Time for 2012," *The Guardian*, February 22, 2010.

a passageway that would scan people: "Smiths Detection Moves Forward with Tunnel of Truth," *Homeland Security Newswire*, November 3, 2006.

"The unsuspecting Britons": Quoted in Eliot A. Cohen, "History and the Hyperpower," *Foreign Affairs*, vol. 83, no. 4 (2004), pp. 49–63.

211 *a national security advisor under Ronald Reagan:* The quotations here are drawn from a conversation with Admiral John Poindexter in November 2008.

213 *In a letter to the U.S. Senate:* "Palmer for Stringent Law," *New York Times*, November 16, 1919. For background on the Palmer Raids, see Stanley Cohen, "A Study in Nativism: The American Red Scare of 1919–1920," *Political Science Quarterly*, vol. 79, no. 1 (March 1964), pp. 52–75.

"There is no time to waste on hairsplitting": "The Red Assassins," *Washington Post*, January 4, 1920.

"In the war in which we are now engaged": Muller, *American Inquisition*, p. 17.

provided assistance in tracking down: J. R. Minkel, "Confirmed: The U.S. Census Bureau Gave Up Names of Japanese-Americans in WW II," *Scientific American*, March 2007.

would leverage another cache of confidential data: Herring, *America's Longest War*, p. 279; John Sbardellati, "Power to Destroy: The Political Uses of the IRS from Kennedy to Nixon" (book review), *Journal of Cold War Studies*, vol. 7, no. 3 (2005), pp. 158–159.

214 *20 percent of all workers in the country:* Ralph S. Brown, "Loyalty-Security Measures and Employment Opportunities," *Bulletin of the Atomic Scientists*, April 1955.

"were authorized to use subterfuge": Theoharis and Cox, *The Boss*, pp. 312–313.

compiling a database of 1.5 million names: Kathryn Olmsted, "Lapdog or Rogue Elephant?" in Theoharis et al., *The Central Intelligence Agency*, pp. 189–230.

covert mail-opening program . . . infiltrated a broad range: Athan Theoharis, "A New Agency: The Origins and Expansion of CIA Covert Activities," in Theoharis et al., *The Central Intelligence Agency*, pp. 155–188.

"dangerously indulgent attitude": Theoharis and Cox, *The Boss*, p. 328.

one out of eight Americans: Theoharis and Cox, *The Boss*, pp. 4–5.

Congress passed the USA Patriot Act, which allows: Larry Abramson and Maria Godoy, "The Patriot Act: Key Controversies," National Public Radio, February 14, 2006.

215 *secretly given license to tap telephone conversations:* James Risen and Eric Lichtblau, "Bush Lets U.S. Spy on Callers Without Courts," *New York Times*, December 16, 2005.

run into trouble in the courts: "Times Topics: Wiretapping and Other Eavesdropping Devices and Methods," *New York Times*, October 19, 2010.

the euphemism for torture that the Roman Inquisition employed: John Tedeschi, "The Status of the Defendant before the Roman Inquisition," in Guggisberg, Moeller, and Menchi, eds., *Kertzerverfolgung im 16. und frühen 17. Jahrhundert*, pp. 125–146.

Roughly 750 detainees: "Times Topics: Guantánamo Bay Naval Base (Cuba)," *New York Times*, updated April 25, 2011.

216 *since the first prisoners arrived:* "The Guantánamo Docket: A History of the Detainee Population," *New York Times*, updated June 13, 2011.

217 *known as Camp Justice:* Andrew O. Selsky, "Guantánamo's Days Numbered, Tough Choices Ahead," Associated Press, June 28, 2008; Charles D. Brunt, "N.M. General Says

Detainees Make Camp Duty Difficult," *Albuquerque Journal*, September 21, 2008; Chuck Bennett, "'Camp Justice' Is Ready to Roll," *New York Post*, January 30, 2010.

only five detainees had made their way through the process: David J. R. Frakt, "Mohammed Jawad and the Military Commissions of Guantanamo," *Duke Law Journal: The Legal Workshop*, March 28, 2011.

frequency with which particular words have been employed: http://googleblog.blogspot.com/2010/12/find-out-whats-in-word-or-five-with.html.

"The Guantánamo Inquisition": http://www.commondreams.org/views03/1128-08.htm.

"Guantánamo's Inquisitors": http://pierretristam.com/Bobst/07/bb010307.htm#gu.

"From the Inquisition to Guantánamo": http://www.flickr.com/photos/takomabibelot/384240795/.

218 *He was on his second voyage, with a fleet of seventeen ships:* Sale, *Conquest of Paradise*, pp. 128, 142.

looking for gold but found only fish: Gott, *Cuba: A New History*, pp. 16, 39–40.

Under the terms of the lease: Carol J. Williams, "Cuba Politics: US Base Serves Political Purpose," *Los Angeles Times*, April 18, 2007.

to map in detail the rapid growth of Camp Delta: Adrian Myers, "Camp Delta, Google Earth, and the Ethics of Remote Sensing in Archaeology," *World Archaeology*, vol. 42, no. 3 (2010), pp. 455–467.

219 *modeled directly on "supermax" prisons in the United States:* Jeffrey Toobin, "Camp Justice," *The New Yorker*, April 14, 2008.

"according to the custom and practice of Castile": Sale, *Conquest of Paradise*, p. 128.

not always clear why many of the detainees were there: Charlie Savage, William Glaberson, and Andrew W. Lehren, "Classified Files Offer New Insights Into Detainees," *New York Times*, April 24, 2011.

One of Francis Walsingham's spies . . . observed a similar phenomenon: Hutchinson, *Elizabeth's Spymaster*, p. 96.

221 *"Detainee began to cry. Visibly shaken":* Philippe Sands, "The Green Light," *Vanity Fair*, May 2008.

222 *medical personnel . . . witnessed the questioning:* Vincent Iacopino and Stephen N. Xenakis, "Neglect of Medical Evidence of Torture in Guantánamo Bay: A Case Series," *PLoS Medicine*, April 26, 2011; "'Doctors' at Gitmo," *The Dish*, April 26, 2011.

improvised as best they could: Philippe Sands, "The Green Light," *Vanity Fair*, May 2008.

That assessment has never been documented: David Rose, "Tortured Reasoning," VF.com, December 16, 2008.

Michael V. Hayden . . . told Leon Panetta: Woodward, *Obama's Wars*, p. 60.

223 *This was the setting in which Stafford Smith:* The quotations here are drawn from a conversation with the author in June 2009.

agreed to an out-of-court settlement: John F. Burns and Alan Cowell, "Britain to Compensate Former Guantánamo Detainees," *New York Times*, November 16, 2010.

7. With God on Our Side

225 *"The Church has no fear of historical truth":* Quoted in Richard Boudreaux, "Putting the Inquisition on Trial," *Los Angeles Times*, April 17, 1998.

"We know you're wishing that we'd go away": Quoted in Mazur, *Encyclopedia of Religion and Film*, p. 94.

226 *that had long been in a state of disrepair*: John Thavis, "No Place Like Home: Papal Apartments Get Extreme Makeover," Catholic News Service, January 6, 2006.

the frescoed walls of what may have been her villa: Alessandra Stanley, "'God's Parking Lot' Is in Conflict With Rome's Ancient Past," *New York Times*, December 3, 1999.

227 *official maps . . . architectural plans . . . Hebraic material*: Cifres and Pizzo, *Rari e Preziosi*, pp. 30–31, 64–105.

hard to believe that any volume in these two catalogues: For a complete list of the works cited in the final edition of the Index of Forbidden Books, see http://www.cvm.qc.ca/gconti/905/BABEL/Index%20Librorum%20Prohibitorum-1948.htm.

Apparitions are reported more frequently than you might imagine: Rick Rojas, "Church Affirms Virgin Mary Apparition in Wisconsin," *Los Angeles Times*, December 15, 2010.

228 *dampen intellectual life*: Baldini and Spruitt, *Catholic Church and Modern Science*, vol. 1, p. 88.

which declared ordinations by the Anglican Church: The papal bull *Apostolicae Curae* ("On the Nullity of the Anglican Orders") was promulgated on September 18, 1896. http://www.papalencyclicals.net/Leo13/l13curae.htm

229 *"a tormented phase in the history of the Church"*: Pope John Paul II, Address to the International Symposium on the Inquisition, October 31, 1998.

"That's not our favorite subject": Interview with David Kertzer, May 2001.

230 *The "pleasant surprises" that Cardinal Silvestrini was hoping for*: Bruce Johnston, "Vatican to Open Up Inquisition Archives," *Daily Telegraph*, January 12, 1998.

231 *"the eye that never slumbered"*: Prescott, *History of the Reign of Philip II, King of Spain*, vol. 1, p. 446.

remembers the moment clearly: Conversation with the author, February 2010.

help people . . . make a confession: Kevin Jones, "New iPhone App Aims to Help Catholics Go to Confession," *Catholic News Agency*, February 4, 2011.

232 *The process began with a pastoral letter*: Pope John Paul II, "*Tertio Millennio Adveniente*," November 10, 1994; "As the Third Millennium Draws Near," *L'Osservatore Romano*, November 14, 1994.

It continued in 1998 with the document: Commission for Religious Relations with the Jews, "We Remember: A Reflection on the Shoah," March 16, 1998.

in a penitential service: Alessandra Stanley, "Pope Asks Forgiveness for Errors of the Church Over 2,000 Years," *New York Times*, March 13, 2000.

"Death to the butchers of the Inquisition!": Kertzer, *Prisoner of the Vatican*, pp. 265–267.

roses are frequently left: Rory Carroll, "Vatican on Defensive as Italian Atheists Honour Their Martyr," *The Guardian*, February 17, 2000; John L. Allen, "The Unofficial Jubilee Year Guide to Rome," *National Catholic Reporter*, October 20, 2000.

mounted a raucous reenactment: Alessandra Stanley, "Honoring a Heretic Whom Vatican 'Regrets' Burning," *New York Times*, February 17, 2000.

King Juan Carlos joined Israel's president: "Spanish Royal Couple Arrive Here Tomorrow," Reuters, November 7, 1993.

233 *periods of "intolerance and persecution"*: Alan Riding, "500 Years After Expulsion, Spain Reaches Out to Jews," *New York Times*, April 1, 1992.

the same status in law: William Drozdiak, "Spain's Inglorious Edict of 1492: Apology of the Nation That Expelled Its Jews," *Washington Post*, March 31, 1992.

to no avail: Isambard Wilkinson, "King Snubs Moorish Appeal for Apology," *Daily Telegraph*, January 20, 2005.

"I support Ferdinand and Isabella": "Former Spanish PM Defends Pope, Says Muslims Should Apologise," Agence France Presse, September 23, 2006.

234 *some 1,271 government organizations . . . deal with national-security concerns:* Dana Priest and William M. Arken, "Top Secret America," *Washington Post,* July 19, 2010.

235 *people cannot discover if their names are on it:* Ellen Nakashima, "Single Tip Can Now Land a Person on US Terrorism Watch List," *Boston Globe,* December 30, 2010.

referred to as a "blurred groin": "Humorist Dave Barry and His TSA Pat-Down," *All Things Considered,* National Public Radio, November 15, 2010.

made to undergo an "enhanced pat down": Mary Forgione, "TSA's Patdown of 6-year-old Girl Draws Anger — and a Call for Change," *Los Angeles Times,* April 19, 2011; Ed O'Keefe, "TSA, Congress to Review Screening Procedures After Pat-down of 6-year-old Girl," *Washington Post,* April 13, 2011.

special prosecutors . . . led to a culture of obsessive investigation: Anthony Lewis, "The Prosecutorial State," *American Prospect,* January/February 1999.

rationalists of the Enlightenment conceived of government: Bosher, *The French Revolution,* pp. 246–247.

"in which everybody is deprived of political freedom": Hannah Arendt, "Reflections on Violence," *New York Review of Books,* February 27, 1969.

236 *The effort was probably doomed:* "FBI Ditches Carnivore Surveillance System," Associated Press, January 18, 2005.

identify some of the thousands of keywords: One such list can be found at http://www.angelfire.com/wa/militia/echelon1.html.

similar initiatives survive: Siobhan Gorman, "NSA's Domestic Spying Grows as Agency Sweeps Up Data," *Wall Street Journal,* March 10, 2008.

The attorney general . . . was in intensive care: Dan Eggen and Paul Kane, "Gonzales Hospital Episode Detailed," *Washington Post,* May 16, 2007.

surveillance of this sort continues: James Risen and Eric Lichtblau, "Bush Lets U.S. Spy on Callers Without Courts," *New York Times,* December 16, 2005; James Risen and Eric Lichtblau, "Spying Program Snared U.S. Calls," *New York Times,* December 21, 2005.

237 *companies will provide bespoke systems:* Christopher Rhoads and Loretta Chao, "Iran's Web Spying Aided by Western Technology," *Wall Street Journal,* June 22, 2009.

"a normal condition of politics": Jack Balkin, "Bradley Manning, Barack Obama, and the National Surveillance State," *Balkinization,* March 17, 2011.

number of state and federal requests for wiretap authorization: "Applications for Orders Authorizing or Approving the Interception of Wire, Oral, or Electronic Communications," Administrative Office of the United States Courts, June 2011.

a graphic display of his personal movements: Noam Cohen, "It's Tracking Your Every Move and You May Not Even Know," *New York Times,* March 26, 2011.

predicting if you're about to jump to another phone company: Robert Lee Hotz, "The Really Smart Phone," *Wall Street Journal,* April 23–24, 2011.

238 *"Computer vision" systems are now employed:* Steve Lohr, "Computers That See You and Watch Over You," *New York Times,* January 1, 2011.

Under the new Texas guidelines: Tom Leonard, "Biblical Values and Confederates Promoted in Texas Textbook Revisions," *Daily Telegraph,* May 21, 2010; Brad Knickerbocker, "In Texas, Social-Studies Textbooks Get a Conservative Makeover," *Christian Science Monitor,* May 22, 2010; James C. McKinley, Jr., "Texas Conservatives Win Curriculum Change," *New York Times,* March 12, 2010.

239 *decreed that profanity was no longer to be used:* Cassell Bryan-Low and Aaron Lucchettti, "George Carlin Never Would've Cut at the New Goldman Sachs," *Wall Street Journal*, July 29, 2010.

Amazon was able to delete those books remotely: Brad Stone, "Amazon Erases Orwell Books from Kindle," *New York Times*, July 17, 2009.

"second-generation filtering": Ronald J. Deibert and Rafal Rohozinski, "Risking Security: Policies and Paradoxes of Cyberspace Security," *International Political Sociology*, vol. 4, no. 1 (2010), pp. 15–32.

240 *managed to shut down the entire Internet in the country:* James Glanz and John Markoff, "Egypt's Autocracy Found the 'Off' Switch," *New York Times*, February 16, 2011.

to collect names and trace relationships: Farnaz Fassihi, "Iranian Crackdown Goes Global," *Wall Street Journal*, December 3, 2009; Evgeny Morozov, "Foreign Policy: Iran's Terrifying Facebook Police," National Public Radio, July 13, 2009.

"What if the liberating potential of the Internet": Morozov, *The Net Delusion*, p. 59.

"exploiting cyberspace for their own strategic purposes": Evgeny Morozov, "Iran: Downside to the 'Twitter Revolution,'" *Dissent*, vol. 56, no. 5 (2009), pp. 10–14.

content it considers inappropriate: Nicholas D. Kristof, "Banned in Beijing," *New York Times*, January 22, 2011.

demanded . . . that he release all the private e-mails: Josh Marshall, "Wis. GOP FOIAs Emails of State University Prof Critical of Gov. Walker," *Talking Points Memo*, March 25, 2011; Paul Krugman, "American Thought Police," *New York Times*, March 27, 2011.

Amazon dropped . . . no longer process financial contributions: "Banks and WikiLeaks," *New York Times*, December 25, 2010; Lauren Kirchner, "Why Amazon Caved," *Columbia Journalism Review*, December 3, 2010; Amy Davidson, "Banishing WikiLeaks?," *The New Yorker*, December 1, 2010.

241 *only one person in six:* "Freedom of the Press 2010: Broad Setbacks to Global Media Freedom," p. 20. http://www.freedomhouse.org/template.cfm?page=533.

"No longer is it easy to hide": Ronald Deibert, "Blogging Dangerously," *Index on Censorship*, vol. 39, no. 4 (2010), pp. 88–90.

search engine called SeekFind . . . site called I'mHalal: Habiba Nosheen, "Religious Search Engines Yield Tailored Results," National Public Radio, September 13, 2010.

"the myth of the separation of church and state": Cathy Young, "GOP's 'Christian Nation,'" *Reason*, July 14, 2004.

242 *Angry rejoinders were instantaneous:* "Fox News Figures Outraged Over Obama's 'Christian Nation' Comment," *MediaMatters*, April 9, 2009.

professed bewilderment: "Sarah Palin's 'Christian Nation' Remarks Spark Debate," ABC News, April 20, 2010.

an army of "prayer warriors": Julian Lukins, "The Faith of Sarah Palin," *Charisma*, January 1, 2009; Michael Joseph Gross, "Is Palin's Rise Part of God's Plan?," VF.com, September 17, 2010; Scott Conroy, "Palin Feels Strength of 'Prayer Warriors,'" *CBS News*, October 22, 2008.

"if the Holy Spirit lives within you": David White, "Gov.-elect Robert Bentley Intends to Be Governor Over All, but Says Only Christians Are His 'Brothers and Sisters,'" *Birmingham News*, January 17, 2011.

laid the blame . . . "pact with the devil": Manya Brachear, "Pat Robertson Blames Haiti Quake on 'Pact with the Devil,'" *Chicago Tribune*, January 18, 2010; "Falwell Apologizes to Gays, Feminists, Lesbians," CNN, September 14, 2001.

the idea of an Islamic facility near "hallowed ground": For good overviews of the controversy, see Lisa Miller, "War Over Ground Zero," *Newsweek,* August 16, 2010; and Will Saletan, "Mosque Uprising," *Slate,* August 9, 2010.

243 *"entitles them to positions":* Fareed Zakaria, "The Real Ground Zero: Let's Promote Muslim Moderates Here," *Newsweek,* August 16, 2010.

"no more mosques": http://action.afa.net/Blogs/BlogPost.aspx?id=2147497353.

Opposition to Islamic facilities: Laurie Goodstein, "Across Nation, Mosque Projects Meet Opposition," *New York Times,* August 7, 2010.

plans to gather copies of the Koran: Chad Smith, "Dove World Told It Can't Burn Qurans," *Gainesville Sun,* August 19, 2010.

"send a message to Islam": Damien Cave, "Far from Ground Zero, Obscure Pastor Is No Longer Ignored," *New York Times,* August 26, 2010.

riots in Afghanistan: Enayat Najafizada and Rod Nordland, "Afghans Avenge Florida Koran Burning," *New York Times,* April 1, 2011; Rod Nordland, "Taliban Exploit Tensions Seething in Afghan Society," *New York Times,* April 5, 2011; Ismail Sameem, "Ten Dead in Afghan Quran Burning Protests," MSNBC, April 2, 2011.

from "the seed of Islam": "Graham: Obama Born a Muslim, Now a Christian," CNN Politics, August 19, 2010.

244 *70 percent of Americans:* "Overwhelming Majority Oppose Mosque Near Ground Zero," CNN Politics, August 11, 2010.

ballot initiative . . . restrict any use of sharia law: Donna Leinwand, "States Enter Debate on Sharia Law," *USA Today,* December 9, 2010; Carla Hinton, "Measure Keeps Courts From Considering Sharia Law," *Oklahoman,* November 5, 2010.

"actual word of God": Frank Newport, "One Third of Americans Believe the Bible Is Literally True," Gallup News Service, May 25, 2007.

had consulted "a higher power": Nicholas Lemann, "The Will to Believe," *New Republic,* February 17, 2011.

245 *god of anger . . . gene of aggression:* Louis Menand, "The Gods Are Anxious," *The New Yorker,* December 16, 1996.

"If there's a one percent chance": Suskind, *The One Percent Doctrine,* p. 62.

247 *"not wholly responsible for the way we are":* Michael J. Sandel, "The Case Against Perfection," *Atlantic Monthly,* April 2004.

248 *"To make mankind just and happy":* Isaiah Berlin, "On the Pursuit of the Ideal," *New York Review of Books,* March 17, 1988.

249 *he came across the manuscript:* M.A.E. Nickson, "Locke and the Inquisition of Toulouse," *British Museum Quarterly,* vol. 36, no. 3/4 (Autumn 1972), pp. 83–92.

"When you see what it contains": Bourne, *The Life of John Locke,* vol. 2, p. 75.

turned on the very idea of uncertainty: Locke, *A Letter Concerning Toleration,* pp. 25–27, 33, 37, 38, 43, 51–54.

250 *he calls the process:* See Searle, *Making the Social World* and *The Construction of Social Reality.*

"to possess but one idea": Boswell, *Boswell's Life of Johnson,* vol. 6, p. 304.

251 *"bright halo of enthusiasm":* Reese, *Inside the Vatican,* p. 251.

BIBLIOGRAPHY

Abelard, Peter. *Historia Calamitatum, The Story of My Misfortunes.* Translated by Henry Adams Bellows. New York: Thomas A. Boyd, 1922.

Aczel, Amir D. *The Jesuit and the Skull.* New York: Riverhead, 2007.

Aicher, Peter J. *Guide to the Aqueducts of Ancient Rome.* Wauconda, IL: Bolchazy-Carducci, 1995.

Alcala, Angel. *The Spanish Inquisition and the Inquisitorial Mind.* Boulder, CO: Social Science Monographs, 1987.

Alleg, Henri. *The Question.* Translated by John Calder. Lincoln: University of Nebraska Press, 2006.

Allen, John L., Jr. *Cardinal Ratzinger: The Vatican's Enforcer of the Faith.* New York: Continuum, 2001.

Amiel, Charles, and Anne Lima. *L'Inquisition de Goa: La Relation de Charles Dellon (1687).* Paris: Editions Chandeigne, 1997.

Anderson, James Maxwell. *Daily Life During the Spanish Inquisition.* Westport, CT: Greenwood Press, 2002.

Arendt, Hannah. *Eichmann in Jerusalem.* New York: Viking, 1963.

Aristophanes. *The Frogs.* Cambridge, MA: Harvard University Press, 2002.

Baer, Yitzhak. *A History of the Jews in Christian Spain.* Philadelphia: Jewish Publication Society, 1992.

Baldini, Ugo, and Leen Spruitt. *Catholic Church and Modern Science: Documents from the Archives of the Congregations of the Holy Office and the Index.* Rome: Libraria Editrice Vaticana, 2009.

Bancroft, Hubert Howe. *A History of California.* San Francisco: The History Company, 1886.

Beinart, Haim. *Conversos on Trial: The Inquisition in Ciudad Real.* Jerusalem: Magnes Press, 1981.

———. *The Expulsion of the Jews from Spain.* Oxford: Littman Library of Jewish Civilization, 2005.

Bethencourt, Francisco. *The Inquisition: A Global History, 1478–1834.* Cambridge: Cambridge University Press, 2009.

Birmingham, David. *Portugal and Africa*. New York: St. Martin's, 1999.

Bishop, Bill. *The Big Sort*. Boston: Houghton Mifflin, 2008.

Black, Christopher F. *The Italian Inquisition*. New Haven, CT: Yale University Press, 2009.

Black, Edwin. *IBM and the Holocaust*. Washington: Dialog Press, 2001.

Blackwell, Richard J. *Galileo, Bellarmine, and the Bible*. Notre Dame, IN: University of Notre Dame, 1991.

Blouin, Francis X., ed. *Vatican Archives: An Inventory and Guide to Historical Documents of the Holy See*. New York: Oxford, 1998.

Boas, Frederick S., ed. *Elizabethan and Other Essays* [by Sir Sidney Lee]. Freeport, NY: Books for Libraries Press, 1968.

Bosher, J. F. *The French Revolution*. New York: W. W. Norton, 1988.

Boswell, James. *Boswell's Life of Johnson*, 6 vols. Edited by G. Birkbeck Hill. Oxford: Clarendon Press, 1887.

Bourne, Henry Richard Fox. *The Life of John Locke*. 2 vols. London: Henry S. King, 1876.

Brown, Ralph S. *Loyalty and Security: Employment Tests in the United States*. New Haven, CT: Yale University Press, 1958.

Budiansky, Stephen. *Her Majesty's Spymaster*. New York: Penguin, 2005.

Bujanda, J. M. De. *Le Controle des Idées à la Renaissance*. Paris: Droz, 1996.

Cahalan, Kathleen A. *Formed in the Image of Christ: The Sacramental-Moral Theology of Bernard Häring, C.Ss.R.* Collegeville, MN: Liturgical Press, 2004.

Camus, Albert. *The Rebel*. New York: Vintage, 1958.

Cannandine, David. *Ornamentalism: How the British Saw Their Empire*. Oxford: Oxford University Press, 2001.

Cantor, Norman. *Inventing the Middle Ages*. New York: William Morrow, 1990.

Carey, Vincent P. *Voices for Tolerance in an Age of Persecution*. Washington, D.C.: Folger Shakespeare Library, 2004.

Carr, Matthew. *Blood and Faith: The Purging of Muslim Spain*. New York: New Press, 2009.

Carroll, James. *Constantine's Sword*. Boston: Houghton Mifflin, 2001.

Caspit, Ben, and Ilan Kfir. *Netanyahu: The Road to Power*. Secaucus, NJ: Birch Lane Press, 1998.

Chadwick, Owen. *Catholicism and History: The Opening of the Vatican Archives*. Cambridge: Cambridge University Press, 1978.

Chapman, Charles E. *A History of California: The Spanish Period*. New York: Macmillan, 1926.

Chávez, Fray Angélico. *Our Lady of the Conquest*. Santa Fe: Historical Society of New Mexico, 1948.

Cifres, Alejandro, and Marco Pizzo. *Rari e Preziosi: documenta dell'eta moderna e contemporanea dell'archivo del Sant'Ufficio*. Rome: Gangemi Editore, 2008.

Coffin, David R. *Pirro Ligorio: The Renaissance Artist, Architect, and Antiquarian*. University Park: Pennsylvania State University Press, 2004.

Cohn, Samuel K., and Stephen A. Epstein, eds. *Portraits of Medieval and Renaissance Living.* Ann Arbor: University of Michigan Press, 1996.

Collins, Paul. *From Inquisition to Freedom.* New York: Continuum, 2001.

Colonnello, Aldo, and Andrea Del Col. *Uno Storico, un Mugnaio, un Libro.* Montereale Valcellina: Circolo Culturale Menocchio, 2002.

Costen, M. D. *The Cathars and the Albigensian Crusade.* Manchester, UK: Manchester University Press, 1997.

Coulter, Ann. *Godless: The Church of Liberalism.* New York: Crown, 2006.

Couvares, Francis G. *Movie Censorship and American Culture.* Washington, D.C.: Smithsonian Institution, 1996.

Crowley, Roger. *Empires of the Sea.* New York: Random House, 2008.

Dalberg-Acton, John Emerich Edward. *Essays on Freedom and Power* (1949). Boston: Beacon Press, 1979.

Damico, Helen, and Joseph Zavadil, eds. *Medieval Scholarship: Bibliographic Studies on the Formation of a Discipline,* Vol. 1, History. New York and London: Routledge, 1995.

Del Col, Andrea. *Domenico Scandella Known as Menocchio: His Trials Before the Inquisition, 1583–1599.* Tempe, AZ: Medieval and Renaissance Texts and Studies, 1997.

Demos, John. *The Enemy Within.* New York: Viking, 2008.

Derrida, Jacques. *Archive Fever.* Chicago: University of Chicago Press, 1996.

Dostoyevsky, Feodor. *The Brothers Karamazov.* Translated by Richard Pevear and Larissa Volokhonsky. New York: Knopf, 1992.

Duffy, Eamon. *Saints and Sinners: A History of the Popes.* New Haven, CT: Yale University Press, 2006.

Duffy, James. *Portuguese Africa.* Cambridge, MA: Harvard University Press, 1959.

Dutton, Paul Edward. *Carolingian Civilization.* Peterborough, ON: Broadview Press, 2004.

Eco, Umberto. *The Name of the Rose.* New York: Harcourt Brace & Company, 1983.

Eisenstein, Elizabeth. *The Printing Revolution in Early Modern Europe.* New York: Cambridge University Press, 1983.

Elton, Charles Isaac, and Mary Augusta Elton. *The Great Book-Collectors.* London: Kegan Paul, Trench, Trubner, 1893.

Emsley, Clive, Eric Johnson, and Pieter Spierenburg, eds. *Social Control in Europe,* Vol. 2: 1800–2000. Columbus: Ohio State University Press, 2004.

Faulhaber, Charles B., and Stephen Vincent. *Exploring the Bancroft Library.* Salt Lake City: Signature Books, 2006.

Feitlowitz, Marguerite. *A Lexicon of Terror.* New York: Oxford, 1998.

Fenlon, Dermot. *Heresy and Obedience in Tridentine Italy.* Cambridge: Cambridge University Press, 1972.

Fijnaut, Cyrille, and Gary T. Marx, eds. *Undercover: Police Surveillance in Comparative Perspective.* The Hague: Kluwer Law International, 1995.

Fredriksen, Paula. *Augustine and the Jews.* New York: Doubleday, 2008.

Gibbon, Edward. *Decline and Fall of the Roman Empire.* 3 vols. New York: Knopf, 1993.

Gibson, David. *The Rule of Benedict.* New York: HarperCollins, 2006.

Giles, Mary E. *Women in the Inquisition.* Baltimore: Johns Hopkins University Press, 1999.

Ginzburg, Carlo. *The Cheese and the Worms.* Baltimore: Johns Hopkins University Press, 1980.

Gitlitz, David M. *Secrecy and Deceit: The Religion of the Crypto-Jews.* Philadelphia: Jewish Publication Society, 1996.

Given, James B. *Inquisition and Medieval Society.* Ithaca, NY: Cornell University Press, 1997.

Given-Wilson, Chris. *Fourteenth-Century England.* Woodbridge, Suffolk: Boydell Press, 2002.

Godman, Peter. *The Saint as Censor: Robert Bellarmine Between Inquisition and Index.* Leiden: Brill, 2000.

Godman, Peter. *The Silent Masters: Latin Literature and Its Censors in the High Middle Ages.* Princeton, NJ: Princeton University Press, 2000.

Goldstone, Lawrence and Nancy. *Out of the Flames.* New York: Broadway, 2002.

Gott, Richard. *Cuba: A New History.* New Haven, CT: Yale University Press, 2004.

Gottfried, Robert S. *The Black Death: Natural and Human Disaster in Medieval Europe.* New York: Free Press, 1983.

Grendler, Paul. *The Roman Inquisition and the Venetian Press, 1540–1605.* Princeton, NJ: Princeton University Press, 1977.

Groebner, Valentin. *Who Are You? Identification, Deception, and Surveillance in Early Modern Europe.* New York: Zone Books, 2007.

Guggisberg, Hans Rudolf, Bernd Moeller, and Silvana Seidel Menchi, eds., *Kertzerverfolgung im 16. und frühen 17. Jahrhundert.* Wiesbaden: Harrassowitz, 1992.

Gui, Bernard. *The Inquisitor's Guide.* Translated and edited by Janet Shirley. Welwyn Garden City, Herts.: Ravenhall Books, 2006.

Guilaine, Jean, and Jean Zammit. *The Origins of War: Violence in Prehistory.* Malden, MA: Blackwell, 2005.

Hackett, Jeremiah, ed. *World Eras,* Vol. 4, Medieval Europe: 814–1350. Farmington Hills, MI: Gale, 2000.

Haliczer, Stephen, ed. *Inquisition and Society in Early Modern Europe.* London: Croom Helm, 1987.

Haliczer, Stephen. *Sexuality in the Confessional: A Sacrament Profaned.* New York: Oxford University Press, 1996.

Hamburger, Philip. *Separation of Church and State.* Cambridge, MA: Harvard University Press, 2002.

Hare, Augustus J. C. *Walks in Rome* (1871). New York: Cosimo Classics, 2005.

Harvey, David. *The Condition of Postmodernity.* Oxford: Blackwell Publishers, 1990.

Harvey, L. P. *Islamic Spain.* Chicago: University of Chicago Press, 1990.

Henningsen, Gustav, and John Tedeschi, eds. *The Inquisition in Early Modern Europe.* Dekalb: Northern Illinois University Press, 1986.

Hentoff, Nat. *Free Speech for Me — but Not for Thee.* New York: HarperCollins, 1992.

Herring, George C. *America's Longest War: The United States and Vietnam, 1950–1975.* Boston: McGraw-Hill, 2002.

Himmelfarb, Gertrude. *The New History and the Old.* Cambridge, MA: Harvard University Press, 1987.

Hogan, David E., and Jonathan L. Burstein, eds. *Disaster Medicine.* Philadelphia: Lippincott Williams & Wilkins, 2007.

Hordes, Stanley M. *To the Ends of the Earth.* New York: Columbia University Press, 2005.

Hsia, R. Po-chia, ed. *A Companion to the Reformation World.* Oxford: Blackwell, 2004.

Hunt, Lynn, Margaret C. Jacob, and Wijnand Mijnhardt. *The Book That Changed Europe: Picart and Bernard's Religious Ceremonies of the World.* Cambridge, MA: Harvard University Press, 2010.

Hutchinson, Robert. *Elizabeth's Spymaster: Francis Walsingham and the Secret War That Saved England.* New York: St. Martin's, 2006.

James, George Wharton. *In and Out of the Old Missions of California.* Boston: Little, Brown, 1905.

Kamen, Henry. *The Spanish Inquisition: A Historical Revision.* New Haven, CT: Yale University Press, 1998.

Kerr, Fergus. *Twentieth-Century Catholic Theologians.* Oxford: Blackwell, 2007.

Kerrigan, Michael. *The Instruments of Torture.* New York: Lyons Press, 2001.

Kertzer, David. *The Kidnapping of Edgardo Mortara.* New York: Knopf, 1997.

——. *Prisoner of the Vatican.* New York: Houghton Mifflin, 2004.

Kessell, John L. *Kiva, Cross and Crown: The Pecos Indians and New Mexico, 1544–1840.* Tucson, AZ: Southwest Parks and Monuments Association, 1987.

Kessell, John L., Rick Hendricks, and Meredith D. Dodge, eds. *To the Royal Crown Restored: The Journals of Don Diego Vargas, New Mexico, 1692–1694.* Albuquerque: University of New Mexico Press, 1995.

Kieckhefer, Richard. *European Witch Trials.* Berkeley: University of California Press, 1976.

King, Ursula. *Spirit of Fire: The Life and Vision of Teilhard de Chardin.* Maryknoll, NY: Orbis, 1996.

Kingdon, Robert M., Thomas A. Lambert, and Isabella M. Watt, eds. *Registers of the Consistory of Geneva in the Time of Calvin.* Vol. 1. Grand Rapids, MI: Eerdmans, 2000.

Knaut, Andrew L. *The Pueblo Revolt of 1680.* Norman: University of Oklahoma Press, 1995.

Kors, Charles, and Edward Peters. *Witchcraft in Europe.* Philadelphia: University of Pennsylvania Press, 2001.

Kübler-Ross, Elisabeth. *On Death and Dying.* New York: Macmillan, 1993.

Kunin, Seth D. *Juggling Identities: Identity and Authenticity Among the Crypto-Jews.* New York: Columbia University Press, 2009.

Kurtz, Lester R. *The Politics of Heresy.* Berkeley: University of California Press, 1986.

La Farge, John Pen. *Turn Left at the Sleeping Dog: Scripting the Santa Fe Legend, 1920–1955.* Albuquerque: University of New Mexico Press, 2001.

Lash, Joseph P. *From the Diaries of Felix Frankfurter.* New York: W. W. Norton, 1975.

Law, Thomas Graves, and Christopher Bagshaw. *A historical sketch of the conflicts between Jesuits and seculars in the reign of Queen Elizabeth: with a reprint of Christopher Bagshaw's True relation of the faction begun at Wisbich; and illustrative documents.* London: D. Nutt, 1889.

Lea, Henry Charles. *A History of the Inquisition of the Middle Ages.* 3 vols. New York: Harbor Press, 1955.

Lea, Henry Charles. *A History of the Inquisition of Spain.* 4 vols. New York: AMS Press, 1988.

Le Roy Ladurie, Emmanuel. *The Mind and Method of the Historian.* Chicago: University of Chicago Press, 1981.

———. *Montaillou: The Promised Land of Error.* New York: Random House, 1979.

Lester, Toby. *The Fourth Part of the World.* New York: Free Press, 2009.

Liebman, Seymour B. *The Enlightened: The Writings of Luis de Carvajal, El Mozo.* Coral Gables, FL: University of Miami, 1967.

Llorente, Juan Antonio. *A Critical History of the Inquisition of Spain.* Williamstown, MA: John Lilburne, 1967.

Locke, John. *A Letter Concerning Toleration.* Edited by James H. Tully. Indianapolis, IN: Hackett, 1983.

Lomeli, Francisco A., and Clark A. Colahan, eds. *Defying the Inquisition in Colonial New Mexico: Miguel de Quintana's Life and Writings.* Albuquerque: University of New Mexico Press, 2006.

Lovato, Andrew Leo. *Santa Fe Hispanic Culture.* Albuquerque: University of New Mexico Press, 2004.

Mackay, Christopher S. *The Hammer of Witches: A Complete Translation of the* Malleus Maleficarum. Cambridge: Cambridge University Press, 2009.

Macrakis, Kristie. *Seduced by Secrets: Inside the Stasi's Spy-Tech World.* New York: Cambridge University Press, 2008.

Marchak, Patricia, with William Marchak. *God's Assassins: State Terrorism in Argentina in the 1970s.* Montreal: McGill-Queens University Press, 1999.

Mazur, Eric. *Encyclopedia of Religion and Film.* Santa Barbara, CA: ABC-CLIO, 2011.

Menocal, Maria Rosa. *The Ornament of the World.* New York: Little, Brown, 2002.

Miller, Arthur. *The Crucible.* New York: Viking, 1953.

Monter, E. William. *Frontiers of Heresy: The Spanish Inquisition from the Basque Lands to Sicily.* Cambridge: Cambridge University Press, 1990.

———. *Enforcing Morality in Early Modern Europe.* London: Variorum, 1987.

———. *European Witchcraft.* New York: Wiley, 1969.

Moore, R. I. *The Formation of a Persecuting Society.* Oxford: Basil Blackwell, 1987.

Moorhead, Max L. *New Mexico's Royal Road: Trade and Travel on the Chihuahua Trail.* Norman: University of Oklahoma Press, 1958.

Morellet, André. *Abrege du Manuel des Inquisiteurs.* Paris: Jerome Millon, 1990.

Morozov, Evgeny. *The Net Delusion: The Dark Side of Internet Freedom.* New York: Public Affairs, 2011.

Muller, Eric L. *American Inquisition: The Hunt for Japanese-American Disloyalty in World War II.* Chapel Hill: University of North Carolina Press, 2007.

Mundill, Robin R. *The King's Jews: Money, Massacre, and Exodus in Medieval England.* London: Continuum, 2010.

Netanyahu, Benzion. *Don Isaac Abravanel.* Ithaca, NY: Cornell University Press, 1998.

———. *The Origins of the Inquisition in Fifteenth-Century Spain.* New York: Random House, 1995.

Nevin, W. W. *Vignettes of Travel: Some Comparative Sketches in England and Italy.* New York: Worthington, 1891.

Oldenbourg, Zoe. *Massacre at Montségur.* New York: Pantheon, 1961.

———. *Destiny of Fire.* New York: Pantheon, 1961.

Orwell, George. *1984.* New York: Harcourt, Brace & World, 1949.

O'Shea, Stephen. *The Perfect Heresy: The Revolutionary Life and Death of the Medieval Cathars.* New York: Walker, 2000.

Pacheco, Allan. *Ghosts, Murder, Mayhem: A Chronicle of Santa Fe.* Santa Fe, NM: Sunstone, 2004.

Parry, J. H. *The Age of Reconnaissance.* Berkeley: University of California Press, 1981.

———. *The Discovery of the Sea.* London: Weidenfeld and Nicolson, 1974.

———. *The Spanish Seaborne Empire.* London: Hutchinson, 1966.

Pastor, Ludwig von. *The History of the Popes from the Close of the Middle Ages.* London: Routledge, 1969.

Patai, Raphael. *On Jewish Folklore.* Detroit: Wayne State University Press, 1983.

Pegg, M. G. *A Most Holy War: The Albigensian Crusade and the Battle for Christendom.* New York: Oxford University Press, 2008.

———. *The Corruption of Angels.* Princeton, NJ: Princeton University Press, 2001.

Pérez, Joseph. *The Spanish Inquisition.* New Haven, CT: Yale University Press, 2005.

Perry, Mary Elizabeth, and Anne J. Cruz, eds. *Cultural Encounters: The Impact of the Inquisition in Spain and the New World.* Berkeley: University of California Press, 1991.

Peters, Edward. *Inquisition.* New York: Free Press, 1988.

———. *Limits of Thought and Power in Medieval Europe.* Farnham, UK: Ashgate, 2001.

———. *The Magician, the Witch, and the Law.* Philadelphia: University of Pennsylvania Press, 1978.

———. *Torture.* Philadelphia: University of Pennsylvania Press, 1996.

———, ed. *Heresy and Authority in Medieval Europe.* Philadelphia: University of Pennsylvania Press, 1980.

Prahlow, Joseph. *Forensic Pathology*. New York: Springer, 2010.

Prescott, William H. *History of the Reign of Philip the Second, King of Spain*. Boston: Phillips, Sampson, and Company, 1857.

Preston, Douglas, and José Antonio Esquibel. *The Royal Road: El Camino Real from Mexico City to Santa Fe*. Photographs by Christine Preston. Santa Fe: University of New Mexico Press, 1998.

Purdie, Albert Bertrand. *The Life of Blessed John Southworth: Priest and Martyr*. London: Burns, Oates, and Washbourne, 1930.

Ranke, Leopold von. *The Ecclesiastical and Political History of the Popes of Rome During the Sixteenth and Seventeenth Centuries*. 3 vols. Translated by Sarah Austen. London: John Murray, 1840.

Ratté, John. *Three Modernists*. New York: Sheed & Ward, 1968.

Read, Piers Paul. *The Templars*. New York: Da Capo, 1999.

Reese, Thomas J. *Inside the Vatican: The Politics and Organization of the Catholic Church*. Cambridge, MA: Harvard University Press, 1996.

Reith, Charles. *The Blind Eye of History: A Study of the Origins of the Present Police Era*. Montclair, NJ: Patterson Smith, 1975.

Rejali, Darius. *Torture and Democracy*. Princeton, NJ: Princeton University Press, 2007.

Robinson, James Harvey. *Petrarch: The First Modern Scholar and Man of Letters*. New York: G. P. Putnam, 1898.

Ross, Dan. *Acts of Faith: A Journey to the Fringes of Jewish Identity*. New York: St. Martin's, 1982.

Roth, Cecil. *History of the Marranos*. New York: Sepher-Hermon, 1992.

———. *The Spanish Inquisition*. New York: W. W. Norton, 1996.

Rowland, Ingrid D. *Giordano Bruno: Philosopher/Heretic*. New York: Farrar, Straus and Giroux, 2008.

Rowling, J. K. *Harry Potter and the Order of the Phoenix*. New York: Scholastic, 2003.

Rubin, Nancy. *Isabella of Castile*. New York: St. Martin's, 1992.

Russell, Jeffrey Burton. *Witchcraft in the Middle Ages*. Ithaca, NY: Cornell University Press, 1972.

Rynne, Xavier. *Vatican Council II*. New York: Farrar, Straus and Giroux, 1968.

Sachar, Howard M. *Farewell España: The World of the Sephardim Remembered*. New York: Random House, 1994.

Sale, Kirkpatrick. *Conquest of Paradise: Christopher Columbus and the Columbia Landscape*. New York: Knopf, 1990.

Saraiva, Antonio José. *The Marrano Factory: The Portuguese Inquisition and Its New Christians, 1536–1765*. Boston: Brill, 2001.

Saygin, Susanne. *Humphrey, Duke of Gloucester (1390–1447) and the Italian Humanists*. London: Brill, 2002.

Scholes, France V. *Church and State in New Mexico, 1610–1650*. Albuquerque: University of New Mexico Press, 1937.

Scholz-Hänsel, Michael. *El Greco*. Cologne: Taschen, 2004.

Searle, John. *The Construction of Social Reality.* New York: Free Press, 1995.

———. *Making the Social World: The Structure of Human Civilization.* Oxford: Oxford University Press, 2010.

Setton, Kenneth M. *The Papacy and the Levant, 1204–1571.* Philadelphia: American Philosophical Society, 1984.

Shea, William R., and Mariano Artigas. *Galileo in Rome.* Oxford: Oxford University Press, 2003.

Silverblatt, Irene. *Modern Inquisitions: Peru and the Colonial Origins of the Civilized World.* Durham, NC: Duke University Press, 2004.

Simmons, Marc. *Spanish Pathways: Readings in the History of Spanish New Mexico.* Santa Fe: University of New Mexico Press, 2001.

Soldatov, Andrei, and Irina Borogan. *The New Nobility.* New York: Public Affairs, 2010.

Starr, Kenneth. *The Starr Report.* Rocklin, CA: Forum, 1998.

Stead, Philip John. *The Police of France.* New York: Macmillan, 1983.

———. *The Police of Paris.* London: Staples, 1957.

Sullivan, Karen. *The Inner Lives of Medieval Inquisitors.* Chicago: University of Chicago Press, 2011.

Sumption, Jonathan. *The Albigensian Crusade.* New York: Faber and Faber, 2000.

Suskind, Ron. *The One Percent Doctrine: Deep Inside America's Pursuit of Its Enemies Since 9/11.* New York: Simon & Schuster, 2006.

Tanner, Joseph Robson. *Tudor Constitutional Documents.* Cambridge: Cambridge University Press, 1930.

Tedeschi, John. *The Prosecution of Heresy.* Binghamton, NY: Center for Medieval and Renaissance Studies, 1991.

Theoharis, Athan, and John Stuart Cox. *The Boss: J. Edgar Hoover and the American Inquisition.* Philadelphia: Temple University Press, 1988.

———, with Richard Immerman, Loch Johnson, Kathryn Olmsted, and John Prados. *The Central Intelligence Agency: Security Under Scrutiny.* Westport, CT: Greenwood, 2006.

Thomas, Keith. *Religion and the Decline of Magic.* New York: Scribner, 1971.

Timerman, Jacobo. *Prisoner Without a Name, Cell Without a Number.* New York: Random House, 1981.

Tobias, Henry J., and Charles E. Woodhouse. *Santa Fe: A Modern History, 1880–1990.* Albuquerque: University of New Mexico Press, 2001.

Trevor-Roper, H. R., *The European Witch-Craze of the Sixteenth and Seventeenth Century and Other Essays.* New York: Harper, 1969.

Udal, John Symonds. *Marriage and Other Poems by J.S.U.* London: Taylor and Co., 1876.

Weinberg, Bennett Alan, and Bonnie K. Bealer. *The World of Caffeine.* New York: Routledge, 2002.

Weiss, René. *The Yellow Cross: The Story of the Last Cathars, 1290–1329.* New York: Knopf, 2000.

Williams, Penry. *The Later Tudors.* Oxford: Clarendon Press, 1995.

Wills, Garry. *Saint Augustine.* New York: Penguin, 1999.

Wolfe, Robert, ed. *Captured German and Related Records: A National Archives Confer-ence.* Athens: Ohio University Press, 1974.

Woodward, Bob. *Obama's Wars.* New York: Simon & Schuster, 2010.

Yates, Frances. *The Art of Memory.* London: Pimlico, 1992.

INDEX

Catholic Church *(cont.)*
    demands anti-Modernist oath, 171
    enforces doctrinal rigidity & social con-
        trol, 169–71
    printing revolution and, 112–14
    prosecutes Albigensian crusade, 30–33
    Queen Elizabeth I and, 70, 111, 193–94
    relationship with civil government,
        21–22
    supporters kill Gov. Rosas, 158
    suppresses Cathar heresy, 9–10, 28–29,
        30–35, 117
"Catholic Church and Modern Science,
    The" (document series), 228,
    229–30
Catholic Encyclopedia (1907): approves
    censorship, 118–19, 170
cell phones: and surveillance, 237–38
censorship. *See also* Index of Forbidden
        Books
    of Abelard, 117
    by Amazon, 239, 240
    America threatened with, 182
    Bellarmine on, 121–22
    Bellarmine threatened with, 123
    and book-burning, 117
    Carroll on, 115
    Catholic Encyclopedia approves, 118–19,
        170
    CDF and, 12, 18, 24
    Congregation of the Index and, 11,
        118–19
    in France, 197–98
    by Goldman Sachs, 239
    Google and, 115
    Hentoff on, 116
    Master of the Sacred Palace administers,
        117–18, 126
    and power of imprimatur, 118, 121, 124,
        160
    under Queen Elizabeth I, 194
    by Roman Inquisition, 69–70, 118–26,
        227, 231
    in Russia, 115–16, 130
    Savonarola promotes, 117
    of self, 126–27
    social damage of, 125–26
    in Spanish empire, 160
    St. Paul approves, 117
    Tedeschi on, 123–24

    by Texas State Board of Education,
        238–39
    in Inquisition archives, 17–18
    of WikiLeaks, 240–41
Chadwick, Henry, 190
CHAOS program (CIA): surveillance by,
    214
Chavez, Angelico (father): on Inquisition
    in New Mexico, 145–46, 159
Cheese and the Worms, The (Ginzburg),
    136–37
Cheney, Dick: "Cheney Doctrine,"
    245–46
    defends waterboarding, 94
China: control of Internet in, 115, 126,
    240
    intellectual freedom restricted in, 126
church and state, separation of: Obama on,
    242, 243–44
    in U.S., 238, 241–44
Cifres Giménez, Alejandro (monsignor):
    administers Inquisition archives,
    15–17, 225–29, 246
civil liberties: national security and,
    210–11, 213
Clement V (pope), 44
Clement VIII (pope): and coffee, 139
COINTELPRO program (FBI): surveil-
    lance by, 214
Collins, Paul: on Inquistion in modern
    world, 170
Columbus, Christopher, 73, 102, 218
    accompanied by *conversos,* 102, 150
    personality & ambitions of, 146–47
Comey, James B., 236
Commonweal, 124
communications revolution: Inquisition
    and, 148–49
Concordia discordantium canonum (Gra-
    tian), 38–39, 55
Confucianism: Catholic Church and, 164
Congar, Yves, 251
Congregation for the Doctrine of the Faith
    (CDF). *See also* Inquisition, Sacred
        Congregation of the Holy Office
    and apparitions, 227–28
    archives of, 4–6, 108
    and censorship, 12, 18, 24
    criticizes Harry Potter books, 18–19
    excommunicates Balasuriya, 179